T5-AGT-998

CARE OR CUSTODY

Community Homes and the Treatment of Delinquency

CARE OR CUSTODY

Community Homes and the Treatment of Delinquency

by
Norman Tutt

Introduction by
HOWARD W. POLSKY

AGATHON PRESS, NEW YORK

© 1974 by Norman Tutt

Introduction © 1975 by Agathon Press, Inc.

Library of Congress Cataloging in Publication Data

Tutt, Norman
Care or Custody
Includes bibliographical references.
1. Juvenile delinquency — Great Britain. 2. Juvenile
detention homes — Great Britain — Case studies.
3. Rehabilitation of juvenile delinquents — Great Britain.
I. Title.
HV9146.T87 1975   364.6   74-9318
ISBN 0-87586-049-4

Contents

INTRODUCTION

by Howard W. Polsky

Care or Custody is the most comprehensive analysis to date of a residential treatment center for adolescent boys in trouble. I use the term *comprehensive* for three reasons: (1) the study is informed throughout by current theories about young offenders and the multiple forces influencing their lives before, during and after detention; (2) it presents a variety of perspectives by successively positioning "Wellside," one of 121 residential institutions for adolescent offenders in England and Wales, from the viewpoints of the boys, the administration, the staff, the instructors and counselors and social workers; (3) throughout this odyssey, a strong and delicate balance is maintained between objectivity and compassion.

Dr. Tutt proceeds cautiously in reviewing the pertinent data from other studies, as well as his own extensive observations, and then weaves these facts into a model of explanation so that the descriptive material is always enhanced by theoretical analysis.

For example, many studies have shown that factors contributing to or concomitant with increases in delinquency are: association with older adolescents in trouble, deterioration of neighborhoods, overcrowding in the home, parents who are unskilled and low-paid or unemployed, irregularity of school attendance, frequent job changes by young people, etc. When these conditions are personalized, as in this book, in the words and feelings of young people, we are given a vivid picture of the coldness of their social and physical environment, the absence of sympathetic adults and peers, and the unavailability of any kind of genuine support within their homes, schools, churches or youth clubs.

But Tutt goes beyond the facts in attempting to assess all of these forces within a theoretical framework. His own research and extensive review of the literature suggest that the major causes of delinquency can be explained by a combination of psychological and sociological theories. Within this framework he zeroes in on the *lack of achievement motivation* among young offenders because of a combination of child-rearing practices and a punishing, depriving social environment. The absence or frustration of the achievement drive that is compulsively encouraged in industrial societies is a crucial factor in the development of delinquency. Those young offenders who are motivated to achieve are usually denied success by society and in their frustration eventually become aggressive toward it.

However, Tutt maintains, the majority of young offenders are not motivated to achieve. Their delinquency can be ascribed not to frustration at the limited opportunities available to them and the consequent development of aggressive drives against society, but rather to the same culturally conditioned desires for material goods that their non-delinquent peers have. Thus the deprived low achievers improve their lot through systematic thievery; it is the smaller number of frustrated high achievers who are malicious toward both people and property. These two kinds of deprivation — material and psychological — lie at the heart of the complex web of forces inducing youngsters primarily from low income families and areas to experiment with delinquent activities.

Particularly useful for Americans in the correctional field is Tutt's clear and precise exposition of England's approach to the treatment of young offenders. He describes a variety of settings within the community as well as the different types of residential centers in isolated areas. These descriptions are placed within the overall political framework of the changing professional and governmental attitudes toward caring and working with young offenders. Tutt shows how certain expectations and attitudes both of the child coming into residential care and of the staff place constraints on the kind of care which is given. The evolving philosophy of treatment based on past experience, both researched and informally transmitted, is carefully reviewed in the context of the accelerating changing patterns of residential care. This is a most useful analysis for our work here in America, where we are undergoing analogous transitions.

Tutt sheds new light on the omnipresent dilemma of custody versus rehabilitation, and punishment versus treatment. This old conflict pervades and informs every aspect of the care of young offenders. But Tutt has gone beyond rehashing all of the old pros and cons. He gives us specific guidelines for measuring the effectiveness of these conflicting aims of residential treatment and provides a yardstick for us not only to measure the accomplishments of our own institutions but also to compare our overall correctional system with that of England and other countries.

The wealth of detail in Tutt's description of a single residential treatment center provides background for his sharp criticism of correctional policies that remove a child from his home grounds, give him specialized treatment, and then return him to an unchanged adverse social environment. The contradictions in this policy are fully bared in Tutt's superb analysis of the central dilemma of the physically isolated residential treatment center.

I could not agree more with Tutt when he maintains that we have created these large residential monsters because of the unfounded fears of the community that if these youngsters are allowed to remain in their home environments ordinary citizens and their children will be endangered. The fact of the matter is that there is a very small percentage of youngsters, perhaps three to seven percent, who are so uncontrollable and violent as to represent a danger to themselves or to others and thus require a secure protected environment. It is because of this small percentage that the much larger group of nonviolent youngsters has also been forced into this unnecessary kind of confinement.

As the recent closing down of the large correctional institutions in Massachusetts has already demonstrated, the overwhelming majority, over 92 percent, of young offenders in the Bay State are now doing quite well in a variety of smaller residential homes in or close to their own communities. These results should shatter for all time the myth that it is necessary anymore to "warehouse" these youngsters in isolated settings and accelerate the movement toward working with them in a host of new, smaller settings, in after-school or all-day group homes and centers in or near the communities in which they grew up. This approach affords professionals the opportunity of influencing not only the youngsters themselves but the adverse social environment that continues to trap them in internally defining stereotyped roles by labeling them as deviant. Being in the community and working with the family, the school, the social center, the peer groups and the neighbors, enables us to relieve many of the pressure points that make it difficult for these youngsters to find their way in society.

Tutt's description and analysis of the institution he calls Wellside will surely be regarded as a classic. Tutt is keenly aware that every school is an organic structure, which, like life itself, develops its own rhythms of change and stagnation. This is the single most important perspective that he brings to our understanding of this and other treatment facilities. He recognizes that every child and every staff member produces a ripple which affects every part of the institution and which can, when sufficiently reinforced, bring about qualitative changes in the ongoing life of the center. From this perspective, Tutt attempts qualitative characterizations of the school, concentrating successively on critical aspects of the overall structure and culture of Wellside, while drawing our attention to the continuous modification and adaptation to each other of the different units within Wellside as well as between Wellside and the larger correctional system and community.

Tutt delves deeply into the structure of Wellside, showing us how youngsters and staff are inducted and socialized into the normative patterns of the institutional culture, the various types of child-caring, counseling and teaching procedures used by the staff, and the effects of differences in language and cultural background both among the staff and between staff and youngsters.

It is typical of Tutt that he not only examines in detail the special quality of treatment procedures — for example, group therapy — but always places the particular modality in the context of the institutional setting and shows the interaction between its effects and the way in which the youngsters and staff live out their lives in the institution.

Thus, Tutt traces the development of a Boys Council at Wellside, shows us in detail how it functions, and then provides his own evaluation of the Council's effectiveness, taking into account both its advantages and disadvantages. So there are no cop-outs here. Tutt is not content merely to present a balanced portrait of the institution; he takes the next necessary step of cutting past the neutral observer's position to give us his unique assessment of what each set of pluses and minuses add up to, of their role in this institutional setting, and of their impact upon the youngsters.

Tutt properly devotes considerable space to transcripts of interviews with staff and youngsters. Three representative staff members, counselors who are on the front line and spend the most time in intensive interaction with the youngsters, tell us in their own words about their background and how that influences their outlook and behavior with the boys. We can conclude, in essence, that many of the counselors, some of them quite able, suffer from the constraints of the institution as much as the youngsters do. They fantasize about working with the youngsters in a much more autonomous fashion. This is important because in the coming era of smaller community group homes, it is precisely these kinds of counselors, supported by more specific training in how to work with young offenders, who can be the pivotal linking point in the transition from the larger to the smaller community-based residential setting. We know now that this approach is better for the youngsters, but it is also clear that the staff would feel much more challenged to work toward genuine care and rehabilitation in these smaller settings.

The interviews with the boys are also revealing. They enable us to understand the confusion these youngsters experience in coming to grips with the authority of the courts, the schools and the institution. Their inability to understand how the systems operate and how to function within them contributes to their failures and conflicts about their own best interests. The alienation from adults makes them compulsively dependent upon their peers; thus the norms of the peer group and its leadership become the crucial influence on individual youngsters. Here Tutt confirms my own studies of the peer subculture, showing how the institution nourishes deviant values and works against the rehabilitative efforts of the staff. The youngsters crave affection, are denied these feelings and strive desperately to gain recognition among their peers, many of whom have been given so little throughout their own childhood that they have little to offer to their buddies going through the same searing experiences of institutional life.

A central theme crucial to both staff and youngsters' lives is the role of authority. Too often a coercive or manipulative authoritarian way of life, buttressed by violence or the threat of violence, has permeated the lives of staff and youngsters. A terrible bind is operative here. Young people who are treated in this unidirectional way in time learn to be familiar, skilled and "comfortable" only with aggressive and authoritarian-manipulative forms of behavior. When they are considered "well" enough to be released, they usually continue these patterns of behavior with their offspring, wives and others. The large impersonal treatment center works against developing consensus on more direct personal bases in which people can give feedback to one another without cutting each other down or threatening one another. There is no shortcut to overcoming authoritarian ways. Unfortunately, people within institutions come to accept that way of life as natural. We must experiment, as Tutt so eloquently writes, to find ways to provide more autonomy and to help the staff and youngsters find ways of relating to each other on bases other than violence, the threat of violence, or unrelenting authority.

Tutt's analysis of the role of the headmaster is penetrating. He concentrates on the headmaster's inability to administer effectively because he has so little information about what really goes on in the institution. This situation can be relieved only by expanding both the responsibilities and authority of the staff lower down on the hierarchical ladder. Often this can be done through feedback sessions in small meetings where staff can communicate in more personal face-to-face encounters.

There is no doubt that undergoing this kind of transition will result in some failures, but in the long run it will help create the kind of environment that is so necessary in an institutional setting to combat the authoritarian history and biases of both the staff and youngsters. Tutt quotes my own analysis of these kinds of institutions where I have tried to show how the residents develop a subculture that mirrors the authoritarian regimen of the staff. One actually reinforces the other, and it is the responsibility of the top administrative staff to unwind this vicious circle.

In a compassionate discussion of the role of the housemaster, Tutt points out that the inadequate resources typical of centralized institutions have an enormously detrimental impact upon the interpersonal relationships between staff and youngsters. Staff and youngsters can identify only with a unit small enough to call their own — their own cottage, cabin or wing, which can be a source of support, gratification and integration. The lack of staff means that several counselors are spread over very large and changing groups, so neither youngsters nor staff can begin to develop the unity and identity that comes out of intensive living together for a period of time.

Tutt does not miss a single important structural dimension in his description and understanding of residential home living. He points out, for example, the importance of women, in Britain usually members of the domestic staff, who help promote a more rounded human social environment. Their nurturing is key among these kinds of youngsters, and, one might add, among the male staff as well. However, there are problems related to sexual rivalries among male staff and between older boys and staff.

In these larger institutional settings there is a marked exploitive division between the front-line nonprofessional staff who do most of the work and the professional and administrative staff who are more removed from the youngsters' day-to-day ongoing life. It is my firm belief that both professionals and nonprofessionals, as well as the youngsters, suffer from these psychological walls of separation. This is one more reason it is so important to begin dismantling the large institutions. Only in smaller settings can those who work closely with the youngsters gain recognition and status for the relentness demands they must respond to and the enormous responsibilities they shoulder.

In small-group community homes residents and staff can learn how to give and take in a constructive way. Working together, they can fairly divide the necessary tasks and in the process learn a great deal about each other both as individuals and as members of different cultures. The group can be a powerful vehicle in helping an individual gain a better understanding of himself, recognize some of his own deficiencies, and be able to work on them so that he can begin to change; but *only* if he wants to.

Tutt shows how these primary groups function at Wellside in very different ways. Each group has an organic rhythm of its own and must find its own unique meaning and identity. Often the administrators are so concerned with control and custodial aspects that they are afraid to nurture the kind of openness that permits a group to define its own identity. But the field of human relations is moving in this direction and the specific proposals and recommendations that Tutt makes on the basis of his study are in the best tradition of social science. He points to possibilities that are both visionary and eminently practical.

To his great credit, Tutt is not trapped by the realities of the institution he has studied, but is willing to explore all the potentials in the system that he has looked at in both micro and macro fashion.

Tutt shows us that it is not only the youngsters who are troubled; staff at all levels are deeply engaged in reexamining the forms of institutional behavior that take over on their own momentum and have become in some instances more of a problem than the problems the institution was designed to resolve. The movement away from the large to the small unit is to be applauded, but we have to understand in intimate detail the dynamics of these kinds of settings, and here Tutt indeed has made a signal contribution. His work will stand as a milestone on the road to the creation of new forms of working with individuals, groups, and communities. This study envisages a new practice for us all.

Howard W. Polsky
Professor, Social Science and Research
Columbia University School of Social Work

Preface

This book is about children in trouble – in trouble with society and, in many instances, in trouble with themselves and their families. Their trouble has been so severe that it cannot be contained within the community and consequently they have been deemed suitable cases for residential treatment. The book concentrates on the type of residential treatment our society offers these children, with specific reference to one such establishment, which I have chosen to call Wellside School. This school has been an Approved School for some thirty years and, in accordance with the Children and Young Persons Act, 1969, is now a designated Community Home. Throughout the book I have used the terms Approved School and Community Home interchangeably. This may be confusing for the reader but it is an accurate reflection of the present situation under which Approved Schools are being integrated into the Community Homes system. Many Approved Schools have not yet realised their new status as Community Homes and consequently both terms are still in common usage amongst professional social workers. Although I firmly believe that the change in name and status will eventually mean radical changes in the function and structure of such establishments, at present Community Homes are still strongly influenced and overshadowed by their historical status, which in many cases stretches back over more than a century of service to delinquent children. If the reader finds this labelling confusing, I apologise, but I feel justified since for the general public the term Approved School will have more meaning than its successor, Community Home.

Wellside School, from which I draw many of my examples, is in many ways not a unique school, except in that it has now been singled out for discussion in this book. This possibly exposes some areas of life within the school which both staff and boys would prefer to remain hidden. The exposure is certainly not done from malice, since my association with the school was extremely happy, but from a desire to make public the manner in which the state cares for children and the pressures engendered for the staff doing the caring.

In this book I state that residential establishments are dynamic organisms and this is certainly true of Wellside, which has undergone many radical changes whilst the book was being written. One of the most important of these has been a major change in the management structure of the school. Until mid-1973 Wellside was a voluntary school managed by an order of Brothers, however, at that time the Brothers decided that their resources were insufficient to allow them to continue managing Approved Schools. Consequently, they decided to withdraw from all such schools in England. At the time of writing the new management of Wellside has not been finally established. The book, therefore, takes on special significance since in many respects it represents an historical chronicle as the experience of Wellside has been repeated throughout the country; the passing of the Children and Young Persons Act (1969) has led to the handing over of Approved Schools from the control of voluntary bodies into the control of the local authorities.

There are many people whom I would like to thank for their help in the preparation of this book. Unfortunately many of them will have to remain anonymous for the sake of discretion. First, I would like to thank the managers, staff and boys at Wellside for their willingness to appear as the subjects of the book. In particular I would like to thank the Headmaster and the three staff and boys interviewed in Chapter VI who inevitably have exposed much of their personal lives and beliefs; their personal honesty and integrity are self-evident from the interviews. I would also like to thank Mr. David Burns of Selly Oak Colleges, who kindly read much of the text and gave invaluable advice and comment, and Mr. Ralph Davies and his colleagues in the Social Work Services of the D.H.S.S. for their encouragement and interest in the project. Ron Lyle, now of Edinburgh University, deserves special mention for his help in compiling the statistical information in the appendices.

Finally I would like to thank my wife, Diana, for her patience and tenacity in typing and retyping the text, and her understanding during the moments of disillusionment and depression that inevitably arose whilst working on this book.

CHAPTER I

Who Are the Young Offenders?

Delinquency has always been a part of childhood – the common stereotype of boys stealing apples is familiar to all – and has generally been accepted as such. But the twentieth century has seen the development of an attitude towards childhood in which it is regarded as a distinct and separate stage in individual development. This has meant that the treatment of juvenile offenders has become more humane – children are no longer punished with the same severity as adults. However, the modern view of delinquency implies that at some point a child will turn into an adult offender. The problems of defining this age of responsibility in legal terms are obvious.

The legal system demands clear definitions. At present the age of criminal responsibility is ten years of age in England. Some of the difficulties involved in defining when a child is responsible for his actions emerged during the passage of the Children and Young Persons Act (1969) through Parliament. Originally drafted and passed by a Labour Government, the Act raised the age of criminal responsibility from ten years to fourteen years. However, the succeeding Conservative Government refused to implement the Act completely and would not accept the raising of the age limit. The legal and penal systems employ two age limits when dealing with juvenile offenders. The legal system provides special courts and legal procedures for children between ten and seventeen years. Similarly the penal system provides Approved Schools, which are not part of the prison service, to deal with offenders of this age group. However, within the prison service there is special provision made for offenders up to the age of twenty-one years. For the purposes of this book, the term 'young offender' will be used to refer to children between the ages of twelve years – exceptionally

1

ten years – and seventeen years of age. The term 'young offender' is used interchangeably with the term 'delinquent'.

It was said earlier that crime is a favourite pastime of youth. It is also a source of fascination for many adults, and a social problem on the treatment of which a good deal of human resources have been expended with apparently little result. Do the hundreds of column inches written about crime in the national press reflect its true extent in society today? The true extent of crime is impossible to calculate accurately. It probably lies somewhere within the range defined by the National Criminal Statistics, at one pole, and the alarmist popular press image of widespread violence throughout our cities, at the other. The best we can do is to make an informed guess about the size of the crime problem. The major difficulty involved in assessing the extent of crime is the fact that the majority of criminal acts are never reported to the police. A good deal of pilfering from places of employment is regarded as 'perks' by the employees, and as inevitable by employers; many instances of assault within the family are accepted as part of the parental rights; much criminal sexual behaviour is seen as an inevitable concomitant of the permissive society. Gibson[1] has shown that over fifty per cent of a sample of 'normal' children will report having committed delinquent acts, and not having been caught. The same sort of thing applies to all of us: how many of us, if we examine our lives, could claim to be like Caesar's wife 'above suspicion'?

With this reservation in mind, the Criminal Statistics[2] can now be examined. There are certain problems inherent in the method of reporting Criminal Statistics which further limit their use. First, the Statistics are presented in terms of the legal classification of offences into indictable and non-indictable offences. Indictable offences are usually considered the more serious offences, and include violence against the person, burglary and theft. I will be concentrating on the aspect of delinquency which involves more serious offences. However, the reader should remember that the concept of 'serious' can be inappropriate, since a non-indictable offence can often involve property of greater value, or the risk of violence. For example, driving and taking away a car is a non-indictable offence, although the car may be worth over a thousand pounds and could prove lethal in inexperienced hands. On the other hand, a burglary involving the theft of a small sum like ten pounds would be an indictable offence. Many non-indictable offences, too, are the very acts which the young find attractive, and which are calculated to

2

arouse the indignation of their elders, like malicious damage and insulting behaviour.

The second problem that arises in using Criminal Statistics is connected with the fact that they give the figures of court proceedings and their results. These show the number of occasions on which proceedings against a person were completed, but not the number of different offenders dealt with during the year, nor the number of offences involved. Thus figures indicating 700,000 court proceedings do not mean that there are that many criminals in society. It could just as well mean that 70,000 criminals appeared in court on ten occasions each, and also had a number of offences taken into consideration on each occasion.

During 1971, the latest year for which statistics are available, there were 1,646,081 indictable offences known to the police.[2] As was suggested earlier, the number of offences actually reported to the police may well be the minority of offences committed. In fact, it has been suggested by some criminologists that for every crime known to the police five are unknown. If this were correct, and it is obviously impossible to validate, it would mean that somewhere in the region of eight million offences were committed in 1971. In the same year, of the offences known to the police 45·4 per cent were 'cleared up' by the police. The term 'cleared up' includes those offences for which a person was arrested or summonsed, or for which he was cautioned; those taken into consideration by a court when the offender is found guilty on another charge; and certain of those of which a person is known or suspected to be guilty but for which, for some reason, he cannot be prosecuted (e.g. he may have died). In real numbers this means the police 'cleared up' 747,475 indictable offences out of a known one and a half million, or out of a possible eight million. These figures are important since much weight is given to the deterrent effect of punitive treatment of delinquency. Deterrence is only possible if detection is certain. Fortunately most of society's deviant members are unaware of the Criminal Statistics and detection rates; if they were they would quickly realise that the odds against being detected for committing a crime are very much in their favour. These odds lengthen if they are applied to specific crimes in specific police areas. It is hopeless to expect that would-be criminals will be deterred by the example of their peers being apprehended. Not only do most delinquents firmly believe that they will never be caught but, in reality, it is statistically very unlikely that they will actually get caught.

Society has been faced with a gradual but relentless increase

3

in crime for the past twenty years at least. To call this a crime wave would be inappropriate, since the analogy of a wave suggests that the figures will build up to a peak, the crest of the wave, and then rapidly dissipate themselves. This is an unrealistic expectation as far as crime figures are concerned. The fact is that with increases in population, and the inevitable increase in urbanisation this entails, crime will continue to increase. The actual past rate of increase is difficult to estimate since often developments in legislation, or changes in methods of reporting statistics, will obscure true changes in the facts. For example, the passing of the Street Offences Act (1958) brought about a rapid reduction in the numbers of young women convicted of prostitution, but it is doubtful whether it actually reduced the amount of prostitution in our cities. Nevertheless, in 1950, there were less than half a million indictable offences known to the police; by 1960 this had risen to approximately three quarters of a million; by 1970 these figures had soared to about one and a half million. These figures, despite the shortcomings of official statistics, indicate a steady rate of growth in the number of indictable offences committed in England and Wales over the period. This increase is a true increase, since the rate of growth is much greater than, and therefore cannot be simply explained by, the rate of growth of the population.

Quantitative Aspects of Delinquency

This book intends to examine the treatment offered to boys aged between twelve and seventeen years who have committed a criminal offence. The reader may well ask, why pick on that group, are they really that important? The answer is quite simply that they are important – not because they eventually become adult criminals, in fact many do not, since their persistant delinquency appears to spontaneously remit in the mid-twenties, in most cases with the onset of marriage! They are important because they provide an indicator to the way in which society deals with its deviants, and particularly its deviant children. And, in turn, this is a good indicator of the level of humanity and compassion within that society. They are also important because those members of the group selected by the courts for residential treatment, form a section of our society whose development within a nuclear family is considered to be inadequate. Instead the state has decided to take on the responsibility for their upbringing, and, as will be shown later, the state is not very effective in this 'parent' role. Conse-

4

quently this group poses an interesting moral question to all of us, namely, by what right does the state decide that an individual's upbringing is inadequate, only to impose on that individual an even less adequate system of care?

However, these ethical problems will be touched on later. Let us first consider the size and type of problem posed to society by this group. Of the offences committed during 1971, 19·3 per cent were committed by boys under seventeen years of age. This percentage is much greater than might be predicted from the actual percentage of boys of this age in the total population. In other words, they commit a disproportionate amount of the crime in society. The peak period for delinquent behaviour is in fact between the ages of eleven and seventeen years. It would seem reasonable to consider delinquency as a predominantly male problem since, during the same period, only 2·1 per cent of offences were committed by girls of the same age.

Table I, below, shows the type of offence committed by boys of this age. The percentage of boys for each age group committing the various categories of offence are given. However, it should be remembered that the National Criminal Statistics are only concerned with principal findings of guilty, consequently each offence category should not be taken as a discrete category. In other words, a boy may at any one time have committed offences in more than one category. That this is more than likely is shown in the Appendix where the boys described have rarely committed only one type of offence, but more usually have committed a number of offences that transcend the arbitrary legal categories.

TABLE I

Showing the percentage of boys aged under fourteen years and under seventeen years committed by the courts for various categories of indictable offence.

Offence	Under 14 years	Over 14 years but under 17 years
Violence against the person ...	1·8	6·7
Sexual offences	0·6	1·4
Burglary and robbery ...	47·1	36·4
Theft and unauthorised taking	41·5	47·3
Handling stolen goods ...	5·7	5·5
Fraud	0·6	0·7
Others	2·7	2·0

From these figures it is obvious that the stealing of other people's property, theft of some form, is by far the most popular youthful crime. It accounts for approximately 95 per cent of the crime committed by boys under fourteen years old, and for 90 per cent of the crimes of boys under seventeen years old. The figures for the older age group, not surprisingly, show an increase in crimes of a violent or sexual nature compared with their younger peers. Crimes of this nature would be expected to correlate closely with developing physical masculinity.

Table II shows the way in which the courts dealt with the above offenders.

TABLE II

The court disposal of those boys aged under fourteen years and under seventeen years found guilty of indictable offences.

Court Disposal	Under 14 years	Over 14 years but under 17 years
Absolute discharge	383	694
Conditional discharge ...	4,512	7,315
Supervision order	5,099	8,338
Fine	3,473	17,100
Detention centre ...	Not applicable	1,415
Care order	2,261	3,394
Attendance centre	2,183	3,202

The meaning of these disposals and their effectiveness in terms of the control of further deviant behaviour are examined in Chapter III. Table II, however, clearly shows that in the vast majority of cases the magistrates apparently did not feel that the offences committed were of sufficient seriousness to merit the removal of the offenders from society. It appears that the magistrates were quite content to deal with the vast majority of the cases by allowing the offender to remain in society. This is important since Short and Nye,[3] working in the United States of America, and using a self-reporting scale of delinquency with the pupils of normal high schools and those of a penal training school, found that, although both groups admitted a surprisingly high number of delinquencies, a larger number of the penal training school inmates admitted having committed more serious offences. This study, along with several others, suggests that the more persistent offenders do eventually end up in institutions. However, the studies also suggest that the delinquent/non-delinquent dichotomy that is popularly assumed to exist is in fact not a dichotomy at all but a continuum; that delinquency is a normal part of adolescent behaviour but becomes viewed as abnormal only when the adolescent is continually appearing in court and, as a result, is institutionalised.

Although for adolescent boys theft is the most popular crime, there are some variations through time of the pattern of offences committed. For example, for 1970 to 1971 the number of boys found guilty of indictable offences under fourteen years declined by 16·1 per cent, and for under seventeen years declined by 2·4 per cent. However, this decline can present a falsely optimistic picture, because during the same period offences of violence against the person increased by 13·5 per cent and 25·7 per cent respectively. (Incidentally, percentages themselves can distort the figures if small numbers are involved, as in this case, in which these increases in real terms were forty cases and six hundred cases respectively.) However, in the same period sexual offences declined by − 24·1 per cent and − 12·6 per cent for under-fourteen-year-olds and under-seventeen-year-olds respectively. It is a matter of debate whether a decrease in sexual offences represents an 'improvement' in the crime figures or not, because there was also an increase in violent offences. These figures do mean that any analysis of criminal behaviour is inevitably very complex. Simplistic generalisations need to be treated with caution and examined closely because they often turn out to be meaningless. For example, the popular general view that crime is increasing needs to be qualified by careful definition of types of crime committed, of the sex of offenders, and their ages.

All these percentages and figures are not only confusing, they are also depressing. So it is important that they be kept in perspective. This can be achieved by comparing offenders with their peers. Thus, for boys under fourteen years in 1971, the number of offenders per 100,000 population of the same age group was 1,177 − a little over 1 per cent of the age group came before the courts; for boys under seventeen years the number of offenders was 4,184 per 100,000 − or a little over 4 per cent of the age group − a considerable increase but still very much a minority. For girls the figures are 188 per 100,000 and 516 per 100,000 respectively. Again girls in trouble measured as a proportion of their peers are in a very small minority, much less than one per cent.

7

It is also important to get the significance of Approved Schools in proportion. The media do tend to exaggerate their position in society. In 1971, there were estimated to be approximately 2·5 million boys between the ages of ten and seventeen years in England and Wales. Of these, some 7,000 were in Approved Schools. These figures speak for themselves but their importance can be underlined by pointing out that, at the same time, there were some 160,000 children receiving education within residential boarding schools, schools for the maladjusted, educationally subnormal and private boarding schools. Of this number, approximately one in five, or 32,000, were supported by finance from their Local Education Authorities. Approved Schools, then, form a minority group among the state's institutions responsible for children.

Qualitative Aspects of Delinquency

So far this chapter has been concerned with quantitative aspects of delinquency, but this obviously does not present the whole picture. We will now examine some of the qualitative aspects of the problem, in order to try to gain some insight into how it feels to grow up in such a way that almost inevitably you come into conflict with the law. We already know that the chances of becoming delinquent are increased if you are an adolescent boy. There are also other important factors which can be identified. In 1951, Ferguson published a detailed study of the homes and social backgrounds of the entire group of Glasgow boys who left school in 1947 at the earliest permitted date.[4] This fascinating study allowed for the collection of important comparative data. In his follow-up study Ferguson was able to identify those boys who became delinquent and then compare their backgrounds with their equally disadvantaged peers in order to identify what specific conditions led to the development of delinquency. His first finding was that delinquency increased as the type of district in which the boy lived deteriorated. So not only is the adolescent boy likely to live in an urban community, he is also likely to live within the slum or 'twilight' area of that community. As well as the siting of the boy's home, the actual size of his home appears to be important. Ferguson found an important relationship between the degree of overcrowding within the home and the incidence of crime. This factor obviously correlates closely with the next: that of family size. Inevitably the larger the family, the more likelihood of overcrowding within the home. He found that the larger the

8

family from which the boy was drawn, the higher the incidence of delinquency and, in general, the greater the proportion of boys with more than one conviction.

But what do these rather cold facts mean in human terms? It means that many of the children who became delinquent are brought up in the most appalling housing conditions, conditions which are often so desperate that they are hard to imagine. Their houses are not only without baths, but completely without sanitation, perhaps a shared cold tap and shared toilet, occasionally no toilet at all, an old dustbin in a stench-ridden backyard serving the purpose. These houses are continually damp; their decorations are impossible to maintain because wallpaper readily peels off and plaster crumbles. Some houses remain standing in pairs, the sole survivors of a demolished and devastated area from which all other families have been rehoused. But no-one is willing to rehouse this particular family because they have been labelled a 'problem family', having fallen behind in their rent. There are houses with more windows broken than intact; inside the rooms are dark and dismal because the cardboard and corrugated iron which have replaced the windows allow no light or air inside.

Cooking in one of these houses is attempted on an open coke fire, because the gas or electric cooker is no longer serviceable: perhaps the supply has yet again been discontinued through failure to pay the arrears, or because the meter has again been broken into, an habitual hazard in the area. What furniture exists is secondhand, badly damaged and abused through years of misuse by many children. The house creates an impression of barrenness since ornaments and pictures, carpets and clocks, are luxuries which are missing and yet create a home. The bedrooms are crowded; there are a large number of children; all the boys have to sleep in the one room and when the eldest comes out of care, or home for the weekend, the younger boys have to share the same bed. Huddled together on a misshapen mattress and covered by an assortment of ragged, threadbare blankets and old coats, sleeping together is an uncomfortable ordeal. In addition many of the siblings will be enuretic.

But then living crowded together, so many in such a small house, has always been uncomfortable, privacy is a luxury enjoyed by other families, you have always known the family intimacies; heard dad come home drunk, beat mum, then vomit and force his undesired sexual attentions on her; you just laid in bed and pulled the covers a little further over your head, bit the blanket and swore that when you were old enough to thrash your dad, you would do so whenever he abused your mum that way. Daytime meant escape from the overcrowding into the streets and demolition sites which were your playground. The street littered with bike tyres and broken glass was your territory, and you guarded it by spitting at the cars of policemen or social workers who were the only people with occasion to enter your territory. Playing in the street was good fun: chasing each other, throwing bricks, getting dirty and rummaging about the demolished houses, occasionally stumbling on people's discarded personal belongings – old photos or old clothes which could be taken home as mementoes. On some really lucky occasions some bits of lead pipe may be unearthed or a copper fitting, this was real 'tat' part of the adult world to be taken down to the scrap yard and traded in for money which could be squandered in the corner shop on sweets and cigarettes. The woman in the shop knew you were too young to smoke but you always said they were for your dad and she didn't bother then, just let you have them. Cigarettes were important because they made you feel big, just like your big brother who was allowed to smoke at home, and who was already fourteen, and came home weekends from wherever it was he got sent away to. But at the moment you are not allowed to smoke at home, so with your mates you sit in one of the demolished houses in a small circle, passing around the cigarette taken from a packet of five Park Drive. Lately, though, you have been getting bolder and the other day smoked a fag whilst walking around the shopping centre and despite your worries no-one had taken any notice, let alone stopped you. That afternoon you had dared your mate to steal a packet of cigarettes from the shop, and he had, which meant you had to steal a matchbox car from Woollies in reply to his dare. That evening when you got home you had been a bit worried but then your mum had hardly noticed your return being too busy with all the babies and as usual you had gone down the Chippy's and bought some chips and come home and ate them in front of the television.

Ferguson's study showed that the incidence of delinquency was relatively low among the children of skilled workers; it was higher among the children of unskilled workers, and especially where there was a parental history of unemployment. He also found that the fact that the mother was out at work had little influence on the incidence of delinquency. The former finding is particularly important in the light of later research, most

10

notably that of the Newsons[5] on the methods of child rearing practised by the different social classes.

The Newsons found quite marked differences in the child-rearing practices of the working and middle classes, even early in life. These differences were particularly marked in those areas of social life which may be assumed to be connected with subsequent delinquency. The most notable areas were: the control of aggression, the rights of property, and the establishment of authority. They found that, for the child in the unskilled working-class family, aggression was often fostered and indirectly encouraged. The child playing with others in the street was expected to stand up for himself and if hit to hit back. The middle-class child was more protected from his peers, and if an altercation occurred he expected, and his expectation was usually confirmed, that his parents would intervene and resolve the argument at a verbal, as opposed to physical, level. Although differences in social class attitudes towards the concept of property were not so marked, the Newsons did find some evidence that middle-class parents showed a greater respect for their children's property than their working-class counterparts. For example, the middle-class mothers placed greater emphasis on apologising to the child after breaking one of his possessions. It would seem that the result of this process would be to encourage the child to respect other people's property. More important, perhaps, are the class differences in telling the child the truth. Mothers are the first and most important authority figure with which the child comes into contact, consequently from his experience of his mother's behaviour in this authority role the child will generalise about other forms of authority. The Newsons found that working-class mothers were more likely to make threats which were impracticable, e.g. threaten to give the child to the bogeyman, or tell downright lies, e.g. say that babies are dug up in the garden, than middle-class mothers. They conjecture that the child eventually reaches an age when he recognises that his mother's statements are no longer true, and that this experience may well give him a jaundiced view of the honesty of all authority figures. The Newsons' work on the differing child-rearing practices would seem to throw considerable light on the kind of upbringing which a future delinquent child is most likely to receive.

Ferguson's figures on schooling and employment are depressing, as we have now come to expect: 'Delinquency was found to increase as scholastic ability deteriorated. Delinquency increased with irregularity of school attendance, especially in the

11

small group where the irregularity was due to truancy. Delinquency rates were high during school life among boys who were employed out of school hours before they left school. Among boys who did not wish to take up skilled work on leaving school the incidence of delinquency tended to be high, as was also the case where some reason other than the interest of work was given by the boy for his job preference. High delinquency rates were associated with frequent change of employer.'

These factors are clearly evident in Barry Hines' novel, *A Kestrel for a Knave,* which tells the very moving story of a disadvantaged boy and his interest in a hawk. In the following conversation between the boy and his schoolmaster Ferguson's findings are given a very real context:

'An' at home, if owt goes wrong on t'estate, police allus come to our house, even though I've done nowt for ages now. An' they don't believe a word I say! I feel like goin' out an' doin' sommat just to spite 'em sometime.'

'Never mind, lad, it'll be alright.'

'Ar it will that.'

'Just think, you'll be leaving school in a few weeks, starting your first job, meeting fresh people. That's something to look forward to isn't it.'

Billy looked past him without replying.

'Have you got a job yet?'

'No, Sir, I've to see t'youth employment bloke this afternoon.'

'What kind of job are you after?'

'I'm not bothered. Owt'll do me.'

'You'll try to get something that interests you though?'

'I shan't have much choice shall I? I shall have to take what they've got.'

'I thought you'd have been looking forward to leaving.'

'I'm not bothered.'

'I thought you didn't like School.'

'I don't, but that don't mean that I'll like work does it? Still, I'll get paid for not liking it, that's one thing.'

This is a truly human expression of the statistics on school and work failure which correlate so highly with delinquency. Let us try to get a more detailed picture of the school and work life of our hypothetical delinquent. In his life school is an irrelevant, but apparently necessary, annoyance. . . .

At first school had been good, you had looked forward to going to

12

primary school, like your big brothers and sisters. Also the primary school was near home and you had enjoyed it because all your family and friends went. The first three or four years had been really good fun and then words like 'eleven plus', 'backward', 'remedial', 'behind in his reading', had begun to filter into teachers' conversations and somehow, intuitively, you knew that they were talking about you. You were then transferred to a class which everyone said was the bottom stream. You knew it meant you were thick, but it didn't matter because there was almost a tradition that your family were in that class. You hadn't played truant much at primary school, there were the occasional days off but your parents had known about those – they had been during the periods when your dad was out of work and then none of the family had got up at all in the mornings. There was no reason then to play truant since you got on well with most of the teachers at school. One in particular had taken quite an interest in you ever since you had gone for P.T. with him and he had noticed the weals on your back – from the beating your dad had given you the night before, with his belt. After that incident your dad, who had promised to stop beating you, had in fact stopped sending you to school until the marks of his beating had healed. One day when you were about eleven everybody at school had been excited and talked about examinations, but this hadn't seemed to apply to you, and yet soon after you were told you were going to the secondary modern school.

It was that year that things began to go wrong, you clearly remember the first day at secondary school; it had proved disastrous. First, when you turned up all the other kids seemed so big, and so many of them and, what's more, they nearly all had a uniform on. That's when it started; this teacher, called your form master, had asked 'Where's your uniform, sonny?' You had wanted to explain that with your dad out of work and the debts at home your mum just had not had enough money to buy one, but somehow you were embarrassed in front of all these new kids in your class, so you had just blurted out 'I must have lost it.' All the other kids had found that funny and burst out laughing, the form master, however, had not and it was then that he made a strange comment 'So you are Johnston's brother, Eh! Regular little comedian, little tearaway eh! But I am warning you now, sonny, you had better not give me as much trouble as your brother did, because I'll have you for it.' You were not certain what this meant but you knew it wasn't good. From that point on school and you began

13

to part company almost by mutual agreement. You had attended regularly at first but then there was an incident with one of the teachers who said you had nits in your hair. That one had really upset you and made you cry in front of the class. That in turn had made you angry, and so you swore at the teacher and ran out slamming the door. Next day when you went back to school they had caned you. You had got knocked about a bit at school, always getting the slipper off the P.E. master because you didn't have a games kit or towel for a shower, and he just refused to listen when you had tried to explain you couldn't afford it.

Anyway by this time you were staying up late at night and doing a paper round early in the morning which meant that you felt too tired to go to school. What is more you weren't allowed to smoke there either, you had to sneak in the toilets or behind the bike sheds. It seemed daft because Mum knew you smoked but didn't do anything about it. Gradually you attended school less and less, and instead spent most of your time down the 'caffs' in the High Street playing the pin ball and fruit machines. There were five or six of you from the same school who met there most days and had a laugh. The biggest of which was lunchtime when some of the school teachers out shopping saw you sat in the 'caff' but never seemed to do anything about it. At the back of your mind you believed they were glad to see you out of school whether legitimately or not. Your little group – it wasn't what you would call a gang – liked a laugh now and again, they really enjoyed messing about. You spent most of your time talking about records, clothes and football, sometimes adults commented that you seemed to have a language of your own but it wasn't really, it was just the names of the latest clothes: Crombies, Channel-seams, Tonik suits, records and football heroes. One bloke in the 'caff', a bit of a brain, a college student, had commented that it sounded like *A Clockwork Orange* and read you a bit which went: 'Our pockets were full of deng, so there was no real need from the point of view of crasting any more pretty polly to tolchock some old veck in an alley and viddy him swim in his blood while we counted the takings and divided by four, now to do the ultra-violent on some shivering starry grey-haired ptitsa in a shop. . .' You forget how it had continued but it hadn't made sense to you anyway. Even if it had, it wouldn't have helped because by now you had given up reading, you had never really learnt to read properly, but it didn't matter you could get by and enjoy life anyway. Soon it would be time for you to

14

get a job and go out to work. In some ways that appealed to you because at last it meant you were an adult, a man, and anyway it would mean the School Board Man, or the Educational Welfare Officer as he called himself, would give over coming round in the mornings to fetch you out of bed. People occasionally talked about jobs but never very seriously, sometimes Mum said 'One day you'll have to get yourself a job, can't do nothing all your life.' But that was about it. Anyway you would get a job, go labouring probably, everybody said that paid good money. What else was there you could do? By now you knew you were no good, a failure, probably always would be. The only thing you were good at was football, mainly because you played all day over the park instead of going to school. You had tried to get a regular game by joining the local youth club but all the other kids had seemed stuck-up some how and although they recognised you as a good footballer they weren't too keen on having you in the team because your kit was a bit scruffy. Also you were supposed to turn up for the other activities, but you didn't fancy those much because they were organised by adults and adults always wanted to push you around – parents, teachers, police, they were all the same.

Ferguson states, 'Where boys were members of such groups as Boy Scouts, Boys Brigade, social and welfare clubs the incidence of crime in post school years was appreciably lower than among lads who were not members of such groups, and the number of lads with more than one conviction was small.' These findings were supported by Morse's study of *The Unattached*. Her most telling comments are given in the conclusion in which she states: 'It has been noted repeatedly that one of the most serious problems of the unattached, whether they recognised it or not, was the absence in their lives of sympathetic adults to whom they could turn for understanding and advice. For a variety of reasons customary sources of adult counsel – home, school, the church, or youth clubs – were not being used by these young people.'

In this chapter I hope I have been able to describe in some measure who the young offenders are and their life style. I now want to move on to examine the hypotheses which have been advanced by adults to explain the development of delinquent behaviour amongst these young people.

CHAPTER II

Why Are They Offenders?

Attempts to answer this question fall into three broad categories (a) the physiological theories: the offender is not physically normal; (b) the psychological theories: the offender is not mentally normal; (c) the sociological theories: the offender's social environment is not normal. Needless to say none of these theories attempts to define 'normal'.

(a) Physiological theories

This group of theories initially stemmed from the work of Lombroso who claimed that many criminals had physical anomalies which bore a striking resemblance to some of the physical features of primitive savages and apes. This theory now appears rather bizarre, but its basic premise – that criminals are genetically 'subnormal' – underlies many other theories in this group. For example, many psychologists, led by Burt,[1] claimed that delinquents were less intelligent than their non-delinquent peers. Later research by Woodward[2] and the McCords[3] suggests that this is in fact not true. Similarly Lombroso's premise underlies much of the work done on the incidence of brain damage amongst delinquents,[4] and the emphasis placed by some researchers on the incidence of electroencephalogram abnormalities amongst delinquents.[5]

The latest example of this school of theories is to be found in the work on chromosomal abnormalities amongst a delinquent population.[6] It has been found that there is a raised incidence of Kleinfelter's Syndrome, i.e. males with an extra male chromosome, amongst the inmates of special security hospitals and psychopathic units.[7] Along with the chromosome abnormality, abnormalities of personality have been noted, i.e. greater aggression and asociability. The inference is drawn from this that the chromosome abnormality leads to abnormal social behaviour

16

in the adult. This work only explains the existence of a small number of very disturbed criminals. The incidence of Kleinfelter's Syndrome among special security hospital inmates is only two per cent of the total hospital population.

Finally, included in this group of theories, is the research by the Gluecks[8] who, following Sheldon's system of somatotyping, claimed that a large proportion of delinquents were of the mesomorphic (athletic) body-type, and of the personality type shown by Sheldon to be related to this. However, against this finding must be set that of Ferguson[9] who, although not directly concerned with somatotyping, found the majority of delinquents to be of smaller physique than their non-delinquent peers.

The physiological school of theories has produced a large body of evidence suggesting that an inherited factor may influence the behaviour of a small proportion of serious and persistent offenders. However, in relation to juvenile delinquency, with which this book is concerned, the evidence for the importance of heredity as a major factor in causing delinquency would appear to be negligible.

(b) Psychological theories

This group of theories can be divided into the *psychodynamic* and the *behaviourist* theories.

The *psychodynamic* theory first, put forward by Freud, suggested that the delinquent suffered the most excruciating neurotic conflicts brought about by the struggle between his *Id* (instinctual drives) and his highly developed *super-ego* (conscience) – the latter being the result of an extremely strict and repressive upbringing. This theory is applicable to only a small proportion of delinquents. The vast majority appear to observers to be free of debilitating anxiety and guilt.

A more likely psychodynamic theory was put forward much later.[10] This suggested that delinquents had a poorly developed super-ego which left the Id unrestrained and unmodified by social considerations, making the individual unloving, guilt-free, impulsive and aggressive. The lack of super-ego development was brought about by child-rearing practices characterised by poor emotional relationships between parents and children. The erratic, inconsistent attitudes of the parents lead to neglect and rejection of the children. This theory came much nearer to what was known by observation about the personality and family background of the delinquent.

The *behaviourist* theories stem mainly from the work of

17

Eysenck,[11] who claims delinquents are of the Extrovert Personality type. This personality type arises from the structure of the reticular formation in the brain. In the Extrovert the reticular formation produces greater cortical inhibition than in the Introvert, making the Extrovert less aware of stimuli and therefore less easily conditioned to any task than the Introvert. Eysenck and his fellow workers produced a large quantity of experimental evidence to support this theory. They related these findings to delinquent behaviour by postulating that the socialising of a child is the result of a long-term and sophisticated conditioning process carried out by the parents and society. This being so, the Extrovert, not being easily conditioned, fails to become adequately socialised and exhibits anti-social or delinquent behaviour.

This theory fails to give a totally adequate explanation since, as West[12] has shown, the excess of Extroverts predicted by Eysenck did not occur in a prison population which was studied. Similarly, since Eysenck claims Extroversion to be normally distributed within the total population, it would be predicted that only the small percentage at the extremity of the distribution would demonstrate poor conditionability and subsequent delinquency. However, as Gibson's[13] study indicates, delinquency is a common part of the maturing process for a large percentage of 'normal' boys.

The psychological theories would appear to be very similar to the physiological theories in that they both go some way towards explaining the existence of a hard core of recidivists but cannot explain the high frequency of delinquency amongst juveniles.

(c) Sociological theories

The proponents of sociological theories regard delinquency as a 'social disease' rather than individual deviancy. This approach does not exclude the physiological and psychological approaches since it could be argued that certain social conditions give rise to an increase in physiological abnormalities amongst children reared in such conditions or, alternatively, that the child-rearing practices of certain social classes are likely to increase the incidence of deviant personalities amongst those classes.

The purely sociological approach is expressed in work such as that of Sprott,[14] who states: 'What we hope to show is that the bulk of delinquents come from certain households and localities, which present traits which are conducive to delinquency and traits which are social rather than psychological.' He continues by introducing the concept of the 'Delinquent Subculture'. This is usually found within the 'twilight' zones of urban areas, the deteriorating slum areas well known to the social welfare agencies as breeding grounds of delinquency, mental illness, alcoholism, prostitution, etc. The social theorists maintain that an individual growing up within this subculture accepts the prevailing standards and norms of his own subculture which are opposed to those of the rest of society.

Mays,[15] working in Liverpool, went as far as to state, 'In the majority of cases delinquency can be regarded as a phase of normal development within a particular evironmental setting.'

However, Stott[16] throws doubt on the efficacy of the concept of the 'Delinquent Subculture' as a total explanation of delinquency by showing that delinquents, whether in high delinquent areas or low delinquent areas, showed greater maladjustment than their peer controls living in these same areas. But he also found that there were more maladjusted boys living in high delinquent areas than low delinquent areas. He concludes, 'The city-ecology proves unfavourable for human development as far as the least privileged sections of the urban population are concerned, the resulting maldevelopment takes the form of the physical, intellectual or emotional impairment of a certain number of individuals.'

Apart from the theories concerning the 'Delinquent Subculture' there are a large number of sociological theories of delinquency concerned with the phenomenon of social stratification. These arise from the observation that delinquency rates are higher amongst the working classes than in the middle-class population. This relationship does not appear to have been artificially produced by greater police vigilance in working-class areas, or by the power of the middle-class parent to intervene on his child's behalf, thereby avoiding court action, but is a genuine relationship which needs an explanation. Explanations for it are numerous and for the sake of brevity are listed below with little comment:

Explanations for the lower rates of delinquency amongst middle class families	*Explanations for the higher rates of delinquency amongst lower class families*
(a) The strict middle-class socialisation of the child inhibits the display of overt aggression by the child.	Erratic and punitive lower class socialisation results in a lack of internal controls.

19

(b) Middle-class parents closely supervise the activities of their children, who therefore do not have the opportunities for exploring deviant behaviour patterns.

Lower-class parents exercise little supervision over their children, who are therefore free to explore deviant behaviour.

(c) The parent-child interaction in middle-class families is egalitarian and affectionate, resulting in the child's ability to develop and maintain affectional bonds with others.

Working-class parent-child interaction is characterised by authoritarianism and a lack of affectional identification, resulting in an inability to develop and maintain affectional bonds with others.

(d) The love withdrawal socialisation techniques of the middle-class inhibit overt aggression within the child. Middle-class values exclude overt aggression, thrills, destructiveness and other focal concerns that promote illegal behaviour.

The focal concerns of lower-class culture include overt aggression, destructiveness, etc., that promote illegitimate behaviour.

(e) Children in middle-class neighbourhoods have neither the incentive nor the opportunity for playgroups to become gangs.

Children in disorganised areas lacking both social and material assets have both the incentives and opportunities for their playgroups to become gangs.

(f) Middle-class children have access to subcultures of religious, learned and professional people, whose values and behaviour reflect wholesome creative expression within rules.

Lower-class children have access to the subcultures of criminals, etc., whose values and behaviour contradict and subvert conventional legal and social norms.

(g) Middle-class children are most likely to obtain legitimately the material goods valued in our culture.

Lower-class children are least likely to obtain legitimately the material goods valued in the general culture.

(h) Since educational institutions are founded on middle-class values, middle-class children are least likely to be frustrated by an inability to meet institutionalised needs.

(i) Delinquency laws reflect middle-class perspectives and, therefore, tend to penalise behaviour different from the characteristic middle-class patterns.

(j)

Unsettled neighbourhoods lacking a sense of community and continuity are more characteristic of lower-class than middle-class areas, the children in such areas are less easily controlled.

Delinquency and achievement-motivation

My own research suggests that the causes of delinquency can be explained by a combination of psychological and sociological theories. My research[17] indicates that an important personality trait, that of *achievement motivation*, is often lacking amongst delinquents because of a combination of child-rearing practices and social environment. Achievement motivation has been defined by David McClelland,[18] the psychologist who has most extensively explored it, as 'competition with a standard of excellence'. He states, 'Most people in this world, psychologically, can be divided into two broad groups. There is that minority which is challenged by opportunity and willing to work hard to achieve something, and the majority that really does not care all that much.' This view of McClelland seems to have particular relevance to delinquency since much previous research on the subject has centred on employment and achievement. For example, Ferguson showed that unemployment or a rapid succession of jobs were contributing factors to reconviction of delinquents. Similarly Wirt and Briggs[19] found that, regardless of social class, delinquent-prone personalities had lower actual achievements, i.e. years at school, school record, job level, than a control group. Also Cohen[20] claimed that the working-class boy, being denied access to legitimate means of achievement through the educational system, seeks an alternative status within

21

a gang. Cloward and Ohlin,[21] Downes[22] and Yablonksky,[23] although offering modifications of Cohen's theory, all saw the frustration of the achievement drive as a crucial factor in the development of delinquency.

The research was begun by giving a standardised interview to thirty adolescent boys with known criminal records who, at that time, were either in a unit for psychopaths or in a Remand Home, having been sent by the courts for Approved School training but awaiting placement. The results of these interviews were compared with interviews with thirty matched controls drawn from a local factory and secondary modern school. The standardised interview used meant that a content analysis could be carried out, and the boys' replies to questions about their status expectations, job aspirations and other topics likely to be linked to achievement motivation could be scored and the two groups compared. The results of this initial pilot study proved hopeful in that they supported the hypothesis that delinquents had lower levels of achievement motivation than their non-delinquent peers. In order to test out this hypothesis more objectively and on a larger scale a test was produced and standardised on a large sample of secondary modern school boys. When this test, which became known as Story Test (B), was shown to be a valid and reliable measure of achievement motivation amongst working-class adolescent boys, it was used as an instrument for measuring the different levels of achievement motivation amongst delinquents in an institution and their controls. This was done by surveying the ninety-four boys who constituted the total population of a Home Office Approved School and comparing their results with those obtained from boys attending a local secondary school. The controls were matched for age, intelligence, social class and religion – all factors which had previously been shown to have a significant relationship with both delinquency and achievement motivation. On obtaining the results of the survey a more detailed interview study was carried out. Each of the eight highest and eight lowest scoring subjects from both the delinquent and control groups were given a standardised interview. This meant that a total of thirty-two boys were interviewed.

The results of the survey, which have been published in full elsewhere,[24] showed that the delinquents had significantly lower levels of achievement motivation than their controls. This finding was firmly supported by the results of the interviews. The interviews with the control group were examined in depth since the lowest scoring controls were much closer in scores to the delinquent group than to their non-delinquent peers. In fact, when the low scoring controls were questioned about aspects of their life which might have connected them with delinquency, it was found that they were deviant in many ways. For example, of the eight lowest motivated controls (who were supposed to be 'normal'), four admitted having committed fairly serious delinquent acts, whereas none of the high scoring controls did. Four of the low scorers had received corporal punishment at school, whereas none of the high scorers had. Six of the low scorers admitted to regular truancy, whereas only one of the high scorers did. Four of the low scorers knew a friend who had been in trouble with the police, whereas only two of the high scorers knew such friends. So, from the interviews with the controls, it appeared that the individual's level of achievement motivation is an important factor in the causation of delinquency, and that boys with low achievement motivation from a 'normal' group are more likely to express deviant or delinquent behaviour than their more highly motivated peers.

The interviews with the institutionalised delinquent group were examined in detail in an attempt to elucidate those factors differentiating delinquent high achievers from delinquent low achievers. The factors considered were: 'broken' home, family size, father's occupation, incidence of delinquency amongst siblings, age of first court appearance, number of court appearances, and previous institutional experience. Of the seven factors considered none differentiated. High and low achievers did not differentiate significantly on the basis of any one of the seven factors. However, there was some evidence to suggest that previous institutional experience lowered an individual's level of achievement motivation. This finding is very important, as will be seen in the next chapter when the effectiveness of residential treatment of delinquency is considered.

LOW ACHIEVEMENT AND CHILD-REARING PRACTICES
From this experimental evidence it appears that the majority of delinquents have lower levels of achievement motivation than their non-delinquent peers. It is possible to explain how this difference arises by examining the different child-rearing practices of the families concerned, and how these practices lead to the acceptance of delinquent or non-delinquent roles.

Winterbottom[25] has pointed out some of the factors involved in producing achievement motivation in children. She obtained achievement motivation scores from a small sample of boys aged between eight and ten years. She also interviewed the boys'

23

mothers about their child-rearing practices. Winterbottom found high and low scores correlated with certain child-rearing practices, the most significant being a concern with early independence training, i.e. the age at which the mother expected her child to know his way around the city, try new things for himself, do well in competition, make his own friends, and attain other similar goals. She also found that mothers of high achievers were more likely to use primary physical manifestations of affection such as cuddling or kissing as rewards for meeting their expectations.

Winterbottom was concerned with long-term parental behaviour resulting in high or low achievement motivation, whereas Rosen and D'Andrade[26] were concerned with the parental behaviour which accompanied the child's involvement in an achievement task. Their sample consisted of forty boys, twenty high and twenty low achievers. The boys, whilst blindfolded, had to construct a tower of irregularly shaped blocks in the presence of their parents who were allowed to advise the boys. The parents were asked to estimate their sons' performances, having been informed that the average performance was eight blocks. The parents of the high achievers established higher levels of aspiration, as measured by the estimated number of blocks, than the parents of low achievers. The parental behaviour during the task was summarised as follows:

Whilst the blindfolded boy worked at the precarious business of piling blocks, parents urged him on, gave him directions, exploded in happy laughter when he succeeded. But there were differences in the character of this behaviour for the parents of the two kinds of sons. Parents of high scorers, especially the mothers, worked up a lot of hopeful encouraging tension over the performance and when it went well poured out happiness and warmth. This is a result consistent with Winterbottom's findings that mothers of high scorers reward accomplishment with hugs and kisses. For low scoring sons there was something distinctive in the father's behaviour. He tended to give them specific directions, and to make decisions for them, to urge them on and react with irritation when things did not go well. It appears that a father who is domineering and authoritarian in behaviour is not likely to have a son with high achievement motivation.

Sprott et al[14] in their study of 'Radby', interviewed working-class families and graded the households on a five-point scale according to the degree of social competence and attitudes displayed. They placed the problem families, chronic social misfits who made no attempt to keep up with accepted standards of honesty, hygiene or household management, in Grade I. The socially aspiring families, people who wanted to better themselves and openly condemned the fecklessness and immorality of their 'deviant' neighbours, were placed in Grade V. The majority of the ordinary working-class families who believed in 'live and let live', trying to preserve reasonable standards themselves while remaining on friendly terms with their neighbours, went into Grade III. Sprott then attempted to highlight the differences between the families at the extremes of the scale.

The Grade I and II families lived in an atmosphere of squalor, possessions were untidy and uncared for, and individual ownership was not prized. The families' leisure was largely taken up with gambling. Irregular sexual unions were frequent and openly discussed, this was reflected in the interviews with the boys:

Quote from Case Study
Are your Mum and Dad at home? Me Dad is back home again now, you know he ran off and left us for three or four months, well he's come back now.

Quote from Case Study
Where is your Dad? I ain't seen him since last Christmas.

Minor acts of physical aggression – mothers clouting children, siblings fighting – were frequent. Parents tended to quarrel openly and violently; the father left the responsibility of bringing up the children entirely to the mother. Children were given pocket money at random to spend as they liked and they were not encouraged to save. This data is supported by the Newsons[28] who found that working-class children received more pocket money than middle-class children, received it in a more random fashion and were compelled to save less. Neither were they encouraged to use their leisure time constructively and they often felt that youth clubs, etc., were too strict or too 'stuck up'.

In comparison, the Grade IV and V families, who were comparable in terms of occupational status and income, took pride in their possessions, and their houses and gardens were carefully tended. They showed little interest in gambling and apparently adhered to a conventional code of sexual morality. They attempted to refrain from hitting their children in temper and parents tried to conceal their disputes from their children. Parents shared responsibility for the children and gave pocket money regularly, encouraging the child to save his money, and

25

use his leisure time constructively by attending youth clubs and church organisations.

It is obvious from the descriptions given above that the child-rearing practices of the Grade I and II families are diametrically opposed to those of the high-achieving families. They place no stress whatsoever on the value of personal possessions, self-denial, hard work, or thrift. They embody more physical punishment than physical praise. They also involve two other important factors, as Wilson[29] showed: the fathers associated with this type of child-rearing practice were more likely to be absent or have poor work records. This would deprive the boys in the family of a successful achievement model with which to identify. Also within large, neglectful, disrupted families the children are more likely to seek to establish their identity within the peer group through playing in the street. The peer group is unlikely to be concerned with social aspirations, occupational status, etc., thereby depriving the child of the learning situation of listening to parents' conversations about what the father did at work.

The differing life styles of the family types described by Sprott lead to different social behaviour by the children. The incidence of convictions for delinquency amongst the Grade I and II families (fifteen out of seventy-two families) was much higher than that amongst the Grade IV and V families (none out of fifty-nine families). Also it is important to note that twenty-two of the seventy-two Grade I and II families and none of the Grade IV and V families had children with poor educational records. These findings are compatible with what is known about the typical delinquent family, which lives in the overcrowded, urban slum area; has a large number of children; exhibits a good deal of parental disharmony – to the extent of the marriage 'breaking up' completely; and suffers severe material hardship, exacerbated by the parents' gambling and drinking habits. In most instances the only method of control demonstrated by the parents in the delinquent family is random physical punishment.

The child reared in the life style of the Grade I and II family is likely to be both a low achiever and a delinquent. My research showed these two things are closely inter-related.

LOW ACHIEVEMENT AND EDUCATIONAL PERFORMANCE

Achievement motivation has always been conceived of as an enduring personality trait, which is laid down within the framework of the child's personality at an early age. The evidence indicating that delinquents were low achievers early in life can be drawn from studies of their academic attainments. The sample of delinquents in my study had an average reading age of approximately ten years. This cannot be attributed solely to low intelligence, and it suggests that the boys were under-achieving when they were in junior school. This finding is supported by Ferguson.[9] Therefore it appears that low achievement motivation is manifested in the form of academic under-achievement prior to the appearance of delinquent behaviour, the peak age for which is fourteen years.

A possible casual relationship between low achievement motivation and delinquency can be seen in the fact that even in the junior school the low achiever is regarded by teachers as a failure; this is supported by the findings of the Plowden Committee.[30] The method of selection for secondary school reinforces this view of the low achiever by labelling him an elevenplus failure. Also, in the competitive atmosphere of secondary school the low achiever is reinforced in his role as a failure through the structure of the school and attitudes of the teacher;[31] this can be seen in two quotes from boys interviewed:

How did you get on with the teachers? I got on well with the History teacher, he was straightforward with you, tell you things not like all the others trying to act posh and all this.

Could you talk to the teachers? Never used to talk to no-one about nothing.

The low achiever by this age is also more aware of the occupational world beyond the school and he realises that he is likely to be a failure in that world also, since he has little of the skills or motivations required to succeed in it.

An observed situation may clarify this point. In an Approved School under study the local Youth Employment Officer was invited to conduct a one day 'teach in' on careers for the boys of school leaving age. Part of the programme was a film strip illustrating four major types of work: work with hands, work with machines, work with people, work with paper. The Officer worked through the strips talking about the jobs involved. Work with hands was concerned with occupations such as joinery, bricklaying, watch repairing, etc. Work with machines was concerned in the main with skilled or semi-skilled jobs in light engineering. Work with people on the whole meant unskilled jobs as shop assistants. Work with paper was concerned with office jobs. The Officer, on reaching the latter 'white collar' group, stopped the film strip and said to the boys, 'These are mainly office jobs, you won't be interested in any of these as most of you won't be able to get them, so I won't bother to show you them.' This is a clear illustration of society placing the low achiever in the role of 'social failure'. The Officer, by his statement, denied the boys right of entry into the status occupations.

Given that the low achiever is forced by society to adopt the role of social failure, why should he opt for the 'delinquent solution'? Although the low achiever is not concerned with job satisfaction or occupational status he is concerned with material gain. This is, in part, a reflection of his early environmental background in which pocket money was given randomly and was to be spent in a purely hedonistic fashion. It is also, in part, a reflection of the society to which he belongs, in which the values of materialism are continually stressed through the mass media. The 'teenage' culture is predominantly a materialistic culture based on clothes, cars, pop records, etc. To quote the Beatles: 'Give me money, that's what I want.' This need for material gain was observed in the interviews with both high and low achievers and is the main reason given by low achievers for not wanting to accept apprenticeships.

Quote from Case Study
Would you like to do any apprenticeship? Don't know.
Why not? Don't know really, because you don't get into the money until you're older, and you might not live that long.

Quote from Case Study
Why wouldn't you like an apprenticeship? Well I'd have a go but I don't think I would stick it, because the money would be no good. I'd start off with about £4 and at seventeen I'd still only be earning £5 and say I give me Mum £3 or £4, I'd only have a £1 left. I want a job that pays well, about £9 or £10 at sixteen, you can get that with the Midland Dairy for a six day week.

The low achiever needs material gain and yet is required by society to adopt a role which makes it impossible for him to satisfy this need through legitimate means, and so he turns to the delinquent solution.

Quote from Case Study
What trouble were you in? Well me Dad used to earn a lot of money being a fitter, and he had this accident, a two ton trailer fell on him and he was in hospital a long while, and when he went back to work he was only earning about sixteen pounds a week and before like he had been earning a lot and I was getting a lot off him. But then when I didn't get as

28

much I started to steal and that and it just went on from there. First time I nicked some toys from Woollies.

This theory would go some way to explaining why criminality has been increasing most rapidly in some of the most affluent countries, as we saw in Chapter I.

Delinquency and the material culture

Criminal statistics provide some evidence in support of this theory, showing that over seventy-five per cent of juvenile crime is some form of larceny. From studies of juvenile case files, it can be demonstrated that the larceny is often of a hedonistic type, namely the theft of clothing, records, sweets, bikes, cars, etc. – the type of property the boys admire and are unable to obtain legitimately. It can be said, then, that delinquents have a high need for material goods but a low achievement motivation which prevents them from satisfying this need through legitimate means, therefore, they opt for the delinquent solution and satisfy the need through illegitimate means.

The above theory can only provide an explanation for low achieving delinquents who commit offences of larceny and, although this is a sizeable proportion of the delinquent population, it is not the total, so other factors must be involved. A possible explanation for delinquency amongst high achievers is that their frustration with society leads to aggression against society. This hypothesis is the basis of Cohen's theory,[20] in which he has argued that the working-class boy, being deprived of status and material wealth in comparison with his middle-class peers, and also being denied access to legitimate means of achievement through the education system, seeks an alternative status within the gang. The gang, by engaging in persistent attacks on middle-class property, enables the deprived boy to hit back at the society which has frustrated him. Studies of gang behaviour have supported Cohen's claim that the gang is a source of status: 'Despite his deficient personality, the sociopathic youth gets caught up in the sweep of a culture dominated by the drive for success and achievement. Deprived of "social ability" and generally blocked from achieving through normal channels many sociopathic youths find the violent gang a most adequate device for successful self-gratification.'[23]

Cohen claims that this theory explains the high incidence of delinquency among working-class boys, the apparent aimlessness of many delinquent acts, and their occurrence within a group setting. Stephenson and White[32] whilst agreeing with Cohen's basic hypothesis, offer an alternative interpretation in terms of distributive justice.

A working-class boy perceives that the rewards of middle-class boys, whom he regards as having the same investment as himself, are much greater. They live in better homes, have more possessions and greater status and generally achieve where he does not. Society flouts the rule of distributive justice; the working-class boys experience anger and resentment. Delinquent acts are attempts to restore justice. For example cheating and stealing may improve the rewards of working-class boys. In addition malicious damage, in the form of destruction of middle-class property, increases the costs of the middle class and, thus, increases lower-class net outcomes.

They proceeded to test this hypothesis experimentally, and their results showed that unjustly deprived boys are willing to take part in delinquent activity (cheating) more frequently than the justly deprived group. In this study deprivation could be conceptualised in the following fashion:

A high achieving boy coming from the 'twilight' area of a city is deprived of opportunities to succeed. Within the twilight areas facilities for education, medical treatment, and social activities are all markedly limited. Given that his range of experience is limited in comparison with boys from middle-class homes, his range of job opportunities is also going to be limited. This is illustrated by the case studies. When asked the question, 'What job would you choose if you could choose any job in the world, regardless of passing exams etc?' with few exceptions the high achievers chose jobs within Classes IV and I, namely jobs within their own range of experience.

Quote from Case Study
If you could choose any job at all what would it be? I'd stay where I am because I know I can enjoy it because I'm enjoying it now. So if I had a choice I'd stay where I am.

Quote from Case Study
If you could choose any job at all what would it be? Any job? I don't know, motor mechanic I think. I've always wanted that, always been interested in motors, and that. I think I'd enjoy it.

In fact only two boys suggested a white collar occupation. This kind of data is reinforced by the conclusions arrived at in

30

a report by the Working Party of the National Youth Employ-ment Council: [33] 'Virtually all the occupations in which the young disadvantaged person covered by Y.E.C. Survey had been employed or sought employment fell into the manual/unskilled category.'

Thus the high achiever desires success but is denied success in terms of status by society, he becomes frustrated with society and eventually aggressive towards it. There is some limited evidence to support this hypothesis. The most likely form for aggression against society to take is that of malicious damage to property. The interviews in my research described above showed that more high than low achieving delinquents were convicted of malicious damage. These figures were not significant but the trend was for high achievers to demonstrate greater aggression against society than low achievers. Although the evidence is suggestive it is in fact very limited since the high achievers who committed malicious damage had also committed larceny, indecent assault, robbery with violence and house breaking.

From the experimental results of this study it would appear that Cohen's theory explains only a minority of delinquent acts. Since the majority of delinquents are not motivated to achieve they are not frustrated by the limited outlets for achievement offered by society, and thus do not need to vent their aggression against society. However, they do have the same desire for material goods as their non-delinquent peers. This division – into frustrated high achievers, and non-motivated low achievers – is ignored by Cohen who refers to status, achievement and increased material rewards as parts of a unitary factor.

The division is half-recognised by Stephenson and White, who claim that working-class boys can restore justice either by improv-ing their rewards through theft, or by increasing middle-class costs by maliciously damaging property. My research, supported by the Criminal Statistics, indicates that the deprived low achiever, who is in the majority, chooses the former means of restoring justice, whereas the deprived high achiever chooses the latter.

Delinquency and Deprivation

Perhaps in this last sentence the crucial factor for the causation of delinquency has been touched on, namely deprivation. Delin-quency is basically caused by deprivation. It may be deprivation within the home – deprivation of the attention and affection of one or both parents through death, illness or marital disharmony.

It may be emotional deprivation caused by parents who are no longer able to love because life has destroyed that ability within them through their own damaged childhood, through the grind of poverty, unemployment and poor housing, or through their desperate attempt to escape via alcohol, or the gambler's dreams of quick riches. It may be deprivation of the opportunities to play and develop as a young child. It may be deprivation of opportunities for creative work or thought because the only work available is mindless, ritualistic toil at a conveyor belt.

Some readers may protest that deprivation does not exist in Britain in the 1970s, but deprivation is relative and this is a basic fact in a capitalist economy; there must be the 'haves' and 'have-nots' or the economy will stagnate. Advertising continually creates demand, often for unnecessary, superfluous items. Thus while a minority of families enjoy central heating, two cars, colour television and dish washers, the minority at the other extreme struggle to find accommodation with a bathroom and indoor W.C., when the 'have-nots' help themselves to goods displayed in shops and garages – goods which politicians and advertisers tell them they have rightful access to – then society proscribes them as deviant and delinquent.

Material deprivation is not the only kind of deprivation which exists in our society. This poem was written by Adrian Mitchell on seeing a case reported in the *Guardian,* on 17 October 1972, in which a mother had allowed her child to starve to death:

SAW IT IN THE PAPERS

I will not say her name
Because I believe she hates her name.
But there was this woman who lived in Yorkshire.
Her baby was two years old.
She left him, strapped in his pram, in the kitchen.
She went out.
She stayed with friends.
She went out drinking.
The baby was hungry.
Nobody came.
The baby cried,
Nobody came.
The baby tore at the upholstery of his pram.
Nobody came.
She told the police:
'I thought the neighbours would hear him crying
And report it to someone who would come

And take him away.'
Nobody came.
The baby died of hunger.
She said she'd arranged for a girl
Whose name she couldn't remember,
To come and look after the baby
While she stayed with friends.
Nobody saw the girl.
Nobody came.
Her lawyer said there was no evidence
Of mental instability.
But the man who promised to marry her
Went off with another woman.
And when he went off, this mother changed
From a mother who cared for her two-year-old baby
Into a mother who did not seem to care at all.
There was no evidence of mental instability.
The welfare department spokesman said:
'I do not know of any plans for an inquiry.
We never became deeply involved.'
Nobody came.
There was no evidence of mental instability.

Children who suffer such extreme cases of deprivation do not
always die, but they grow up into adolescents whom society
brands as 'disturbed', 'delinquent', 'deviant' and society then proceeds to deprive them of their liberty.

CHAPTER III

How Are They To Be Dealt With?

The Objectives of Residential Treatment

The term 'to deprive them of their liberty' is emotive but very accurate since this is exactly what happens to the small, 'hardcore' of persistent juvenile offenders. If the past decade, from 1959 to 1970, is examined (and this period is particularly relevant since some of the sections of the Children and Young Persons Act, 1969, were finally implemented on 1 January 1971), it is found that the number of children in Approved Schools remained fairly constant but with an overall slight downward trend. In 1959 there were 8,022 children in Approved Schools; in 1961 there were 8,377; in 1964 there were 8,698; in 1967 there were 8,213; and in 1970 there were 7,227.[1] All these figures were recorded on the 30th of June in each year, so overcoming the problem of seasonal variations in number. The numbers grew annually until a peak was reached in 1964 since which time they have decreased. And yet, as was shown in Chapter I, the figures for criminal offences generally over this period have increased rather than decreased. The idea of treating the offender within the community appears to have begun to gain ground about 1966, and has been greatly encouraged by the Children and Young Persons Act, 1969. So that in April 1972, fifteen months after the introduction of the Act, there were 5,986 children in Approved Schools, compared with over 7,000 immediately before the Act (the figure was 6,557 on 31 March 1973 so that even then the numbers were beginning to increase).

However, these figures may well prove to be extremely misleading in retrospect since the fall in the Approved School population did not mean an increase in community care but merely a transfer of numbers from one type of residential treatment to another. For example, the latest available official statistics show that the Borstal population of fifteen-year-olds expanded considerably in 1971, when the Act came into force, rising from 189 at the end of 1970 to 253 at the end of 1971. Similarly during this period a section of a senior Detention Centre was converted for use as a junior centre accepting 14 to 17-year-olds; this increased the capacity of such centres by 25 per cent, or by over six hundred places. When it is considered that children are sent to Detention Centres for either three or six months, thus allowing for a 'through-put' of over a thousand additional offenders, whereas the Approved School, whose average length of stay is seventeen months, has a much lower 'through-put', it may prove that the number of children receiving residential/custodial experience of one form or another is not in fact declining but that changes in magisterial procedure are merely causing a reallocation of numbers.

This view is certainly supported by statements from Magistrates which appeared in a series of articles on the Children and Young Persons Act, in *The Times* newspaper.[2] One Magistrate said, 'You cannot give these children therapy if they are not there to receive it.' The implication of this is that the children need to be placed in secure accommodation of some form. This comes from the same source, 'As Professor Winifred Cavanagh, Chairman of Birmingham Juvenile Magitrates, has put it "The panel felt it of the greatest importance that children should be prevented from adding to their criminal experience after the first finding of guilt, if they were not to mature into hardened criminals. Adequate provisions must be made in the plans which are now being drawn up if the work of the juvenile court was not to be, to a considerable extent, defeated." Professor Cavanagh believes, in particular, that it is essential that some secure places should be provided to house young offenders.'

It begins to appear that there is a small but persistent number of young offenders that society at large, and as represented by the Magistrates' Courts, is not prepared to tolerate, and in consequence their removal from the community into some form of residential establishment is prescribed. If this is so, it is important to examine the kind of treatment offered to those offenders who are not removed from society, since those who require residential treatment do so because other forms of treatment have been offered and have failed. It also inevitably affects the expectations and attitudes of the child coming into residential care and also, to some extent, affects the expectations and attitudes of staff offering such care and, by implication, places constraints on the type of care which they can offer.

35

Juvenile Court procedures for dealing with delinquents

The Juvenile Court has a range of procedures with which it can deal with young offenders. This range in reality operates on a form of sliding scale, rising with each court appearance. The scale of procedures was, with minor variations, constituted as follows: absolute or conditional discharge; a fine; probation or supervision order; Attendance Centre; Detention Centre; Fit Person Order; and Approved School order; but this has been changed by the passing of the Children and Young Persons Act. These alternatives would probably be interspersed with periods in remand homes. The operation of this unofficial scale meant that the child had often become habituated to treatment by the time he arrived at Approved School. It should be noted that there are in fact wide regional variations within the range of court disposals. For example 26 per cent of first offenders aged 12-13 years received conditional discharges from the Juvenile Court in Glasgow, whereas only 4 per cent of their contemporaries in the Metropolitan Police District received the same disposal.[3] Similarly there are wide differences in the way one court deals with boys of varying ages. In the study quoted, Glasgow Juvenile Court granted absolute discharges to 42 per cent of 8-11 year-old first offenders, but to only 26 per cent of 12-13 year-old first offenders. Despite these variations an analysis of boys' previous histories as shown in a later chapter does demonstrate a reasonably clear and consistent pattern of disposals.

ABSOLUTE AND CONDITIONAL DISCHARGES:
This disposal is basically the issuing of a severe warning to the first or minor offender by the court. The conditional discharge is a warning which is taken into consideration if the child reappears in court at a later date charged with further offences. This disposal can be effective with an offender who is apprehended in an act of 'normal' adolescent delinquency. The presence of the police and the court appearance can impress upon the child the severity with which the community views his behaviour.

FINES
There are limitations on the level of fine which may be imposed on juveniles. In most instances, especially with younger juveniles, the fine is likely to be paid by the parents, in fact this is always the case in children under fourteen. Fines are effective because they often serve to shock the parents into facing up to their responsibility towards the child. However, with the severely

deprived families from which most persistent delinquents come it may well only serve to reinforce the anti-authority attitudes of the parents and cause them to further reject their offending offspring.

PROBATION

A probation order involved the child being placed under the direct supervision of a probation officer for periods varying between one and three years. The probation officer was expected to establish a case-work relationship with both the probationer and his family and, through counselling, help the child and his family resolve the interpersonal problems which were assumed to have given rise to his delinquency. The probation officer could also liaise with the child's school and might later help him find employment. In general he was expected to be an understanding, supportive adult acting as a stabilising influence in the child's damaged life. Unfortunately, this was rarely more than a hope since the probation officers nearly always had extremely heavy case loads and supervision often became nothing more than a monthly visit by the probationer to the probation office for a ten minute interview. Probation officers found that, because of pressure of work, they often only saw their clients when crises arose and then it was often too late. It is very difficult to evaluate the success of probation since there are inevitably so many variables present, not the least of which is the quality of the supervision given. Any institutional treatment can be assessed in terms of current behaviour control and post-institutional behaviour (and the closed penal establishment has, as shall be seen later, extremely good current control, but little post-institutional effect). However, probation orders alone had very poor current control; the young offender was still living within the community and was open to the total range of family, peer group and environmental pressures. Hammond[4] found that probation was no more effective than imprisonment when expected reconviction rates after both types of treatment were compared. And both markedly ineffectual in contrast with fines, the effects of which exceeded expectation for all groups of offenders.

ATTENDANCE CENTRES

Attendance at an Attendance Centre was one of the new forms of treatment for young offenders introduced by the Criminal Justice Act 1948. It is important because it is perhaps the first overtly punitive experience the young offender may receive, but it is also the fore-runner of the intermediate treatment envisaged in the Children and Young Persons Act (1969). The court is able to commit a young offender to an Attendance Centre for between six and twenty-four hours, depending on his age. Attendance Centres are usually run by the police on Saturday afternoons and attendance is compulsory. It is therefore non-custodial but punitive in that it was deliberately established to deprive the offender of his leisure. Supporters of Attendance Centres also claim that it teaches boys a constructive use of their leisure time by offering classes in physical education, motor maintenance, road safety, first aid, etc. Attendance Centres have two major advantages over other forms of treatment; they are inexpensive to operate, and reasonably effective with adolescents with very limited delinquent history.[5] Their major disadvantage is that attendance is impossible to enforce. Once a youth has been committed to a centre, if he fails to attend on three consecutive occasions he is returned to the court for further action. The amount of non-attendance at these centres constitutes a serious disadvantage of this method of treatment, affecting approximately 15 to 20 per cent of those youths committed.

FIT PERSONS ORDER
A Fit Person Order, which obtained until the child reached eighteen years of age, was aimed primarily at those children whose delinquency was obviously the result of deprivation of reasonable care and affection, and who therefore needed personal attention rather than punishment. The 'fit person' referred to in the title was, in the majority of cases, the local authority Children's Department. Their actions varied but usually involved removing the child from home and placing him or her in a foster home, children's home or, where appropriate, a hostel. Although this action was not seen by the authorities as punitive it was often interpreted as such by the child, as will be illustrated in later chapters. The importance of this disposal lies in its historical influence, since it does in fact form the basis of the more recent legislation dealing with delinquent children.

DETENTION CENTRES AND APPROVED SCHOOLS
These institutions represent the first extensive experience of custodial treatment for most young offenders. However, they are based on entirely different precepts and offer very different treatment. The Detention Centres are administered directly by the Home Office Prison Department and in consequence have much in common with the Borstal and prison system. They are highly disciplined and overtly punitive, and were originally devised as a

'short, sharp, shock' – boys being sentenced for periods of three or six months. They are secure establishments; staff wear uniforms as do the inmates; the day consists of hard work, physical education and militaristic discipline. These institutions often build in minor irritations in order to increase the punitive element; for example, smoking is strictly forbidden, television watching is closely limited, no sugar is allowed in tea, etc.

The success rates of Detention Centres have never been very impressive especially as they have a comparatively naive intake in that the delinquent experience of the offenders is not as great as those entering Borstal.[6] And yet they have often been strongly advocated as the solution to juvenile crime – basically because they satisfy the retributive/punitive element in society. In the eyes of society, and of many magistrates, they offer a system in which 'young thugs are made to conform'. In this they are regarded as an adequate replacement for National Service. However, for many of the damaged children who pass through them, they merely underline the experience of deprivation which society in general seems to offer them.

Approved Schools are the subject of the rest of this book and will consequently be discussed at length below. However, it is important to point out that a child was sent by the Juvenile Court to an Approved School under an approved school order. Basically this stated that the child would be detained within an Approved School for not less than six months, and not more than three years. He could be released at any time during this period at the discretion of the school's managers.

BORSTAL TRAINING
Borstals offer custodial treatment to juvenile offenders over fifteen but under twenty-one, who must be sentenced by the Higher Court, often on the recommendation of the Juvenile Court. They, like Detention Centres, are administered by the Prison Department of the Home Office, and consequently have much in common with their fellow establishments. Borstals vary enormously, from open to secure establishments, to those offering special facilities for boys of above average intelligence and/or those with psychiatric difficulties. Later in this chapter the effectiveness of Borstal training will be examined along with that of Approved Schools.

CHILDREN AND YOUNG PERSONS ACT 1969
This then was the situation before 1 January 1971, when the Children and Young Persons Act 1969 came into being. This

Act, which was hailed by many as the most significant break-through in the treatment of delinquency in this country, altered the position radically. Unfortunately the Act itself came at an inopportune moment in two important ways. Firstly, between the passing of the Act and its implementation there was a change in government, and it soon became obvious that the new government had no intention of fully implementing certain sections of the Act, in particular those sections raising the age of criminal responsibility. Secondly, the effectiveness of the Act was dependent in many ways on the local authority Children's Department since it was based on the assumption that trained and experienced social workers could offer suitable care to children in trouble and thereby allow them to remain in the community. However, some of the main provisions of the Children and Young Persons Act (1969) were implemented on 1 January 1971, and in April of the same year the Children's Departments underwent a massive and far-reaching upheaval as the Local Authority Social Services Act 1970 came into being. This Act established generic Social Services Departments in the Local Authorities on the lines of the Seebohm Committee recommendations. These departments are responsible for an extremely wide range of human problems including mental health, physical handicap, old age, and children in trouble. The Children's Departments were incorporated into the new Social Services Departments and much of the expertise they had developed was diluted throughout the whole range of social services. A situation developed, and is as yet unresolved, which caused *The Times* to comment, 'This meant that the methods and continuity of the Children's Departments were broken at exactly the time the Government needed their expertise most. It has been estimated that now less than 50 per cent of the official workers charged with the delicate task of coping with often deprived and neglected children in trouble are trained for the job.'

Despite these difficulties in implementation, the Act offered many unique opportunities to break with tradition and develop novel approaches to treatment. These are spelt out in detail in the White Paper *Children in Trouble*[7] – which the Act closely followed:

> The aim of the changes described is to increase the effectiveness of the measures available to deal with juvenile delinquency. Effectiveness means helping children, whose behaviour is unacceptable, to grow up, to develop personal relationships, and to accept their responsibilities towards their fellows, so

that they become mature members of society; in some cases it also means firm control of anti-social behaviour. In order to achieve this aim it is necessary to develop further our facilities for continuing treatment, both residential and non-residential. Increased flexibility is needed so as to make it easier to vary the treatment when changed circumstances or fuller diagnosis suggest the need for a different approach. Organisation changes are also desirable so as to provide a setting for closer cooperation between the services concerned.

Three main changes in the power of the juvenile court will be made for this purpose. First, the approved school order will be abolished; an order for the compulsory removal of a child from home will in all cases take the form of a committal to care of the local authority. Second, provision will be made for the development of new forms of treatment, intermediate between supervision at home and committal to care. Third, all supervision of children under 17 will be by the local authority.

The first two changes had the greatest impact on the treatment of young offenders as it existed previously. The abolition of the Approved School order has meant that the distinction between deprived and delinquent children is also no longer legally recognised; the old distinction between a Fit Person Order and an Approved School Order distinguished the types of treatment offered to the two groups. Under the C.Y.P. Act (1969) all children in need will be placed in the care of the local authority, who will be responsible for placing the child in the residential establishment best able to meet his or her need. This statutory action embodies the concept that delinquents are in fact deprived children and should be treated as such.

The White Paper continues,

Local authorities will be responsible for developing a comprehensive system of residential care and treatment for the children received or committed into their care who are not boarded out with foster parents. . . . A considerable variety of provision will be needed within this system, which will be described for legal purposes as the public system of community homes for children and young persons. The needs of the great majority of children will be met by homes which, as now, will care for them as nearly as possible in the same way as a good family, making use of the education, health and other services which are generally available. . . . Even in the long term, however, there will remain a substantial minority of children whose needs cannot be met in this way. There will thus be a continuing need for some establishments providing education and treatment on the premises. In some cases this will be with the limited aim of preparing for an early return to the use of the normal services. In others the first priority will be a therapeutic approach to social education. Some of these children, particularly those whose behaviour is most difficult, will also need control in secure conditions, or very specialised forms of treatment.

Thus the White Paper acknowledges society's need for institutions in which to place those members whose behaviour deviates from the cultural norms to a degree where society is no longer able to tolerate it. The residential institution, therefore, acts as a social control, guaranteeing that extremes of behaviour are removed from society, thus re-establishing equilibrium. The White Paper, although recognising that the child has become deviant through deprivation, then attempts to remedy this deprivation by removing the child, rather than rectifying his deprived environment. In other words, the victim of social ills is further 'scape-goated', thereby avoiding the need to examine and redress those social ills. This argument will be extended later, but it is necessary first to briefly discuss the intermediate forms of treatment.

Returning to the White Paper, *Children in Trouble*:

Intermediate treatment will fall into two categories. The first will involve temporary residence, attendance or participation, for a period or periods totalling not more than one month during each year of supervision. . . . Possible instances are attendance for a number of evenings, or weekend afternoons or entire weekends, at a place of training, treatment or recreation; or taking part in a specified total of hours or days in some organised work project, or social service or adventure training. There are many other possibilities. The aim will be to bring the young person into contact with a new environment and to secure his participation in some constructive activity.

The second category will involve residence at a specified place for a fixed period of not more than three months, beginning within the first year of supervision. . . . This type of treatment will be available for use where the basic need is for help and supervision in the home, but a short period away from home also seems desirable.

Intermediate treatment should prove to be one of the most interesting developments in the treatment of young offenders, since for many years workers in this field have stressed the need for some form of intermediate treatment between supervision in the home and residential treatment. The C.Y.P. Act (1969) should give social workers the opportunity of treating the offender while he still retains his links with the community, if he does not actually remain within it. At present intermediate treatment is very much in embryo and is scarcely beyond the planning stage, and it will be many years before plans are implemented, established and evaluated.

Community Homes

However, to return to residential treatment: basically the new Act has abolished the Approved School Order, and consequently Approved Schools. Instead the Juvenile Court places the offending child in the care of the local authority, who then place the child in whatever situation it deems suitable, one of the situations being a Community Home, the successor of the Approved School. What should Community Homes offer? The Department of Health and Social Security in their booklet, *Care and Treatment in a Planned Environment,* have attempted to answer this question. They state, 'The aim, in our view, should be to provide community homes whose scope is such that a child's entire needs may be provided for within the treatment programme offered by the home to which he goes.' Of meeting the child's needs the same publication continues,

> For healthy development it is important not only that a child's basic physical needs should be met adequately, but also that he should experience satisfying personal relationships, both with adults and with other children, and should have the opportunity for satisfactory identifications. It is through this experience that a child can grow up with a realisation of his own worth. He needs the underlying sense of security that it gives if he is to learn to cope with his impulses, to be able to postpone immediate gratification and to develop self-discipline. A child must feel safe enough to make mistakes, and to be able to learn from them without undue anxiety; he has to be helped to appreciate the needs and feelings of others, and to learn to share and to give and thus acquire habits of socially acceptable behaviour. He needs opportunity to acquire skill in making choices and must be encouraged to develop a concept of right or wrong. A growing ability to communicate with others and an increasing sense of satisfaction through achievement are fundamental to healthy development.

Certainly if this is the new task for Approved Schools it is very different from that stated in 1963, seven years earlier:

Approved schools are residential establishments approved by the Secretary of State under section 79 of the Children and Young Persons Act 1933 for children and young persons whom the courts consider to need not only removal from home but also a fairly long period of *residential training*.

Treatment – or Punishment?

The definition of Community Homes is also far removed from the public's expectations of Approved Schools, as expressed by the Magistrates' Association when referring to disciplined residential treatment. This division of opinion between those ultimately responsible for the management of Community Homes and those committing children to their care has led Greenwood-Wilson to write,

This is the logical muddle which confronts the residential social worker in his daily task. They are called upon to be agents of punishment in so far as they are the visible persons who deprive the child of his or her liberty, freedom of will, and customary environment; and at the same time they are the agents of therapy who, by fostering a close relationship and applying the best teachings of social science as they understand it are striving to cure the psychological illness which they believe to be the cause of the delinquency. I am suggesting that this basic paradox inevitably militates against sucess.[8]

This is the crucial conflict within any institution dealing with deviant members of society, and particularly within these dealing with offending children since society also has expectations that adults should protect and care for children. The conflict is twofold and although the two parts are not mutually exclusive they are perhaps better considered separately. The dilemma is one of custody versus rehabilitation, and punishment versus treatment.

The Effectiveness of Residential Treatment

The conflicting aims of residential treatment provide us with a pointer towards the way in which we should measure its effectiveness. It is essential to remember that a number of aims are involved because this is not a unitary task. Effectiveness can be measured in four major ways: first, if a major component of

44

residential treatment is custody, as I hope I have shown, then it is possible to examine effectiveness in terms of the current behavioural control of the institution; secondly, if rehabilitation is a major task, the 'success' rates, or the quality of post-institutional behaviour, can be examined; thirdly, if punishment is a significant factor, any detrimental outcome from the institutional experience will be relevant; finally, if treatment is important, it is possible to examine differences between overtly treatment-orientated and traditional authoritarian regimes.

CUSTODIAL EFFECTIVENESS

As research on absconding illustrates Approved Schools latterly have not been very good at providing custody. In 1968 there were approximately 11,000 abscondings from the 121 Approved Schools. There is little doubt, too, that these figures are now sadly out of date and that the present figures would prove to be very much higher since, as Clarke and Martin show,[9] the figures for abscondings over the previous twelve years until 1968 showed a clear and accelerating growth curve. The transition to Community Homes with their stress on openness reduced supervision and regimentation, and more involvement with the community will no doubt increase the opportunities for absconding and consequently the absconding rate.

Absconding is extremely important since the child is placed into the *care* of the institution and each absconding poses very dangerous and specific risks to the child. As will be shown when the population of a specific school is examined, persistent absconding is the most frequent reason for a boy's transfer to another institution, and each transfer underlines to the child society's rejection of him, and increases the probability that he will fail to adjust to society. Each time a child absconds he is 'at risk': both boys and girls are sexually exploited, and they are more likely to commit further offences, often to survive, stealing food, money and clothing. Clarke and Martin see delinquency as learned behaviour and in this context absconding becomes of vital importance since each offence committed in the course of absconding further habituates the child to delinquency. They state:

> If the suggestion that absconding predisposes a boy to further offending after release is correct, and the evidence in its favour is strong, absconding from approved school assumes an even more serious perspective. For if absconding is largely determined by the factors in the school environment, then it follows

that the environment in some schools is leading more boys (and possibly more girls as well) to fail than might have been the case had they been sent to other schools.

The ineffectiveness of Approved School custody may well be working to the detriment of the child. It is important that effective custody should not necessarily entail closed, secure accommodation. Probably the most effective custody is that established when small groups of children live in close contact with adults and develop close relationships with them, as well as being under their close supervision, in comfortable congenial surroundings. To introduce this type of custody generally would necessitate greatly increasing the staff/child ratio and increasing the material resources available to schools. The best deterrent to absconding on a cold winter's night (January is the peak season for absconding) is to be able to sit in a nice warm room and make a pot of tea with an adult who is interested and concerned with your welfare and is prepared to talk to you.

It can be stated that current behavioural control is not effective in open Approved Schools at present. This statement is reinforced by the fact that in the year 1970, when there were approximately 7,150 boys in approved schools, 558 boys were dealt with by the courts for offences committed during their period of Approved School training. This figure is a gross underestimate of the number of boys actually committing offences during their residential treatment, since it does not include boys being given a conditional discharge by the court, nor boys who are not taken to court by the police on the understanding that the offence w̶ ̶ be dealt with by the internal discipline of the school. Th ̶ two latter methods of dealing with boys who offend whilst a̶ ̶ dy in an institution are by far the most common.

REHABILITATION 'SUCCESS RATES'
The effectiveness of rehabilitation or post-institutional behaviour can be estimated by the well-known 'success rates' of Approved Schools, Detention Centres and Borstals. The 'success rate' is based on the number of children found guilty of an offence during a three-year follow up. For Approved Schools in the last five years for which statistics are available, from 1963 to 1967, the figures make depressing reading; the average percentage of reconvictions for boys was 66 per cent and for girls 22 per cent. The figures for Detention Centres and Borstals are no more cheering – 61 per cent and 68 per cent respectively for boys. Figures for girls from such establishments are not very meaningful

because they are a comparatively small number. The effectiveness of institutional rehabilitation for boys can claim success rates of the order of only 30 per cent to 40 per cent, and this on the very dubious assumption that all boys were otherwise certain of reconviction. In other words, the 30 per cent to 40 per cent may well represent a spontaneous remission of delinquent behaviour rather than the success of residential treatment. The success rates – perhaps more accurately described as failure rates – of residential treatment have been severely criticised by those working in the field. They argue that immediate success rates do not matter and that the important aspect of success is whether ultimately the child will become a responsible adult able to care for his own children, and thereby avoid the perpetuation of delinquency. Alternatively, they argue that if a boy is admitted for offences of violence and after treatment is convicted of petty larceny he appears statistically as a failure but he may be less of a threat to society and therefore a success.

These arguments are obviously valid but they are irrelevant to a consideration of the effectiveness of the rehabilitation factor in residential treatment. For boys it can be said that the effect of residential treatment in reducing delinquent behaviour is minimal. For girls, however, its effect is much greater. Why this should be so is as yet unknown, but it may well prove to be unassociated with the type of residential treatment given and have more to do with the earlier marriage of girls.

DETRIMENTAL PUNITIVE EFFECTS
The punitive factor in residential treatment tends to manifest itself in detrimental effects on the child resulting from the residential experience. Mapstone of the National Children's Bureau, recently described the characteristics of 314 children who had spent part of their life in the care of a local authority or voluntary organisation children's home.[10] She found that these children as a group were at a disadvantage compared with the general child population in almost every respect, e.g. general health, physique, educational progress, and a wide range of other factors, such as ability to make positive relationships, ability to adapt to environment of home, school and neighbourhood, emotional stability, ability to give as well as take. Her survey was on children's establishments designated as non-punitive and caring by society which still appear to have a devastating and disastrous effect on the children in their care – although it should be stated that the influence of inherited factors cannot be ruled out.

A survey of drug taking among girls, carried out at Cumberlow Lodge Remand Home,[11] showed that girls who had experienced periods of residential 'care' were more likely to become drug dependent than their controls. An eight-year follow up of upward of 900 young offenders (equally representative of Detention Centres, Borstal and prison) showed that the best predictor of failure in terms of reconviction after release was either number of previous convictions or amount of previous institutional treatment.[12] In other words, the paradoxical situation has arisen that the more residential treatment a child gets because he is deprived or delinquent, the more deprived or delinquent he is likely to become. During the past decade a good deal of subjective and objective research has brought out the debilitating and damaging effects of institutional treatment on the individual. There is no deliberate policy of punishment on the part of the institutions but unfortunate side effects develop if a child is removed from his nuclear family and, although the policy is to care for the child or offender, the outcome is invariably detrimental to the recipient.

TREATMENT EFFECT

It is difficult to examine the treatment effect of residential institutions since research into differences between overtly treatment-orientated regimes and traditional authoritarian regimes is fraught with difficulties, some of which have been described by Clarke and Cornish.[13] However, such an evaluation is essential, if only on economic terms – therapeutic regimes usually require higher staff ratios and more professional support and are therefore more expensive to operate. Clarke and Cornish, however, found no significant difference in results from an acknowledged therapeutic community and a traditional authoritarian unit in an Approved School. Their experience has been repeated throughout the Borstal and prison service. H.M. Prison Grendon provides specialist psychiatric treatment for both adult and young offenders, although the latter are in the minority. The percentage reconvicted within two years of discharge was the same for a group of young offenders, and a matched group from elsewhere in the Borstal system.[14] This result parallels that for adults: 'The most striking result must be the absence of any evidence that Grendon patients do any better after release than other groups of prisoners who have not received treatment at Grendon.'[15] A similar pattern exists for establishments which are not strictly penal. Work by Sinclair on Probation Hostels[16] shows that failures during the period of residence in the hostel seemed to be related

48

primarily to the quality of the hostel itself. But reconviction after hostel treatment did not reflect differences between hostels. In addition, the three years reconviction rate for Sinclair's sample was 69 per cent, a figure comparable to that for Borstal and prison.

To sum up: residential treatment, as it exists at present in the Community Homes system, remembering as yet that this is relatively unaltered, except in name, from the Approved School system, is failing badly on three major counts and succeeding only unintentionally on a fourth. It is failing on the counts of custody, rehabilitation and treatment, and succeeding on the count of punishment in so far as its effect on the client is detrimental.

Residential treatment fails to achieve its objectives because its objectives are unclear and muddled. It is often expected to carry out two diametrically opposed tasks and as long as such confusion persists it is doomed to failure. It also fails because it is often asked to perform an impossible task. It is accepted that the cause of much delinquent behaviour is the adverse and depriving social environment of the child. If this is so it is nonsense to remove the child from that environment, give him specialised treatment for an indeterminate period of time, and then return him to the unchanged adverse environment and expect the effects of residential treatment to persist against overwhelming odds. A simple example is the problem of unemployment which has been consistently shown to be a causal factor in delinquency. The Community Home may well succeed in motivating a boy to work and in teaching him the necessary skills but none of this will be of any use if he is returned to a city where 10 per cent of school leavers are unemployed. Social 'diseases' need radical social policies if they are to be eradicated.

Why is it then that residential treatment is allowed to continue when it is extremely expensive and yet ineffective? The estimated total net expenditure on Approved Schools for the year 1970-1971 was £11,773,122. The simple answer is that society needs or thinks it needs it. Most residential treatment of young offenders is carried out in 'total' institutions, these institutions are characterised by the eixstence of barriers to social intercourse with the outside world. Goffman[17] groups total institutions into five rough categories:

First, there are institutions established to care for persons

49

felt to be both incapable and harmless; these are the homes for the blind, the aged and orphaned. Second, there are places to care for persons felt to be incapable of looking after themselves and a threat to the community, albeit an unintended one; T.B. sanitaria, mental hospital and leprosaria. A third type of total institution is organised to protect the community against what are felt to be intentional dangers to it, with the welfare of persons thus sequestered not the immediate issue; jails, penitentiaries, P.O.W. camps and concentration camps. Fourth, there are institutions purportedly established the better to pursue some worklike task and justifying themselves only on these instrumental grounds: army barracks, ships, boarding schools, work camps. . . . Finally there are those establishments designed as retreats from the world even while often serving as training stations for the religious.

Of these categories all but the fourth can be conceived of as agents of social control, removing those persons whose physical or mental health or behaviour deviates too widely from socially accepted norms. The dullest members of our society are placed in subnormality hospitals, the most able in universities. The extremely bad are put in prisons, the extremely good in monasteries, and so on. The validity of this concept is perhaps best illustrated when society's norms change through changed circumstances and a redefinition of what is deviant behaviour occurs. Thus in peacetime very aggressive persons are placed in prisons, in wartime they become heroes and passive persons (conscientious objectors) are put in prison.

Society needs total institutions for social control. However, when the position of Communty Homes is examined, the issue is found to be clouded. In Goffman's Scheme, Community Homes are a mixture of categories one and three; they contain children, i.e. a group of persons designated incapable, and yet the children appear to have intentionally endangered society by their offences. Society needs and will continue to need Community Homes because some children are orphaned, or rejected and abandoned by their parents, and they will not all be fostered, for various reasons, and will need residential care. Also there will always be a small minority of very violent children whom society will not allow to remain free. Finally, there will always be a group of children – and these are the majority in care – whom society will 'scapegoat', and make an example of, in a futile effort to deter their peers. This group will be the most defenceless group in society, the deprived and underprivileged who are unable to comprehend and manipulate the legal system for their own ends, and who do not have the ability to protest and protect their rights. Given that this group exists, and will continue to exist because of the exploitative nature of society, how are they to be treated? In the following chapters a specific Community Home will be examined in detail in an attempt to begin to answer this question.

CHAPTER IV

Wellside

Residential treatment facilities for children

In 1969 Wellside was one of a hundred and twenty-one Approved
Schools in England and Wales. Of these, thirty were girls' and
the remainder were boys' schools. Some of these schools were
managed by religious bodies, like Wellside, some by voluntary
organisations, and others by committees of interested local people
or directly by the local authority.[1] They all professed the same
basic aim, 'The primary objects of approved school training are
readjustment and social reeducation in preparation for return
to the community,'[2] and yet set about achieving this in many
different ways. The regimes within the schools varied widely,
phrases such as 'casework-orientated', 'permissive – therapeutic',
'traditional', 'structured', 'paternalistic', 'warm,' 'strict', occur in
studies which have attempted to analyse the variations in
regime.[3, 4] Three of the boys' schools specifically offered nautical
training as a means of rehabilitating the boys.

Physically the schools varied enormously too, some being in
large rural manor houses and others in purpose-built, house-
units in suburban areas. Some had large spartan dormitories
where fresh air appeared to be a vital therapeutic ingredient,
and others had single, pin-up festooned bedrooms comparable
with university halls of residence. Some had proudly displayed
heated indoor swimming pools, whilst others bemoaned cramped,
damp classrooms. Some proudly boasted of their openness and
freedom, and others shyly displayed a secure detention room,
saying, 'Well it's rarely used now-a-days, of course, occasionally
a boy will ask to be put in there himself, that's the only time
it's used.' One girls' school had masses of barbed wire, secured
windows and locked doors, all 'To keep intruders out', of course!

Since the passing of the Children and Young Persons Act, 1969,
the Approved Schools, along with the local authority Children's

52

Homes, Remand Homes and Reception Centres, have become integrated into a comprehensive system of Community Homes, offering a range of services to children in need. The passing of an Act by Parliament does not in itself bring about change, but it does make change a statutory possibility. Inevitably there is a time lag between the passing of the Act in Parliament and any discernible changes at the grassroots. This is the current position in the children's services; change is possible, and is beginning to materialise, but it will be many years before the attitudes of staff working the system readjust and accept the concepts embodied in the Act. This situation has already been discussed.

The diversity of residential treatment facilities for children means that in describing Wellside one is merely describing a small part of the whole picture. The children's residential services have no unifying factors, unlike the Borstal and prison service which has a centralised programme of recruitment and training, and a system whereby officers are rotated among the various institutions. This to some extent guarantees a uniform system with only limited variations. The children's residential services, however, have no centralised recruiting; each establishment recruits to meet its own needs; training is carried out by bodies detached from the service, namely universities, polytechnics and local colleges of further education; and staff are not transferred from one establishment to another. Thus each establishment has developed its own autonomous structure and ethos, usually based on the ideas and philosophy of its head, under the guiding hand of the Home Office Inspectorate. The latter have now become Social Work Service Officers of the Department of Health and Social Security, offering much the same service but across a wider spectrum.

A description of a specific school may be representative neither of the total residential services, nor, indeed, representative of itself. A school is an organic structure, which, like life itself, is in a constant state of flux. Each new boy admitted changes the school slightly; he may be a pro-authority, peer group leader willing to help staff in their task; he may be extremely disturbed and disruptive, putting staff and boys under great stress by his continual outbursts of aggressive behaviour; or he may be a persistent absconder who triggers off a contagious outbreak of absconding, forcing the staff into more repressive measures. Similarly, each new member of staff alters the overall composition of the school; he may be quiet and introverted, but capable of thinking up ideas for the development of the school; he may be enthusiastic and keen, continually encouraging others to greater activity; or he may be a focal point for staff room 'grousing', continually complaining about the boys' behaviour and staff's working conditions. Similarly, changes in community attitudes may radically affect the school: a prospective Member of Parliament, seeking a popular local cause, may start demanding greater security in the Community Home in his constituency in order to protect the property of his constituents; a local parent may complain about the boys' language and behaviour at the swimming baths and start campaigning for them to be banned. Innumerable factors can affect the school.

Therefore a detailed description of a school at any specific point in time cannot illustrate its development, nor give any clues to the continually changing kaleidoscope of interpersonal relationships between boys and boys, boys and staff, and staff and staff. Instead, what I hope to offer is a characterisation of the school, concentrating on certain aspects representative of the overall ethos and aims. These aspects themselves are continually being modified and adapted, but within them is embodied the basic attitude on which the school is founded, namely that of respect for the child, through which the child learns respect for the staff.

Wellside

The actual buildings of Wellside testify to the changes in society which have occurred in the last century and a half. Starting life as a magnificently positioned Georgian rectory of mansion proportions, it became the home of a wealthy Midlands industrialist, only to revert to the Church at a later date (1940) in a completely new role – that of providing a home for deprived and underprivileged urban children. The property was bought by the Superiors of a religious teaching order of Brothers. In 1940 they took over the large rambling manor, together with stables and a collection of nissen huts, and two Brothers and some forty boys moved from the war-endangered south of England to the comparative security of the rural Midlands. The school has completely changed now. Where nissen huts once stood a private road passes ten semi-detached staff houses, all of mock-Georgian design to match the imposing manor at the end of the drive. Facing the manor across an attractive floral roundabout is another large mock-Georgian house: the community house for the Brothers, who originally lived in the nissen huts with the boys. The stables which once housed somebody's prized hunters now vibrate to the throb of the juke box, the drone of a television set, the gentle thud of billiard balls, and the clack of table tennis, all accompanied by the shouts and cries of wrestling, chasing, arguing, playing boys. Extended beyond the stables are the classrooms. Initially one may be puzzled as to what age group occupy them. There are junior school charts on the wall alongside lino-cuts of pin-ups and carefully painted posters declaiming 'We are the Birmingham Boot Boys', this together with home-made radios, burglar alarms and electric motors.

Bounded on two sides by the classrooms and the main house and on a third by the gym is the 'yard', a large tarmaced area with five-a-side goals marked at either end on the wall and fencing, and some minimal flood lighting. The yard is a kind of social centre/forum for the school, and figures prominently in the institution's jargon.[5] Boys say menacingly to each other, 'Wait till I see you on the yard!' Staff say to boys, 'See me later on the yard and we'll talk about it.' Harassed staff call 'Back on the yard for assembly.' Whenever boys are 'on the yard' plastic footballs appear and a game starts, soon to be interrupted by dialogues like:

'Can I join in?'
'Yeah, you're on our side.'
'No he's not, you've already got seven and we've only got six.'
'Yeah, but look who you've got, and you're already winning.'
'Well if he's on your side I'm not playing.'
'Oh shut up, you big baby, and get on with it.'
'No, I'm not, come over here and say that.'
'Alright I will.'

And so football is temporarily forgotten, to start up again when the major transfer of players has been settled amicably. Somewhere in the vicinity of the yard and its adjoining buildings a man will be seen walking slowly, his progress impeded by a circle of six or more clamouring boys. He appears to be involved in a soliloquy of random phrases.

'Look you two, if you are going to fight do it outside.'
'No I don't think there was a letter for you.'
'Yes I'll be taking you to the dentist today.'
'Who do you want me to phone, your sister? Right!'
'Look I've told you two once, go and fight somewhere else, you're ruining those pullovers.'
'I'm not sure when your review meeting is, I'll check and let you know.'

55

'No I haven't got a light, I'm sorry, ask John W . . . he took my last match.'

This is the housemaster on yard duty.

On the third side of the yard is the gym with showers and changing rooms, and the boys' toilets and washroom, which are beautifully tiled and fitted and, as the boys will proudly tell you, all done by the boys and opened by the headmaster in a satirical public opening ceremony, complete with white ribbon and scissors. The boys' toilets are their territory. This has not always been so; at one time staff used to patrol them in case a boy was in there smoking, or, even worse, masturbating! But the legalising of smoking within the school has changed all that and the toilets are the boys' territory where clandestine deals are discussed and occasionally vicious subcultural punishment meted out.

The beautifully fitted and equipped gym looks out on to the gardening department with its four large, commercial hen houses, two for battery chickens and two for deep litter broilers. Its large commercial green-houses are stocked with pot plants, lettuce, cucumber and tomatoes. Its brick implement shed, again built by the boys, is a scene of constant activity. As a boy driving a tractor pulling a wagon loaded with carrots from 'over the field' pulls into the shed, others start unloading, sorting and bagging the carrots in preparation for Friday's run into the local market.

To the side of the garden department are the department workshops, the builders' appears to be a cross between a building supplies stores and a youth club. In their workshop, alongside sand and bricks and carefully kept tools, stands a superb model railway layout, a large old record player with piles of Reggae discs, a couple of old but workable televisions and boxes of postage stamps, all ready for the evening activities. Next to the builders' is the joiners' workshop, containing an array of impressive and dangerous looking industrial joinery machines, with some boys making a huge window frame to replace the rotted sash windows in the old house, whilst others work carefully on tea trolleys to take home. After the joiners' comes the painters', its occupants busy in white, paint-bespattered overalls, carrying scaffolding up to the main house, others with pots and rolls of wallpaper.

Adjacent to the yard is a covered yard lined with small lockers on one side full of football boots, and in one corner a pile of large logs, some four feet long and more than a foot in diameter. Here boys with axes hack away, others, with more intent and preoccupied look, work diligently on a log with Surform and electric sander: 'I'm doing another totem pole, did you see the last one? It's in the headmaster's office.' Behind the heap of logs is the pottery room, where boys fashion in clay animals, nudes, abstract designs, etc. Around the walls, with a background of unfinished murals of Hells Angels, sleepy Mexican villages and portraits, are shelves loaded with the finished, fired and glazed products. All interesting, some looking as though they should be in an Art college, others a junior school.

In the administration block again, as the boys will tell you, built by them, although none of the current population of the school were involved, there is a continuous stream of boys:

'I just want to see the headmaster about my weekend.'
'A. can I show you my scrapbook about horses?'
'Mr. F. has got my jacket in his office.'
'Mr. P. can you just sell us ten fags?'

The whole school area, some fifty acres of playing field, sheep grazing and market garden, and all the buildings are dominated by the main house. This impressive three-storey Georgian mansion is the hub of the school, and rightly so, since it is where the ninety-five boys live. The chapel, the boys' dining room, the staff room and the Lulu room (a general purpose room so named because of the ten foot high photo of Lulu which is a feature of its décor) all lead off the oak-panelled entrance hall. The impressive staircase, beautifully carpeted, leads up to a large landing which has been turned into a pleasant lounge for the boys, with books in cases around the walls, contemporary chairs and matching occasional tables. From here stairs lead to the top storey, and doorways lead into the dormitories. These appear so prim and tidy one finds it difficult to believe boys really live here. Polished Sapele floors glisten, a neat strip of carpet tiles runs up the centre of the room deadening the sound of footfalls; either side of the carpet are carefully ranged old iron beds with bright coloured counterpanes covering mattresses misshapen with use; every so often a bed is stripped and its blankets folded – these are occupied by boys who are enuretic and they have to make them with clean sheets every night. Beside each bed there is a simple locker with perhaps a comic or pair of pyjamas visible; nowhere is there a photo of home or other personal possessions on display. At the end of the dormitory is a wardrobe, one door open showing it to be empty except for a dirty sock in one corner. The dormitories are all bright and interestingly decorated, some have attractive wallpaper, but the

57

majority are painted with murals depicting pirate scenes or a frenzied table tennis match, or the scoring of a climactic goal. The dormitories vary in size. The majority have twelve or so beds but two smaller ones with only three beds are notable and somehow seem 'warmer' and more acceptable. Further along the corridor can be seen a row of washbasins and an array of pegs each with a numbered towel.

On the ground floor is the boys' dining room with its ten to fifteen plain tables crammed in together; table cloths and condiments are noticeable by their absence. When ninety-five boys sit down to eat one notices the poor acoustics which magnify the clatter of knives and forks to such an extent that, together with the noise of the serving boys moving about, conversation is inhibited.

Along the corridor from the dining room are doors labelled 'Surgery', 'Matron's Store', 'Matron's Dining Room', and 'Suit Room'; it is the latter which explains the empty wardrobes in the dormitories. Behind this locked door hang the boys' clothes, protected from theft and malicious damage. So much of the boys' personal clothing was stolen by other boys when it was kept in the wardrobes that the only solution seemed to be to keep it locked up and it is only handed out by a member of staff when asked for by a boy. But somehow that seems to make it 'impersonal' clothing.

The most striking thing about the main house is its silence and orderliness in comparison with the rest of the school. Why is this? Well it is quite simple, the boys live here but they don't live here. The boys sleep here, to be more exact, and from 'risings' to bedtime they don't go into their dormitory, it is not allowed. Thus the main house, apart from meals, is hardly used by the boys. This would seem to detract from an important aspect of the boys' life in Wellside, since:

'His bed space is the only place within the community home which the individual child sees as his own, and this has to be recognised in its planning. We should like to emphasise that its use should not be limited to sleeping and dressing; it should be a private place but one with a wide variety of uses. These might include washing, display and storage of personal possessions and clothing, reading and studying – and just day dreaming. Some children may want to practise musical instruments in the bedrooms and others may like to spend time on hobbies. Space needs to be provided for children to display photographs, newspaper cuttings, pin-ups and so on.'[6]

58

This is the physical structure of Wellside at the present time; what happens within this setting I hope to illustrate by reference to various specific aspects of the life there. I am not going to describe the 'routine day' at Wellside, since much of this will emerge in the following chapters. In the physical description of Wellside no mention was made of secure perimeter fencing; that is because none exists, the school is completely open, no doors are locked to keep the boys in. The school's entrances open on to a main trunk road, or on to open countryside. Given this situation absconding obviously occurs and this is the first aspect of school life with which I wish to deal.

The Problem of Absconding

The importance of absconding from Community Homes needs to be re-examined and perhaps re-emphasised, because in the past few years there has been a tendency to 'play down' its importance. This has been done by heads, partly in an attempt to reduce staff's anxieties, but also partly because of a woolly-minded concept of social work which maintains that if the child needs to abscond he should not be discouraged. In fact, a head of a special unit for persistent absconders once remarked, 'The unit is here to meet the child's needs, if she needs to run away this is where she can run from.' However, the small amount of research aimed at examining absconding in depth does not bear out these ideas. In the first place, absconding from Approved Schools has risen sharply in the past decade: the numbers of boys and girls absconding (including bounds breaking) from Approved Schools in 1956 were 2,682 and 1,317 respectively. In 1968 these figures had risen rapidly to 8,884 for boys and 2,144 for girls.[3] During this period the actual number of boys and girls in Approved Schools had remained fairly constant at approximately 6,500 and 1,100. Since absconding appears to be determined by environmental factors rather than by individual personality differences, it would appear that this massive increase is due to changes in the attitudes and regimes within the schools rather than changes in the population entering the schools.[3]

Secondly, absconding is important because of the effect it has on the individual child's treatment. As pointed out before treatment is dependent on the physical presence of the recipient. Consequently the impact of any form of treatment offered by the institution is greatly reduced if the child persistently absconds. However, of even greater importance is the effect the act of absconding has on the child's prognosis. Wilkins[7] showed a clear

59

association between frequency of absconding and increased likelihood of direct committal to Borstal from Approved School. The explanation for this relationship is quite simple: an absconder is more likely to commit further offences to assist his survival, i.e. stealing cars, bicycles, food, breaking into unoccupied houses for shelter, etc. Wilkins went on to show that a clear association existed between absconding and the likelihood of committing further offences on release from Approved School. There is no obvious reason for this association but Clarke and Martin[3] suggest that absconding is itself a delinquent act, so that by absconding the boy becomes more confirmed in delinquency. This learning process results in the increased likelihood of offending after release.

Thirdly, the absconder is vulnerable and endangered in many ways. This is true of both boys and girls, but girls are particularly open to sexual exploitation. Consequently girls often return from absconding having contracted venereal disease or occasionally have become pregnant; similarly, boys may return having suffered an homosexual assault.

It is obvious from the evidence presented that absconding needs to be reduced, to further treatment of the individual, to protect him or her, and to protect society. The situation at Wellside was reaching worrying proportions and accordingly some steps were taken to reduce abscondings. The situation is best summarised by quoting from the Headmaster's report to the Annual General Meeting of the Managers, 1971:

Absconding continues to be a problem with which we have yet to come to terms. It is fair to say that at any one time absconding does not affect the majority of boys in the school, nor does this phenomenon create in staff the anxieties that it did formerly. During the last twelve months there have been 183 instances of absconding, this figure is very high but in order to see it in perspective the following facts must be borne in mind. 61 boys were responsible for this figure, which means that over the period of twelve months 69 had not absconded at all. Furthermore, 23 boys absconded once, 12 boys twice and 7 boys three times, making a total of 111 boys for whom absconding did not become a significant problem. Finally four boys between them were responsible for 55 abscondings.

The high rate of absconding should be noted because this was one of the major problems facing the school at that time. The rates of absconding for all schools tend to remain stable through time; it is 'breaking through' this high rate of absconding that

60

is the problem because the school builds up an unofficial tradition of absconding amongst the boys. The boys become aware of the high rate of absconding and absconding becomes a matter of peer group status. In interview, a large number of boys refer to their first instance of absconding as almost compulsive behaviour, i.e. they felt they had to do it just to see what it was like. On return to school the absconder becomes the centre of attraction and is able to talk a good deal about his great adventures whilst out of the school, and this presumably raises his status within his peer group. It was against this background that the reception procedure was adopted within Wellside. The procedure was orginally established, not as a measure to reduce absconding, but as the result of staff discussion. The staff recognised that entering an Approved School is a traumatic experience for any child, and staff have a responsibility to attempt to lessen this trauma. Intuitively the staff felt that if one could lower the child's anxiety on admission this would enable him to settle down and establish close personal relationships with the staff earlier in his career.

At about the same time Clarke and Martin,[3] drawing on their research, gave certain practical suggestions aimed at reducing absconding. These included reduction of the boy's anxiety in the period following admission because it is in this initial period after admission when the boy is at greatest risk. Their suggestions included the studying of each newcomer in a consciously clinical manner so as to place him in the dormitory, classroom or workshop best fitted to his needs; the deployment of extra staff to familiarise the boy as quickly as possible with the school routine; and the establishment of effective communications with the boy's home.

THE RECEPTION PROCEDURE AT WELLSIDE

The reception procedure started prior to the boy's arrival at the school, since the local authorities, when requesting admission for a boy, sent the relevant case papers to the school for consideration. This gave an opportunity for staff to study the case papers before making a decision. In most cases where the admission appeared to be 'routine' the case papers were seen and discussed by the headmaster, the deputy headmaster, the third in charge and the psychologist. However, when the information available suggested that the prospective new boy was likely to prove extremely difficult, either to the school or himself, the case papers were discussed by a full meeting of the staff. The decision having been made to accept the boy the following pro-

61

cedure was adopted. A group of staff was made responsible for receiving boys 'into care'. This 'reception committee' consisted of the matron, the headmaster's secretary, the third in charge, who was a housemaster, and the psychologist. The committee was selected as far as possible to cover all facets of receiving a boy; thus the matron was concerned with his clothing, the third in charge with his dormitory, and the secretary in dealing with the correspondence and actually receiving the boy into care – this is interesting because someone who is usually seen as an auxiliary member of staff was in fact playing a vital therapeutic role.

It was the responsibility of the reception committee to have studied the boy's case papers prior to his admission and to have informed all other members of staff of his arrival and the salient features of his case. The aim of this was to enable staff to help the boy settle as quickly as possible and to avoid upsetting him by broaching topics which he may have been particularly sensitive about, for example the staff would be aware of whether the boy's parents were alive and living together, divorced or deceased, and could avoid embarrassing a boy by asking questions about his parents. The reception committee was responsible for contacting the boy's family and child care officer prior to his arrival and arranging where possible for one or both of the boy's parents and his child care officer to accompany him, or to be at the school on his arrival. One day of the week was fixed for receiving boys. Thursday was chosen since it enabled the boy to see the routine of the school, both at work during the week and at play at the weekend, in the shortest possible time. As far as possible new boys were admitted individually. This was important as Clarke and Martin have shown: 'The rate of admission to a school might have an important bearing on the ease with which staff could make relationships with newcomers, boys admitted in close proximity seem much more likely to abscond than boys admitted at longer intervals.'

When the boy arrived he was met at the front door by a member of the reception committee, rather than being taken to the headmaster's office or the administration block. He was then taken to a quiet sitting room for a cup of coffee with that member of staff and another member of the committee and two boys from the school, who had been selected previously as being the same age and from the same area as the new boy. In the majority of admission cases it proved possible to select boys who had known the new boy previously. After the initial informal cup of coffee the boy and his parents were shown around the school by the two boys selected, and on their way round would

62

be introduced to the headmaster for a chat. The group then assembled for lunch in a dining room separate from the main body of the school. This lunch period proved extremely valuable, being a time in which staff and boys could talk to the new boy and allay many of his fears about the school.

When the parents had seen around the school and returned home the new boy was taken care of by his two guides. They were responsible for him for the rest of the day, helping him to make his bed, sitting him at their table in the dining room, etc. In the period after admission the boy was allowed to wear his own clothes until such time as he asked to wear school clothes – usually within the first two or three days. Finally a weekend at home was arranged for the boy during the month following admission.

Having established this reception procedure, which involved the deployment of a number of staff, it seemed imperative to check whether the procedure was effective. This could be done by assessing what effect it had on absconding. This was done by comparing the figures for absconding amongst the boys admitted within the four months from September to December 1969 with those admitted during the same period in 1970. The latter group had undergone the reception procedure described above. By matching the two periods important variables such as holidays and darker evenings could be controlled. The study was not extended beyond December 1970 since the Children's and Young Persons' Act 1969 came into being at that time and may well have affected the type of boy admitted to the school. The boys were followed up for twelve weeks after admission and the number of boys becoming absconders was recorded, the figures were as follows:

For the 1969 period twenty boys were admitted, of these eleven became absconders in the twelve-week period.
For the 1970 period eleven boys were admitted, of these only one absconded.

If these figures are statistically analysed using Fisher's Test of Exact Probability it is shown that the 1970 figures are significantly lower than the 1969 figures. The probability of these figures having occurred by chance is low, less than twice in 100. The figures are summarised in Table I.

The figures for the incidence of absconding, i.e. the number of times boys ran away as opposed to the number of boys who ran away, for the two groups were: seventeen abscondings in the 1969 period, and only one absconding in the 1970 period.

63

TABLE I

The Number of Boys Admitted During a Four-month Period in 1969 and 1970, and Whether or Not they Became an Absconder Over a Twelve-week Follow Up.[8]

	Absconders	Non-Absconders
No. of boys admitted in 1969 Period (N=20)	11	9
No. of boys admitted in 1970 Period (N=11)	1	10

p=·013 using Fisher's Test of Exact Probability

It is important to remember that these figures are only for those boys admitted in that period and take no account of the incidence of absconding for the remainder of the boys in the school. From these figures the only certain conclusion that can be drawn is that the figures for new boys absconding in the 1970 period was lower than those for the 1969 period. The difference cannot be said to be entirely due to the establishment and implementation of the reception procedure, since there were obviously many other variables which remained uncontrolled. The most obvious of these is that the 1970 group contained less boys who had previously proved to be persistent absconders – none of the boys in either group were described as potential absconders by their classifying schools, nor were any of the group transferred to Wellside from other institutions for persistently absconding, as occasionally happens. Another important variable is whether the boys were exposed to the influence of confirmed absconders early in their career. To some extent this variable could also be controlled by checking the number of abscondings for the total school during the two periods. The number for the two periods were not significantly different: 73 for the 1969 period and 64 for the 1970 period. These figures suggest that the 'atmosphere' of absconding for the two periods was similar.

Although it cannot be said with certainty that the reception procedure does reduce absconding it appears that it does have some influence on it. However, it is impossible to distinguish the factors involved in the reception procedure which have the greatest influence, since it may well have been that the spacing out of admissions had the greatest effect, and it should be noted that approximately half the number of boys were admitted during the same period of time in 1970 as in 1969. The admissions were more widely spaced in 1970; on three occasions two boys were admitted simultaneously, otherwise all boys were admitted

64

individually. In 1969, however, on one occasion four boys were admitted simultaneously, and on two occasions three boys, otherwise all boys were admitted individually. Of these ten boys, seven absconded in the follow-up period, so it does in fact appear that spacing out is important.

The deployment of staff and boys to help settle the new boy into the school by reducing his anxiety cannot be shown with absolute certainty to be a crucial factor in the reception procedure. However, it did seem to have a positive face validity since all boys were observably anxious, and some were able to verbalise their fears and fantasies about the school. The sort of interchange that went on between boys was as follows:

New boy: 'Are there alarms on these windows?'
Old boy: 'Don't be stupid.'
New boy: 'Well how do they stop you escaping?'
Old boy: 'You don't escape, you just walk out if you want to.'

Similarly the boy's fear that he was going to be locked away from his family was dealt with by having his family present and by talking about the frequency of leave; this was later demonstrated by an early weekend at home. The parents' anxieties were allayed, because on looking around the school and seeing the freedom the boys enjoyed, meeting staff and assessing staff's interest in the children they soon came to realise that their preconceived image of Approved Schools as harsh, secure, repressive, institutions was wrong. This helped the child to settle much quicker by reducing his own anxieties.

I have dealt with the reception procedure at some length because it is important. Goffman[5] has shown, in his study of asylums, that the effect of the reception procedure that an individual undergoes on entering any institution is of vital importance. Goffman talks of the individual having to role-change, of being stripped of his own personal role and being offered an institutional role. The procedure followed at Wellside was an attempt to get over some of these problems. It was obviously by no means infallible, and a certain amount of 'institutionalisation' occurred. However, it was a long way from the harsh reception procedure so often described in personal recollections of prison experience. For example, Brendan Behan in *Borstal Boy*,[9] gave a graphic description of a degrading reception procedure in which boys were brought in, stripped, showered, heads checked for lice, and then issued with Borstal clothing, losing the whole of the identity associated with their life outside and having to accept the identity offered by the institution.

Staff Selection Procedure

It is interesting to compare the reception procedure for the boys with that for accepting staff into the school. Staff at Wellside came from many different backgrounds, some of which will be discussed in a later chapter. The procedure for their appointment had much in common with that of the boys. Their application forms were initially sorted by the headmaster, the deputy headmaster, the psychologist and the third in charge, but were available to all staff for their perusal. Whenever possible the applicants were invited to come and look round the school and spend a day, or a weekend, within the school, so that staff could get to know them and they could get to know staff. In this way they could also see how the school operated and decide for themselves whether they wanted to proceed with their applications.

The selection committee then drew up a short-list of applicants who were invited for the selection day. The selection day was a vitally important part of the organisation of Wellside. The idea started with the appointment of the psychologist, when applicants for the post of psychologist were invited to attend for a weekend, during which they were asked to present a case study of one of the boys in the school to the staff, having previously interviewed the boy. They also had to present a paper on some aspect of child care to the staff and – speaking personally, the most arduous part of the procedure – they were asked to take a group of boys for a general discussion in which the boys gave the applicant a thorough interview. They were finally interviewed by a panel of professional advisers and by the school managers. This lengthy selection procedure has been written up elsewhere.[10] After the appointment of the psychologist the basic idea was retained for the selection of staff, but the procedure was shortened somewhat.

The normal selection procedure for staff was that applicants arrived for the day and began by having coffee and a brief chat with the headmaster. They then proceeded to look around the school if they had not already done so. They met all the staff informally in the staff room over a cup of tea, and the staff then had an opportunity of discussing fully with the applicants their roles within the school, their relationships with other staff, and their special interests. They were then asked to take a group of boys for a general discussion, which all the applicants did quite willingly. After the discussion the boys were asked for their opinions of the applicants. The applicants then went on

66

to have a much more detailed interview by the headmaster and managers. An appointment was finally made, based on the staff's, the boys', the headmaster's and the managers' opinions, information being collected from all groups involved and collated to help to make the appointment.

This procedure is exceptionally interesting because it was one major area where the boys participated in decision making within the school. They responded well to this responsibility. At no time did they exploit the situation. Their comments were often extremely shrewd, for example: 'I think he would be too soft with the boys,' or 'I think this person is a bit of a bully, he'd try to push us around.' They knew exactly what sort of member of staff they wanted and how to identify the right qualities in applicants. This procedure has often been misinterpreted as boys having the right to 'hire' and 'fire' staff. This was not the situation at all; the boys were asked for their opinions and these were given equal weight with the opinions of other groups. The situation did not arise where boys chose an applicant whom the staff considered unsuitable or vice versa. The staff and boys were always in close agreement. Had such a situation arisen the headmaster's decision would have overruled the boys, as he is responsible for the behaviour of staff after their appointment. The important thing to note is that the boys were involved in the selection of staff, and at a time when university students were clamouring to be given this right.

Once the boys and staff had arrived at Wellside, how did they interact? Something of the network of personal relationships that existed between staff and boys is demonstrated in the interviews reported below, but in this chapter I want to concentrate attention on two structures within the school which were aimed at facilitating the development of relationships. These structures were the programme of group counselling and the boys' council.

Group Counselling

In a Community Home, treatment is the responsibility of each member of staff, for specific treatment, i.e. intensive psychotherapy or drug therapy, is not only in very limited supply, but can have only limited impact on the total life of the child in the institution. The treatment offered by the staff is the provision of acceptable and appropriate models of human behaviour with which the child may identify. This treatment is offered on the basis of the knowledge of normal child development. The normal child, growing up in a family situation, identifies with the

67

appropriate parental figure, incorporating facets of the parental personality into his own immature personality. Identification may take place through imitation or through learning based on rewards.[11] From normal child development it is known and appreciated that children identify with what people do and are, rather than with what they say. For example, it is known that the use of physical punishment is not effective in eliminating aggressive behaviour because aggression is being used to overcome aggression.[12] In other words, in terms of identification, how can one expect a child to control his aggression if the model he is offered is one of uncontrolled aggression?

For treatment through identification to succeed opportunities for identification must be available. In most institutions these opportunities are very limited. In the school, staff members were usually in a role with which the boy could not readily identify – the boy being presented with a model of a teacher, housemaster, etc. Counselling groups provided the opportunity for the boys to identify with the model of a 'person'.

In the counselling group the staff member had to shed much of his normal 'in-school' role, although obviously it was not possible to shed the total role, because the individual was still a member of staff. This was not easy for staff to do since they had to shed the authority attached to their normal roles and instead deal with boys on a personal level, stating how they felt and what they thought as an individual. This left them open to questioning and criticism from the group and it was essential, therefore, that they felt secure enough to allow themselves to be questioned. Many staff were worried that this process would be carried over from the counselling situation into the 'in-school' situation, and that the group members would question their authority outside the counselling situation. This did not occur because the boys were able to identify the change in role and appreciated that the new role was specific to the situation. In fact, the situation was not unlike that of extraneous duties, when teachers and trade instructors were on duty in the evening and at weekends taking various activities. At these times they inevitably 'changed role', being more relaxed and less 'instructional', and the boys were able to recognise this change in role and modify their behaviour accordingly. Also it must be remembered that a boy was expected to change role in the counselling situation too, from that of 'pupil', with its accompanying attitude of not 'telling tales' and of viewing the teacher as omniscient, to that of group member willing to reveal his personal problems, and knowing that he was unlikely to get a definitive answer to them. It was essential to discard the authority role if interaction within the group was to succeed.

It was important to define the staff's model from the beginning of the group meetings. In the first group meeting the staff member demonstrated that he was not omnipotent by clearly stating the terms of reference of the group. This was done by pointing out that there were certain social and school rules over which staff had little or no control, and although the group might wish to discuss these, it was unlikely that they would be able to change the rules. These topics included length of school holidays, pocket money, school meals, etc.

By accepting the role of group member, a member of staff accepted that his contribution to the group was of equal value with that of the other members, no greater no less. This meant that staff were not able to dictate their own ideas and attitudes to the group even when these were thinly disguised as pseudo-rational arguments, such as 'You're young yet but you will soon find out what life is like', and 'You'll find things are different when you have a wife and kids of your own.' Remarks like these constitute an attempt to deny the child the right to think for himself. In the same way, branding the child's statements as anti-social – 'typical of you lot' – or selfish, is to deny him the right to explore and develop his own ideas. This does not mean that the group's statements went unnoticed. Instead the staff attempted to interpret back to the group how the individual's feelings and attitudes were relevant to them and affected them. In doing this staff would at times be faced by some members of the group 'acting-out' their feelings. This was to be expected when working with a population of boys who are notoriously bad at verbalising their feelings and thoughts. Occasionally a boy would physically threaten another member of the group, or burst into tears. This 'acting-out' behaviour allowed staff an opportunity for interpretation back to the group and was dealt with in this way rather than by punishing the aggressive behaviour, or attempting to be compassionate with the tearful behaviour. The 'acting-out' behaviour proved the ideal point from which to interpret how one individual's behaviour influenced, either positively or negatively, another individual's behaviour.

Interpretation demanded that the staff, although members of the group, were in some way set apart from the group in that they tried to adopt an objective stance. This was essential since at times the group tried to make staff act in collusion with them against other members of staff. Obviously collusion by the staff members with the group would have made inter-staff relationships intolerable, and would have been extremely damaging to the model presented to the child. Failure to collude with the group demonstrated a model which showed that feelings could be overcome in order to conform with one's role, i.e. for a member of staff it was imperative that he work with other members of staff even though personally he might disagree with them. Similarly, failure to collude demonstrated that the model was able to accept the existence of individuals with differing attitudes and opinions and, what is more important, their right to exist. This also points up the sort of relationship that must exist between staff and boys if treatment is to be successful.

These were the basic principles behind the establishment of a programme of group counselling. The practical organisation of the programme took many turns. Initially each boy in the school was randomly allocated to a group, each group consisting of an average of six boys of varying age and intelligence, one member of staff and the psychologist. By this means each boy and each member of staff was allocated to a group and, although it soon became obvious that some boys were unable at their present stage of development to take part in intensive group work, this system was retained in order to avoid divisions within the school between 'nutters' and others, as described by Lumsden Walker.[13] Each member of staff was allocated to a group since it was agreed that the staff would be the 'group therapists', and be responsible for their groups. However, it was notable that although each member of staff was said to be responsible for his group, the groups rarely met in the absence of the psychologist, indicating that staff saw the groups as primarily his responsibility and not theirs. None of the staff were specifically trained in group work and, as with the boys, it soon became obvious that some staff were unable to cope with intensive group work and opted out, using difficulties in timetabling as a useful rationalisation.

At a later date the groups were re-organised and based on the existing groupings within the school, namely the classes and trade departments. This had the effect of reducing the variation in age, and the respective teacher or instructor became the group leader. This was done to allow the intensive group work to support, and work in conjunction with, the existing group work.

The use of group counselling as a therapeutic technique has been advocated by many workers.[14, 15, 16] The difficulties involved in transferring this technique, which was developed for use with voluntary adult patients, to conscripted children have also been described.[17] Few workers have attempted to evaluate group counselling in terms of successful or unsuccessful outcome, and I am not about to join their ranks, because I would predict that the programme of group counselling operating at Wellside would have little permanent effect on the boys. An individual boy would be in a group meeting for one hour per week, so in a year he would attend at a maximum forty meetings, the other weeks being taken up by holidays and unavoidable absences. As the average length of stay at Wellside is twenty-three months it is highly unlikely that a boy would be involved in more than eighty hours of group counselling. Obviously it would be absurd to presume that eighty hours of group counselling out of a period of two years was going to radically affect a boy's behaviour, especially when one considers the massive contrary environmental influence of the peer group.

The prediction that group counselling would not be effective in changing behaviour in the institutional setting described does not invalidate it. There are other important aspects of the process which are beneficial to the individual, and the first of these is linguistic development.

LINGUISTIC DEVELOPMENT

Bernstein[18] has shown that the difference in language usage between the working-class and middle-class child is not in vocabulary or syntax, but in what he calls the use of particularistic and universalistic orders of meaning. Particularistic orders of meaning are closely tied to a given context and do not transcend it. This is probably best illustrated by the following example taken from Hawkins: [19] the child is given a series of four pictures which tell a story, and he is invited to tell the story himself. The first picture involves boys playing football to which the typical working-class child's particularistic response is:

'They're playing football and he kicks it and it goes through there, it breaks the window and they're looking at it and he comes out and shouts at them because they've broken it and so they run away and then she looks out and she tells them off.'

Universalistic orders of meaning transcend the limits of context, and they would be used by a typical middle-class child telling the same story:

'Three boys are playing football and one boy kicks the ball and it goes through the window the ball breaks the win-

71

dow and the boys are looking at it and a man comes out and shouts at them because they've broken the window so they run away and then that lady looks out of her window and she tells the boys off.'

With the last story the reader does not have to have the four pictures which were used as the basis for the story, but in the case of the first story the reader would require the initial pictures in order to make sense of it. The second story is free of the context which produced it, but the first story is closely tied to the context.

In the group counselling situation the boys were often involved in recounting personal anecdotes out of context, for example the happenings on home leave, adventures whilst absconding, etc. Within the group only the story teller knew the context in which the story took place. If he used language with particularistic meanings it was unintelligible to the remainder of the group, even though they were of the same social background and used this form of language themselves. The group soon responded by saying they didn't understand and forced the story teller to keep repeating the story until he eventually put it into universalistic language which all could comprehend. This process is much more effective in teaching language skills than a teacher continually saying to a child, 'Repeat yourself more clearly, I can't understand you,' and is less likely to make the child surrender and say nothing.

The advantages of teaching these language skills are twofold. First, they will help the child's general education, since the school is necessarily concerned with the transmission and development of universalistic orders of meaning. The school is concerned with making explicit, and elaborating through language, principles and actions as these apply to objects and persons, thus the child who is using particularistic language is severely handicapped. Development of universalistic language within the group counselling setting should enable the child to take better advantage of his classroom teaching. Secondly, universalistic language skills are vital in two major areas of life: the interpersonal area, in which the child is made aware of affective states, his own and others; and the regulative area, of authority relations, in which the child is made aware of the moral order and its various reinforcements. The ability to use universalistic language can, therefore, regulate the child's behaviour. Through language he can become more sensitive and aware of his own feelings and those of others, and is therefore less likely to abuse

72

others. He also becomes more aware of the value of moral codes and of linguistic rather than physical means of resolving differences. This should lead to a reduction in violent and aggressive behaviour and acting out, because 'the child learns to talk in code instead of act in code.'[16]

COMMUNICATION BETWEEN STAFF AND BOY CULTURES

Much has been written about the existence of subcultures within institutions dealing with delinquent children.[20] It has been generally accepted that the 'official' view, as presented by managers, headmasters, and staff, of the type of regime operating in an institution is often grossly at variance with the one which is actually operating amongst the children. The 'official' view may be that status is accorded to boys who are willing and able to accept responsibility, whereas status within the boys' subculture may depend on physical prowess or delinquent criteria.

Group counselling can be an effective means of bridging the gap between the two cultures, both by increasing the awareness of the existence of two cultures, and by ensuring the participation of the alienated subculture in the making of decisions which affect it. If the group situation is sufficiently relaxed, and the boys feel that their confidence will be respected, they will readily begin to talk about their culture. The staff are then made aware of what life is really like for the boys in their charge. This awareness alone is often sufficient to modify the staff's system of working and their attitude to the boys. For example, it became obvious through group discussion at Wellside that older boys were manipulating the dining room situation so that they obtained larger meals at the expense of younger boys. The staff's awareness of this problem enabled them to re-organise the dining situation in order to guarantee a fairer distribution of food.

It is important to recognise that this process was handled carefully by staff, in order to preserve group confidentiality. Staff action, therefore, was limited to altering the system within the school rather than dealing with individual boys. If it had been mentioned within a group that a particular boy, not present in the group, was bullying other boys, it would have been disastrous for the member of staff to confront the bully, since the source of information would soon have become obvious. The groups would then have been seen by the boys as a ploy by staff to gain information, and they would have consequently 'clammed up' and refused to talk except on the most mundane of topics. However, it is obvious that if staff are made aware of problems within the subculture they will become more 'vigilant'. The confidentiality of the group at times needed to be broken, but only with the group's consent. If in a group meeting the boys mentioned that one of their number had been involved in offences when on an extra-mural activity, and these offences were undetected, then obviously the group leader could not treat this information passively. However, it was imperative that he gained the group's permission to act on the information. This he often did by asking the group why they had given him the information, since they were aware that he was bound to act on it. It soon became clear that the group wanted some action taken, and readily agreed to the member of staff passing on the information while still preserving the confidentiality of the group.

Group counselling is also a useful means of involving the boys in decision-making within the school. At Wellside the headmaster had a meeting once a week with all the boys to inform them of various ideas for development within the school. For example, he explained to the boys that he was considering allowing boys to go home for weekends more frequently, but unfortunately, because of financial constraints, only a limited number of boys might be able to go home. Given this situation, the groups decided to discuss the problem of how the weekends were to be allocated; should every boy go home on a rota basis? Should weekends be used as a privilege awarded for good behaviour? Should only those boys who lived near to the school go, thereby reducing the expenditure on fares? What was to be done about boys who had no homes? The boys were, therefore, involved in the decision-making and made aware of the reasoning behind decisions which otherwise might have appeared quite arbitrary.

In some instances, discussion within the group affected the institution as a whole. For example, one group spent several meetings discussing the possibility of organising a leaving party for three of its members who were being released. The group in these discussions ironed out several of the problems involved, i.e. venue, number of boys invited, provisions, etc. When this point was reached they were able to go to the headmaster, present their ideas, have them agreed, and organise the party. This is an example of the boys initiating ideas, participating in decision-making and accepting responsibility for implementing their ideas.

ATTITUDE CHANGE

Lewin[21] has shown that participation in group discussion is more effective in bringing about attitude change than traditional 'lecturing'. The influence of peer group behaviour on delinquency is also well documented.[22, 23] The group counsellor is faced with a two-edged sword; peer group discussion is an effective way of changing attitude, but the attitudes existing within this specific peer group are predominantly delinquent. Thus, unless the situation is handled with skill, group counselling may well have the effect of consolidating delinquent attitudes. The group may well divide and polarise over specific attitudes, the division being between boys and staff. Such a situation can be dangerous because it merely strengthens the subcultural divisions already existing within the institution. However, if the group is manipulated successfully it can have a profound effect on an individual's attitudes. A detailed example of how effective the group can be is as follows:

The group consisted of a class of ten boys, the teacher and the psychologist. The day before the group meeting one of the boys, who had only been in the school about two weeks, had been refusing to work in class. The teacher, after a good deal of coaxing, had failed to interest the boy and consequently decided to leave him and concentrate on the remainder of the class. The boy set about disrupting the rest of the class and was soon involved in a heated verbal exchange with the teacher, which culminated in the boy calling the teacher 'a rotten bastard', and then withdrawing to a corner of the classroom. This incident was brought up in the group, a good deal of discussion centred on factors antecedent to the incident. The boy concerned mentioned that when he was in a junior school he had sworn at a teacher and had immediately been sent to the headmaster, but had run home before arriving at his office. Another boy promptly asked if that meant he had intended to abscond if Mr. X. had sent him to the headmaster the previous day, to which he replied 'Of course'. The group were then asked how they had felt at the time of yesterday's incident. The universal reaction was one of anger, best illustrated by one boy's comment to the effect that the new boy had better hurry up and learn that in this school you treat staff decently. The new boy was astounded; by swearing at the teacher, instead of gaining status amongst his peers, as he had expected, he succeeded in alienating their support.

If the group leader is faced by a group with a coherent delinquent attitude then he must perforce change his tactics. Janis and King[24] have shown the effectiveness of role-playing in a group situation on attitude change. This can be carried out in group counselling by the group leader selecting another member, preferably that member most expressive of the delinquent attitude, and asking him to role-play. He is asked to argue the opposite point of view to the one which he has been expressing. He is given a few minutes in which to prepare his ideas and then a few to argue his point to the group; he must then support it in the ensuing discussion. In this situation the selected individual will become more committed to his new viewpoint as the discussion continues and, if he is in fact a peer group leader, he will soon influence the opinions of the other members of the group. Janis and King suggest that such an experience brings about permanent changes in attitude. It is also a technique which avoids a clear division and subsequent confrontation between staff and boys.

PERSONALITY DEVELOPMENT

The rationale of group therapy is basically that man can only know himself through others. We may believe that there is somewhere a 'real me' but in fact there is a 'multi-faced me' which puts on the faces appropriate to varying social situations. Thus we have a father-face, a husband-face, a staff-face, a son-face, etc. We therefore only develop an identity in a social situation, our 'social identity'.[25] A small face to face group allows us to examine our social identity in detail through interaction with others. We can examine in the 'here and now' how our feelings and behaviour affect others and, consequently, our social identity.

In the small, group counselling situation described here there are other important factors, one of which is that of the group as a supportive structure. The boy who is taken into care at an early age because of parental rejection feels totally isolated and that he is the only person to have suffered in this way. In discussing his situation within the group he will gain a great deal of support from others who have suffered similar deprivations. He will also hear of family backgrounds which are far different from his own idealised concept of family life and will gain support through this. The effectiveness of such self-support groups has been shown with a range of behaviour disorders: Alcoholics Anonymous and Drug Addicts at Synanon are two of the most notable examples of such groups. Similarly, when members of the group discuss factors in their personal backgrounds which appear to them significant in precipitating their delinquent behaviour, they will soon discover other boys who experienced similar traumatic events but who adopted different techniques to cope with them.

76

ASSESSMENT

Unfortunately in the past assessment has often been seen as the prerogative of the classifying school and of little importance in the training school. This is obviously nonsense. Assessment must be an on-going process parallel to treatment, providing 'feedback' on the efficiency of the treatment and helping to construct criteria for decision-making in treatment. The group counselling programme provides an on-going system of assessment in a small group situation. In such a situation it is possible to assess subjectively the individual's potential for leadership, relationship and authority, ability to participate in group activity, relationship with peers. It also is possible to use sociometric techniques, such as sociograms, to objectify one's observation. With an intimate knowledge of groupings within the school it is possible to place new boys into groups with which they will be compatible. This clinical consideration and placing of new boys may well be effective in reducing absconding.[3]

LIMITATIONS IMPOSED ON GROUP THERAPY WITHIN THE INSTITUTIONAL SETTING

The process of group therapy has been well documented. Here I wish to discuss the limitations imposed on this process within a total institution. There are limitations upon the effectiveness of group counselling as a means of personality development because of the very nature of the population. As described earlier, the boys involved in group counselling suffer from constraints in their linguistic behaviour which work against discussion of feelings and emotions. There is also a cultural constraint on these boys: talking through problems with understanding sympathetic adults, whether they be clergy, psychologists, psychiatrists, or social workers, is predominantly middle-class, adult behaviour. Working-class boys find this process extremely difficult and culturally unacceptable even at a relatively neutral level (see *Kes,* by Barry Hines, for a superbly accurate description of an encounter between a working-class boy and a Youth Employment Officer.[26]) The boys are also limited by intellectual factors. In the groups described the range of intelligence was from I.Q. = 66 to I.Q. = 125. Low intelligence *per se* is not necessarily a limiting factor but in groups with such widely varying intelligence one is necessarily working at two levels. If intellectual development is seen in Piagetian terms, then the boy of fifteen with an average I.Q. will be able to deal with abstract, logical concepts, whereas a boy of the same age with an I.Q. in the E.S.N. range is only able to deal with concrete, operational concepts.

Not only are there limiting factors in the constitution of the population but limiting situational factors also exist, the most important of which is the confidentiality of the group. Boys resist discussing personal problems and details out of fear – first, of what the staff will do with the information, and second, of how the other boys will use it. Boys in Approved Schools (despite their new name of Community Homes) still see the residential experience as punitive, and see themselves as 'doing time'. The indefinite 'sentence' used by most schools means that the boy has no idea when he will be released except that it must usually be by his eighteenth birthday. He is in his opinion, therefore, permanently on the edge of his release, and consequently he is very unwilling to give information which may affect his release. From the boy's point of view, if he starts talking about problems at home or his worries about adjusting to life, then the staff may well use this information against him by further deferring his release. The boy's first aim is to deny the existence of all problems since, if he has no problems, he is presumably more likely to be released. This is a difficult situation to resolve, since information gained from the group counselling situation *is* likely to affect decisions about the boys' treatment. However, as far as possible, staff should attempt to allay the boys' fears, otherwise the group meetings can become a sterile ritual.

When group counselling is part of a total living situation the participants are inevitably wary of each other and of how others will use information. Pairings that develop in the group are just as easily destroyed in the 'yard', and information which was given in confidence in a therapeutic situation is likely to be turned round and used as insults and abuse. In a residential institution it is very easy for a boy to build up an idealised picture of home and to use this picture for his own comfort and as a protection against others. Normally this idealised picture is inviolate because the interaction between home and school is small; the occasional visits from relatives are not enough to give the other boys a clue to the real picture of home. In group counselling the boy is expected to discard the idealised picture and attempt to come to terms with the reality of the situation. This can only be achieved when there is 'trust' between the members of the group. This 'trust' is difficult both to attain and to maintain because of fluctuations in the membership of the group, through boys being admitted, absconding, being released, being sent home for leave, etc.

From this description of the programme of group counselling established at Wellside it is obvious that its effectiveness in resolving intense personal problems was limited, the advantage of such group work was that it made staff more aware of the boys' problems, and therefore more likely and more able to help the boys individually to deal with their problems. The groups were also important in intensifying existing personal relationships between staff and boys by showing the boys another side of an authority figure. This process was even more marked, however, in the Boys' Council, for it was here that boys came to experience authority for themselves.

Boys' Council

The development of the Boys' Council at Wellside provides a good illustration of the organic nature of a school. The idea of the Boys' Council arose from two sources. The first source was the staff training and development programme which included visits to various other special schools. One of these visits was to schools in Scotland, one of which had a Boys' Court. This Court was punitive in the main, dealing with minor misdemeanours committed by the boys. In the majority of cases the sentences issued by this Court consisted of extra work at weekends. At the school boys went home regularly at weekends. If they were given extra work it meant that they missed the school transport into the neighbouring city and had to make their own way, consequently arriving home later. Staff at Wellside saw this in action and, in discussing the visit on their return to the school, the general feeling was that it was an interesting idea but not applicable to Wellside at that time.

Some two years later some of the boys, whilst studying the Humanities Curriculum Project pack on Law and Order, came across a reference to a Borstal which had its own inmates' court. This reference was in a paragraph in a long article on the Borstal system. The boys picked this paragraph out as being of particular interest and discussed it at great length. They discussed whether or not such a system would be possible at Wellside. There were boys arguing both for and against the idea. The arguments put up against it were that boys would be bullied into not telling the truth; if one of the boy judges passed sentence on another boy, that boy would then 'sort him out' at a later date; boys would bring counter charges against others; if a boy was unpopular other boys would rig charges against him. Other boys argued that all these problems could be overcome because courts worked reasonably efficiently in society generally although similar problems could arise in any judicial system. Discussion of this topic extended throughout that Humanities period and the next, and the particular class involved became very interested in the idea, and asked the teacher if such a system could be set up in the school. After much discussion the teacher brought up the subject at a staff meeting and suggested that the establishment of a Boys' Council be considered. The idea of a Council as opposed to a Court was advocated since it was felt that a Court restricted the range of activities to trying misdemeanours and meting out sanctions or punishments, whereas a Council could operate as a forum for staff and boys. Council members could be taken to be representative of the boys, and the Council could act as the medium for the discussion of topics between staff and boys. This system could be particularly useful in that discussion with the total school was difficult at times, as there was a staff of some thirty people and ninety-five boys, and any meaningful discussion with such large numbers was not possible.

The staff were divided into three main camps over the issue. First there were those who supported the idea and felt that this was a useful addition to the treatment facilities at Wellside. Secondly, there were those who were opposed to the idea and who felt that they would be relinquishing their authority to the boys, that they would no longer be able to reprimand boys and, moreover, that boys might be able to bring them up in front of the Council and question them in front of the whole school. The third group was unable to see how the Council was going to work; they felt that there were too many practical problems involved; what boys would be on the Council, what sort of punishments could they issue, would they deal with all offences, etc. This group felt that more discussion of the idea was needed.

After two or three staff meetings, in which this topic was discussed, it was decided that each staff member should return and discuss it with his group to try to assess the feelings of the boys. The supporters of the Council were quite emphatic that the Council should only come into being if the boys wanted it. It had to be their idea; a Council imposed by the staff would obviously not be a *boys'* Council. So each member of staff went back and discussed it, and this is where the overlapping and interlocking nature of various structures within Wellside becomes obvious, since the place for discussion was the group counselling sessions.

The boys were also divided, some seeing this as an extremely good idea enabling them to have some responsibility for their behaviour, others seeing it as a terrible idea because they felt

80

that they would be picked on and wouldn't receive any justice from the boys. They wanted the staff to be the authority figures because they felt this gave them somebody to dislike. If the boys were the authority figures it was a much more complicated business to dislike and spurn your own peer group. The interesting, but expected result, when members reported back to the staff meetings, was that the staff who were opposed to the idea reported that their own groups were equally opposed to it, and the staff who supported the idea reported that their groups were in favour of the idea. This finding of the 'rank and file' professing the same ideas as the authority figures has been reported by other workers, though in entirely different circumstances, for example, nurses' attitudes have been shown to depend on the attitudes of the medical director.[27]

At this point the matter of the Boys' Council was put in to cold storage for several months, although it was still being generally discussed amongst the boys and by certain members of staff. At one point a representative from each class and department went to see the headmaster to discuss the possibility of starting the Boys' Council. It was interesting that of the representatives chosen some were in favour of the Council and some were against it. The headmaster felt that at this time he could not take any further steps, since the boys were still divided and there was no general consensus. However, through the enthusiasm and energy of one member of staff the matter eventually came to the fore again. This member of staff, who was strongly in favour of the Council, decided to establish amongst the class boys, who were also in favour of the Council, a mock Council.

When they got together to discuss the idea fully, they decided that they wanted a tribunal of four people to represent the Bench, plus a member of staff as Clerk of the Court – a person who would give guidance on general precedents of law. They also drew up a list of possible sanctions the Council could use and set about acting this out on one or two occasions a week. It was a mock Council in that the sanctions issued by it were not carried out. However, the cases referred to it were real cases of misdemeanours by boys brought up by other boys. Having established this Council, the member of staff involved then began to invite other groups to attend as observers to see how the procedure worked; one week he would have the garden department in, and another the joiners, and so on until every boy in the school and all members of staff had seen the mock Council in action. The topic was then brought up again at a staff meeting. By this time the consensus of opinion amongst the staff had gelled; people had seen the Council in operation and felt that it could be useful, and so it was decided to extend it to the whole school and it was also decided that sentences issued by the Council would be carried out. However, some members of staff felt that the various sanctions produced by the boys were far too punitive and that this was a retrograde step for the school, so it was decided that a group of staff and the elected representatives of the boys should meet to decide what sanctions were acceptable. Before this could be done elections were held by the boys for the posts of Councillors, each boy and each member of staff was asked to nominate the four boys whom he would like to see on the Council. The eight boys with the most votes were appointed, and four boys served at any one time. During any particular session a Councillor might have to step down either to be a witness or to be a defendant, in which case another elected member took his place. It was decided that the Council should operate every Monday and Thursday afternoon for an hour.

Perhaps the best way of describing what occurred is to quote from the transcript of one of the Council's sessions, since this illustrates the type of case that arose and the Council's procedure for dealing with it. Also it illustrates the tremendous depth of insight the Councillors showed into their peers' behaviour and the way in which they attempted to offer guidance rather than merely impose punitive sanctions.

In the transcript 'C' signifies Councillor. No attempt has been made to differentiate between the comments of the four Councillors. In two instances the Councillors' (Bench) discussion is quoted in full to illustrate the amount of consideration given by the bench to each case before reaching a decision.

TRANSCRIPT OF COURT PROCEEDINGS

C. First case by Mr. X. against John for burning holes in the jumper of Mike. Will John come forward please. Sit down. Can we hear what you have to say Mr. X.

Mr. X. This lad was accused by Paul, Mike and Jimmy for burning holes in their jumpers. They have shown me the holes in their jumpers, the burns had gone through to their shirts, and in a couple of cases through to the skin, resulting in a very bad burn. I think this is a very serious charge. Will the lads who were burned come out to the bench and show the boys their jumpers please.

C. Will you also show the rest of the boys. Silence please. Do you plead Guilty or Not Guilty?

John Guilty.

82

C. Right, the second case, I'm charging you with threatening to beat up Paul over the incident of lighting a fire. I'll have to stand down. One day last week I was coming into the Table Tennis room and the corridor was open, I seen a load of boys down the corridor, I went down to see what was going on. John had Paul up against the wall and I asked him why he was going to hit him, and he said he had legged [informed] on him about lighting the fires, I told Paul to go out and I wrote it down as a case.

C. Do you plead Guilty or Not Guilty?

John Guilty.

C. John is also charged by Steve for smoking after being banned by the Court. Can we hear what Steve has to say.

Steve It was on Tuesday, John asked Terry for a roll-up and he said no. Then when Terry threw his dog-end away John picked it up and said thanks and started smoking it.

C. Thank you. Do you plead Guilty or Not Guilty?

John Guilty.

C. Will Terry stand up please, when you threw the fag down did you throw it away or chuck it to John?

Terry I'd finished with the fag and just threw it on the table.

C. Why on the table?

Terry Don't know.

C. Why didn't you put it in the bin?

Terry Because Alan had asked for it.

C. Well no need to go on because you've already pleaded guilty anyhow. John charged by Steve for leaving Table Tennis room without permission [previous Court decision]. Will Steve stand up please.

Steve I was in the Table Tennis room and John was running round, he ran out of the room and ran into Mr. Y and said 'Please can I go to the toilet?' Mr. Y. said nothing and John just said thanks and kept running. Laurie is a witness.

C. Do you plead Guilty or Not Guilty?

John Not Guilty.

Mr. X. I have something to add. John came up to me and said a couple of lads were picking on him and if he just put his head outside the door they were saying they'd report him for leaving the room, he was upset by this because he felt they were trying to get him into trouble deliberately.

C. Thank you. Will you leave the room, John.

Bench discussion

Well he's guilty of three of them and not guilty of the other

83

– I think we should send him to the headmaster over burning the jumpers – No I think we should deal with it and then send him to the Head. I think he should have to pay for the jumpers – That's too much, he couldn't out of his pocket money – I suggest he pays so much a week but the Head decides how many weeks he must pay for. – How much a week do you reckon? – About a shilling. – We can ask the Matron how much the jumpers cost, she's here. – We can get her to tell all the boys how much the shirts and jumpers cost, they might look after them better then. – So it's a shilling a week till the Head says stop. What about the case last week with Paul and Alan burning jumpers, we'll have to mention that. – What about the other cases. – Well he says a lot of boys are picking on him and they are. – Well what shall we do about him still smoking, that's contempt of Court. We must do something about that. Bullying Paul I reckon he should just be warned, but about the smoking I reckon he should be stopped. – You can't do that, it didn't work last time. – He's not guilty on Steve's charge, he's got to be allowed out sometimes, and it's Mr. Y.'s fault he should have answered the question. – So on the first charge he's guilty and got to pay a shilling a week until the Head says stop. – The next one he gets a warning if he threatens any boy for telling the truth. – The next, smoking after being banned. – Tell Mr. Z. not to sell him any fags. – But he'll still get them. – No he won't, last time nobody gave him any. – Well, he didn't really smoke it was only a dog-end. – I think it's too hard stopping him smoking. – So we have got to hit him hard. I think we should ban him over the weekend and anybody who gives him a smoke will be charged as well. – That's stupid because some people can't just stop like that. It's hard not to have a smoke. – I think if we let him smoke but confine him to the yard areas and fine him a shilling a week for the jumper, that's enough. – That's O.K. with a warning that we could hit him harder.

C. Call John back in. Quiet please. Will Matron stand up please. Can you give us the cost of the shirts and jumpers damaged.

Matron The jumpers cost £2.47 each and the shirts £1.50.

C. Can you tell us how much they would cost to repair?

Matron Not easily, but I suppose it would take about an hour to repair them, so it would cost about a pound.

C. Thank you. Can we have Paul and Alan [previous offenders

for same offence]. We find you all guilty of burning holes
in jumpers and fine you all a shilling a week until the
Headmaster tells you to stop. We think we are letting you
off pretty lightly because we could make you pay the total
cost of the jumpers and so we are also, John, confining
you to the yard areas; here again we're being light because
we could stop you smoking again, but we won't. You are not
guilty of the fourth offence, but if you are brought up again
for threatening other kids we will send you to the headmaster. Have you anything to say?

C. Next case. Mr. A. charges Mike and Kevin with playing
snooker with the cue rest. Can we hear the evidence.

Mr. A. I went into the billiard room last night after giving these
two permission to go in there, although it wasn't their
night. As I went through the door Mike was using the rest
to play snooker with and was doing this several times. Kevin
had the balls arranged in front of him and was just blasting
at them with the cue. It seemed to me a misuse of the table
and that the cloth was in danger of being damaged.

C. Do you plead Guilty or Not Guilty?

Both Guilty.

C. Right wait outside please.

Bench discussion

C. We find you guilty of mucking about in the snooker room so
you will dust the snooker room and wash it out during your
own free time on Sunday. You will either come to one of us
or to the member of staff on duty to check it is alright.
Have you anything to say?

C. Mike and Brian are charged by Tony for shouting after lights
out. Mike and Brian come out please. Tony can we have
your story.

Tony It was last Monday night about half past ten, I couldn't
get to sleep but most of our dorm was asleep and I heard
someone shouting, this was after Mike had just come back
off the bunk [absconding]. Someone was shouting and I
thought it was Mr. X. at Mike, anyway they kept on
shouting so I got up to have a look and it was Brian and
Mike shouting at each other.

C. How do you plead?

Both Guilty.

C. Will you leave the room then please.

Bench discussion

85

C. We find you guilty of shouting in the dormitories and we think a warning will be enough, but next time we will be much harder on you, if it is for making a noise in the dormitories again.

C. Next case. Martin and John charged by Neil for smoking in the toilets in class time. Come up here please. Stand up and tell us.

Neil I went to the toilet about twenty past ten and these two were smoking in the new washrooms. It was yesterday.

C. Whose class should you have been in?

Both Mrs. B.

C. Why didn't you go?

Martin I just went to the toilet for a smoke.

C. Would you do that with one of the men teachers?

Martin Yes, I've done it plenty of times before.

C. Guilty or Not Guilty.

Both Guilty.

Bench discussion

C. You two will change your housework so that you work in the toilets, tomorrow morning for one day and you will have to pick up the dog-ends with your hands, the same as the regular boys have to since you cause them along with some others that haven't been caught yet.

This then was the Boys' Council at Wellside.

The question that needs to be asked is: Was it in fact a therapeutic structure or just a gimmick? I personally think that it did have a great deal more than gimmickry about it and I will now try to bring out something of its importance and value. This can be described under two headings: therapeutic value and social education value.

THE EXPERIENCE OF AUTHORITY

It is almost a truism to say that many of the children in residential establishments such as Wellside have problems with relationships with authority and this can be explained, as it is in *Care and Treatment in a Planned Environment,* as follows: [6] 'While most children come to a satisfactory understanding of authority and responsibility by the give and take of family life and the image projected by their parents, many of the children with whom we are concerned would not have had this sort of experience.'

The onus is on the residential institution to give the child experience of authority which is neither exceptionally punitive nor exceptionally indulgent. In the vast majority of cases this is done through the identification process discussed earlier in this chapter. However, the Boys' Council offered a different situation in which the boys could experience authority. The Councillors were placed in a clear-cut position of authority which they could use constructively or destructively, but their actions were always observed by their peers. The opportunities for using their position of authority destructively were minimal because of this close observation by their peers, who soon reprimanded the Councillors if they attemped to use their authority partially. For example, on one occasion, when one of the members of the Bench asked the boys for silence, one boy from the body of the meeting immediately leapt to his feet and demanded that the Bench also ask the staff to be quiet since they were also talking. He said that the boys should not be singled out for the reprimand: it should apply to the total 'public'. Members of the Council were able to experience authority under the supervision and with the support of a member of staff – the person acting as Clerk of the Court, whose job was to attempt to make sure that the boys were neither too repressive nor too indulgent, that they didn't show favour to their friends nor disfavour to their enemies, but used authority responsibly. This learning experience was invaluable to some of the boys. In Chapter VI, one boy who had served a term as a particularly effective Councillor is interviewed and his feelings towards this position are analysed in detail, and much of his reported experience appears to have been of value to him.

Since there were eight members elected to the Council, each one served at some point during the term, and elections were held each school term, the number of boys who actually experienced the authority by being on the Bench was in fact quite large. The whole school benefited from this, not just the Councillors. As mentioned earlier, peer group counselling is found to be more effective than counselling by an adult. Consequently counselling offered by the Bench was more effective than reprimands issued by staff. The main body of the boys also benefited from the Council's efforts in breaking down staff-boy barriers. In my time at Wellside a division of the school into a hardened boy subculture and an alienated staff culture was never prevalent. In fact, there had been a continual growing together of the two cultures, and the operations of the Council certainly quickened this growth. The main body of the boys were no longer able to stereotype the staff into punitive, authoritarian persons who merely meted out reprimands and punishments, because the whole issue was altered by the Boys' Council, where the boys took on the responsibility of their own discipline under the guidance of staff. Certainly many of the particularly anti-authority boys within the school found this situation rather threatening. Their stereotype of 'black' authoritarian staff was no longer tenable and they found this quite frightening. Boys reported on several occasions that they didn't like the Council. They wanted the staff to do the sanctioning because then they knew where they were, and they knew whom they hated, but when they had a friend who was on the Bench it was very difficult to decide whether they hated him or not.

SOCIAL EDUCATION

The other important aspect of the Boys' Council was that of social education. The Council provided a valuable method of educating boys about certain social structures – the obvious example being the elections. The boys began to understand the responsibility of a vote. They realised that, having voted for a representative, they had to accept his authority or demand a further election. They also understood the working of the judiciary; the importance of building up a body of case law; what contempt of court meant; what problems were involved in proving a case if no witnesses were available. All these aspects of social education were carried out through the medium of the Boys' Council. An example of how this social education worked occurred when a solicitor visited the school from the local town. He was asked if he would observe the Council and comment on its procedure. The boys found this an invaluable experience because they learnt that procedures which they had developed in their own Council were in fact very similar to procedures existing in the judicial system. The solicitor was also able to offer valuable advice. For example, one of the structures of the Boys' Council which had developed was that of an appeal court, whereby a boy could appeal either against the verdict or sentence. The appeal court consisted of the Headmaster together with the elected Councillors, who discussed the case in the presence of the boy and decided whether the appeal was founded or not. However, the Council was faced by the problem, which inevitably arises where an appeal court exists, that if there is a possibility of appeal and no possibility of further sanctions, an appeal is an attractive gamble. The Council had been bothered by this for a while, because every boy who was found guilty, or any boy who was given punishment, immediately said he was going to appeal. In the discussion with the solicitor it was decided that the way to overcome this problem was to charge boys whose appeals failed an extra 2½p; this reduced the numbers of appeals drastically.

DISADVANTAGES OF THE COUNCIL

These were the advantages of the Boys' Council. However, there were certain disadvantages which may well be rectified in the future. The biggest disadvantage was that although the institution was set up as a Boys' Council it was in fact a Boys' Court, and the Councillors had to take on a fairly repressive authoritarian role. This alienated them from the vast majority of the boys, and maintained an unrealistic and one-sided view of authority. Authority is not only punitive, it is also indulgent, and the school needs to look closely at whether the boys on the Council should be allowed to hand out 'goodies' – perhaps award weekend leave to boys who have been particularly well-behaved – because authority has the power to be benevolent. The main body of boys would then see the Councillors in a more realistic light, representing both sides of authority. Again, in the interview in Chapter VI, one has this sense of alienation from Gerry, the boy interviewed, and certainly the Councillors came under tremendous pressure at one point from the boys, who regarded them merely as creeps and lackeys of the staff.

This was Wellside. Certain aspects of the school have been extracted and described in an attempt to give a clearer picture of its atmosphere and ethos. In the next chapter a closer look will be taken at the people within the school, the staff, the boys and the roles they both play.

CHAPTER V

Staff and Boys

An institution like Wellside is not only a continually changing organic structure but also possesses other 'physical' attributes. An institution is a molar organisation, a homogenous unit built up from the constituent molecules. At Wellside these are the boys, professional staff and domestic staff. Each of these molecules is in turn built up from a collection of atoms, namely the individual persons. The institution reflects the aims and attitudes of all its members, staff and boys. Each individual (atom) brings his own personal experiences and views into the school; he then clusters with similar individuals to form the major subgroups (molecules); these in turn have a common set of attitudes and behavioural norms which in part reflect the constituent individuals' norms, but only in part; each subgroup also has well-developed group mechanisms by which they deter individuals from deviating too widely from the group norm and thereby splitting the group. The subgroups interact to form the institution itself (molar structure) which constantly struggles to form a cohesive unit which adequately reflects the norms of the subgroups.

Norms of the Institution as a Whole

In this chapter I hope to illustrate this process by first describing the molar norms, those common core features of Wellside that bind the various subgroups together (sometimes in an unhappy union). Then I shall outline the features common to the two major molecules, the staff and boys. Finally, I shall examine the atoms of the institution – individual staff and boys. The reader will notice that often the views expressed at the atomic level are at variance to those expressed at the molar level and this is an important characteristic of institutions. When an individual commits himself to an institution, either voluntarily, as with staff, or involuntarily, as with most boys, he must relinquish some of

90

his own identity to the total identity of the institution. We shall see later that this is often a difficult, painful and unsatisfying experience.

The most obvious molar attitude arises from the simple fact that all inhabitants, staff and boys, of the institution are also members of a wider society. As I have shown in Chapter III, the wider society has certain expectations about Community Homes: that they should be custodial, to some extent punitive and that the inmates are perverse. These expectations are also held, to a lesser or greater extent, by the inhabitants of the institution, and greatly effect their behaviour within the Home. Goffman puts the 'labelling' process involved as follows:

> The interpretative scheme of the total institution automatically begins to operate as soon as the inmate enters, the staff having the notion that entrance is prima facie evidence that one must be the kind of person the institution was set up to handle. A man in a political prison must be traitorous; a man in a prison must be a lawbreaker; a man in a mental hospital must be sick. If not traitorous, criminal or sick why else would he be there.[1]

A common attitude that develops amongst the inhabitants is that the inmates are delinquent and that the task of the institution is to stop delinquency. Therefore the introduction of the 1969 Children and Young Persons Act was greeted by the same response from both staff and boys: that if boys 'in care' were mixed with 'delinquent' boys the 'care' boys would turn delinquent. This argument (as well as having face value) has a firm social/psychological basis since, if the prevailing attitudes within the institution are delinquent attitudes, then it would be predicted that 'non-delinquent' members would soon accept the group norm of delinquency. However, this view is extremely negative because it denies that the staff have any significant impact on the attitudes within the institution. Indeed in some institutions this is the reality of life, as Polsky[2] has shown. In the institution he studied the two subcultures were clearly disassociated and the peer subculture was the major influence in the lives of the children. This need not be the situation and there is in fact some evidence, given in Chapter IV, to suggest that the situation at Wellside was radically different.

Nevertheless, the basic premise, accepted by both staff and boys, of the inmates' delinquency and the institution's task of arresting this delinquency produced certain behaviour within the institution. The most important aspect of this behaviour was the staff's failure to accept as normal much of the boys' normal behaviour – having labelled the boys as delinquent, it followed that any behaviour that was seen as unacceptable or disruptive by the staff was cited as further evidence of the boys' delinquency. Thus talking in the dormitories at night after lights out, an inevitable and natural result of having twelve boys sharing the same bedroom, became a major institutional 'offence', and was given the forbidding title of 'causing a disturbance in the dormitories'. This natural, childish behaviour gave rise to a great deal of concern amongst staff, mainly because it was inconvenient to the institution's timetable, and a good deal of staff effort was directed at solving this thorny problem. However, the situation really became absurd when this institutional 'offence' at times took on greater importance than 'true offences' – so that the situation could arise that a boy who had been talking in the dormitories was sanctioned as heavily as a boy who had committed a larceny on weekend leave.

This process, in which socially normal behaviour is misinterpreted by the inhabitants, is clearly illustrated in the institutional language which uses quasi-legal terms to describe normal behaviour. At Wellside, before the boys were allowed to smoke openly, having a packet of cigarettes in one's pocket was described as 'being in possession of smoking materials'.

This process concentrates staff and boys' efforts on examining and modifying only institutional behaviour, much of which was quite irrelevant to the boys' environmental behaviour. A boy who may be admitted for having committed a series of quite serious offences may soon be recognised by all as a 'good boy' because his institutional behaviour conforms to certain expected norms. This process also militates against change in the institution. When capital developments at Wellside were discussed, and it was suggested that the boys should be accommodated in small units of approximately twelve boys, each boy having a single bedroom and each unit being provided with adequate bathrooms, kitchens, lounges, dining rooms, etc., many staff voiced the anxiety that it would be counter-productive to 'give the boys too much'. The headmaster then pointed out that the proposals being made would only provide a setting similar to ordinary household life. The idea of 'giving too much' extends throughout institutional life; the boys are perceived as delinquent and, consequently, as manipulative and exploitative, so any extension of their liberty is often seen by staff as merely providing further opportunity for delinquency.

A similar logic maintains amongst the boys. They also see

92

the task of the home as deterring them from future delinquency, so they continually suggest to staff that the establishment should be more repressive in certain areas. The logic of their viewpoint is that if being separated from one's family is an effective treatment for delinquency, then allowing one home frequently is going to reduce the effectiveness of one's treatment. This often leads to an odd symbiotic relationship between staff and boys. For example, staff were often heard to say that corporal punishment should be reintroduced because the boys preferred it to other sanctions, such as the stopping of pocket money. Similarly, boys would argue for the reintroduction of corporal punishment because some staff members had implied that they needed it, it would do them good, and anyway they deserved it.

This attitude towards corporal punishment leads on to another common core attitude much more widely held by staff and boys, and one which is common to the common backgrounds of staff and boys. From Field's study[3] of boys in Approved Schools, it is obvious that the vast majority of boys come from working-class backgrounds, skilled, semi-skilled and unskilled, and very few boys come from white collar, professional or managerial families. They share this working-class background with the staff, as shown by the Dartington Hall Research Team.[4] From this shared background an attitude arises which is apolitical, materialistic and functional. Staff and boys see themselves as manipulated by the hierarchy and the intellectuals; they do not see themselves as part of a political society able to exert pressure for change. Staff will complain that they are short of resources, are asked to perform an impossible task, and are continually criticised and constrained. They see the people 'at the top' phasing out corporal punishment but not prepared to try and deal with the children themselves or able to offer any constructive alternative. And yet, although they hold these views, often with valid reasons, they are not prepared to state their case publicly or align themselves with pressure groups pushing for a change in conditions. This position is analogous to the situation of the boys and their families.

Similarly boys and staff share the same materialistic attitude; staff enjoying low-cost housing soon accumulate an impressive array of cars, colour televisions, deep freezers; the boys long for the good life when as adults they too will be able to enjoy the comforts of a house and car.

This attitude is closely connected to the functional attitude of staff and boys – that work is essential to obtain money, and that money should be spent on useful things. This attitude rules out whole areas of social life. Art, music, literature are all seen as non-functional and therefore irrelevant niceties. One reads and studies to pass exams; once they have been passed, reading and studying ends. People are regarded as useful or non-useful. Thus outside professionals – psychiatrists, psychologists, etc. – are treated with suspicion. They are non-useful in that they are not seen to work, except when they can perform a direct functional service to the institution, such as arranging the transfer of a particularly difficult boy to another establishment. Similarly, boys view outside professionals without interest unless they are capable of arranging their 'release' or getting them more frequent holidays.

One final attitude which arises from what Goffman calls 'people-work' is that the staff and boys have statuses and relationships in the outside world that must be taken into consideration. Goffman states: 'Kin as critics present a special problem because, while the inmates can be educated about the price they will pay for making demands on their own behalf, relations receive less tutoring in this regard and rush in with requests for inmates that inmates would blush to make for themselves.'

This problem is obvious as far as the boys are concerned since interested parents will make demands on the institution which the institution often finds difficulty in accepting, and which the boys may find embarrassing. However, the situation also operates in reverse. If the boys have opportunities of viewing the staff with their families, they see staff in a different role, often to the embarrassment of the staff. This process is often highlighted by elaborate institutional mechanisms aimed at disguising any obvious close relationship between staff members. Thus in one children's home, where a newly married couple were employed, the head of the home insisted that when at work they referred to each other as Mr. and Mrs. . . . a more artificial situation is difficult to imagine. This problem of outside relationships is overcome by staff and boys tacitly agreeing to reduce family contact to a minimum. Although the institution may extend visiting times and facilities the boys will not openly encourage visitors, for the reasons mentioned by Goffman. For similar reasons, although staff's wives and families live within a hundred yards of the staff's place of employment, they will only rarely venture forth to the area of interaction between the staff and boys, except for specially arranged institutional events when the code of conduct is allowed to lapse for a clearly defined period of time. The odd party will be given, when staff families and boys interact; the boys dancing with wives and chatting-up daughters, but after the event the tacit agreement is reinforced.

94

Residential Social Workers – attitudes and training

At the molecular level, initially, residential social workers will be examined by looking at the training they receive and the attitudes they hold. However, it is important to remember that in Wellside residential social workers are a minority group amongst staff and their influence is consequently small. This will be discussed more fully when the staffing is examined. It is important that the position of residential social workers be examined in depth since they are an important influence in most Community Homes and will also prove to be important in the future at Wellside (see Chapter VII). It is difficult to define the task of residential child care because there is no generally agreed optimum way of helping 'deprived' children. The Home Office in the 1960s saw the task in Approved Schools as trying to help each child in the group to become a better educated, more considerate, more worthwhile character. They (staff) will be concerned about each boy's or girl's private worries, disabilities and family, and will try to find for the children some interest on which they can build a better kind of life. As Approved Schools became Community Homes the definition of the task of the staff became more sophisticated – even if the actual task was not noticeably different. In *Care and Treatment in a Planned Environment* it is suggested,

> that the residential community worker should be responsible for creating and maintaining an environment which provides some of the positive experiences of good home life and a supportive framework for individual treatment, and which is also in itself therapeutic. In such an environment every aspect of the child's day is used to help to heal the effects of past damage and to promote emotional and social growth. The purpose of training is to enable him to fulfil these responsibilities.[5]

We shall examine how these job descriptions match up to the actual job later, but now it is important to examine the training offered to residential workers. Before doing so an important caveat must be stated; this is that, proportionately, very few residential workers are actually trained. It is recognised that the job of caring for deprived children is both complex and demanding, but the vast majority of people carrying out this job have no professional training or qualification whatsoever. A survey, carried out by the Association of Children's Officers, of staff in post in residential establishments on 1st January 1958 showed that 9 per cent of the staff, or 239 out of a total staff of 2,778, held the Home Office Certificate in the Residential Care of Children. By the mid-sixties the situation had improved only fractionally. A survey carried out by the same body revealed that in 1964, 10¼ per cent of residential staff had the professional certificate. By 1968 further improvements in the availability of training had brought the figure of trained personnel to approximately 15 per cent. It is important to point out that these figures do not refer to teaching staff, who would be qualified before appointment. Nevertheless, it is debatable whether the qualification for certificated teachers is sufficient to allow them to cope adequately with the teaching of deprived children, and it is certainly of little help to them in their child care role, both in the classroom and, more particularly, for taking extraneous duties. It is perhaps significant that since local education authorities have taken over responsibility for schools within hospitals for the mentally subnormal, certificated teachers are expected to take a further year's qualification in order to fit them for the task of teaching the mentally subnormal child.

I am placing so much emphasis on training for three important reasons: first, because detailed knowledge is gained during professional training; second, because of the effect such training has on an individual's attitudes within his occupation; and, third, because of the security it offers an individual attempting to carry out a difficult task with little formal support.

The greater part of professional training in child care is carried out by colleges of further education and polytechnics. The course lasts for one year. Approximately two-thirds of the course is spent in study at the college and the remainder in practical training in homes or schools. The courses are designed to produce residential child care officers capable of playing a full part as members of a professional team of social workers, teachers, psychologists, and other specialists. They are planned to help students to equip themselves with some of the skills needed for recognising and responding to the varied and changing needs of children who are living away from home.

The majority of courses fall into a very similar pattern since they all offer the same ultimate qualification, that of the Central Training Councils' Certificate in the Residential Care of Children. A small number of Universities also organise a one year course leading to the Advanced Certificate in Residential Child Care. The Central Training Council's overall responsibility allows for some variations between courses, but in fact there is very little variation. The courses include an introduction to psychology and, in particular, a detailed study of human growth and development, which inevitably concentrates on childhood and adolescence. This section of the course usually contains some rudimentary health education with the emphasis on ailments that are common in childhood. Principles of social work, as one might expect, occupy a large section of the professional training, and include an examination of social work practice, concentrating particularly on the task of residential social work. The course will also include some theoretical and practical group work designed to give the students a greater understanding of group dynamics. A section is also included on social administration and social policy, outlining the development of the social services and their organisation. Further sections on sociology and criminology are offered at a fairly superficial level – inevitable through lack of time. Most courses also offer facilities for creative studies to allow the student to develop an interest and some skill in art, drama, music and outdoor pursuits.

The intake for most courses normally has a fairly wide age range, with a mean age of about thirty years. This means that many of the students have little formal academic qualifications. Many of the younger entrants, however, will have 'O' levels; a smaller number 'A' levels; and occasionally a student may have a degree or comparable high qualification. With an intake of this composition and a duration of only three terms the courses generally take on a conservative, vocational training aspect rather than an academic aspect.

I would submit that the task residential workers are now asked to undertake necessitates a much more rigorous, though necessarily still vocational course, but with an increased academic content. This would help to produce the understanding and ability necessary to analyse the complex concepts involved in residential child care. It is interesting that the Williams Committee recommendation of a basic two-year course for residential staff has only been adopted by a minority of colleges.[6] However, there are signs that the status of training in residential social work will soon be improved. In 1973 the Central Council for Education and Training in social work advocated a minimum qualification based on a two-year part-time course leading to the Certificate of Proficiency in Social Work, and a higher qualification, the Certificate of Qualification in Social Work – a two-year, full-time, college-based course. It still remains to be seen if their recommendations will be implemented. It is important to note that teacher training and the training of psychiatric nurses are both of three years' duration, and the tasks of these two groups are in many ways analogous to that of residential child care.

It is now recognised that in the interaction between social worker and client the attitudes of the social workers are as important as those of the client. Consequently research workers have now begun to investigate the values and attitudes held by social workers. Aldridge-Morris for example suggests that, 'In contrast to the popular social worker stereotype, they are not especially kindly, nor high in conscience or will-power, nor especially resilient to stress or neurosis.[7] However, Ballard stresses the differences between social workers functioning in different situations. He sees field workers stressing concepts of emotional deprivation, love, security and permissive relationships; and residential workers stressing discipline, reality, and punishment for misbehaviour.[8] Similarly my own research (Tutt, 1972)[9, 10] suggests that residential social workers are more conservative in their attitudes than field social workers.

There is some evidence from other sources to support this hypothesis. The Dartington Hall Research Team point out that some staff gave disillusionment with the 'permissiveness' of ordinary schools as their reason for taking up Approved School work.[4] From the same source, they point out that headmasters discussing selection of staff stressed the need for staff who can keep 'good discipline', a phrase which is often synonymous with authoritarianism. These two factors would tend to 'filter' staff coming into residential work, especially Approved School work, guaranteeing the selection of more conservative staff. Once in post, staff will opt to use more authoritarian methods of control for two main reasons: first, they appear superficially to be the most rational, thus if a boy abuses given privileges then it seems logical to remove the privileges. These aversive techniques are prevalent throughout the Approved School system. Second, staff will soon conform to the conservative staff norms of the institution. Since the majority of institutions have comparatively small staffs any deviant member of staff either becomes totally isolated or conforms to the general group norm.

Composition of the Staff

However, as intimated earlier, residential social workers were a very small minority at Wellside and this in turn had important implications for the ethos of the institution. At Wellside, at the time of writing, the staff structure consisted of sixteen professional staff (as opposed to domestic and maintenance staff). Of these sixteen, eleven were 'contact' staff responsible for the boys from waking to going to bed. Of these eleven, eight were certificated teachers and three were residential social workers, of whom only one was professionally qualified. The remaining five professional staff consisted of the headmaster and his deputy, a matron and her deputy and the psychologist. How these roles functioned and their relative importance is discussed in a later chapter, but what most obviously emerges from this staffing structure is that Wellside had ten certificated teachers and only three child care staff – four, if the psychologist is seen as child care staff. This imbalance amongst staff meant that Wellside was most obviously a school and not a home, in that the ethos of the establishment was heavily biased towards education rather than social work. Furthermore, if length of service within the school is examined it soon becomes clear that the trade instructors, men who originally qualified in their trades and only later in life have gained their teachers' certificate, as a group have worked much longer in the school than either the teachers or housemasters. This finding has also been reported by the Dartington Research Team. The consequence of this is that the instructors have a disproportionate effect on the ethos of the school above and beyond their actual numbers.

In *Care and Treatment in a Planned Environment*, it is said, 'We think that in a Community Home they [staff] should be seen as a single professional group, which may include residential child care officers, social workers, teachers and instructors.' This is certainly a laudable aim and one which was attempted at Wellside. But the staff structure ensured that Wellside was much more a boarding school than a Community Home with educational facilities. This was reflected in the physical facilities of the institution: financially well-endowed and well-equipped classrooms and trade departments, and comparatively sparsely furnished accommodation and paucity of clothing and simple toilet articles such as combs and toothbrushes.

Another important fact is that the training of teachers is aimed at inculcating a different set of attitudes from that of social workers. Teacher training emphasises the importance of maintaining distance between the teacher and child. Colleges of education recommend that the teacher first establish discipline and control over his class before showing any signs of relaxation. Teacher training fails to emphasise the importance of the child's home background, and the current lack of parent-teacher associations in many state schools underlines the antipathy most teachers feel for greater contact between school and home. The teacher-pupil relationship is basically a vertical, authority relationship with the teacher seen as the person who 'knows' what is right and best and who is expected to be in control and obeyed. This relationship is essentially different from that required in successful social work, in which the relationship should be horizontal, with the social workers and client working together. A principle of social work is said to be the importance of being 'non-judgemental' in one's dealings with clients; the same certainly cannot be said about teaching, where so much emphasis is based on grading and judging pupils' performances.

Finally, the teaching ethic is concerned mainly with problems of learning. Personal problems only become of importance when they hinder the learning process. This again is fundamentally different from the social work attitude which is focused entirely on personal problems. These differences in attitude of teachers to a greater or lesser extent affect the attitude of teachers at Wellside and, through them, the overall ethos of the school. Until this is overcome Wellside will continue to remain primarily a school and not a home.

Some idea of the training and experience of the boys of Wellside – complementary to the account I have given of the staff's experience – can be found in the Appendix to this book (p. 213).

CHAPTER VI

Case Studies of Staff and Boys

Case Studies of Staff

The following three case studies are transcripts of interviews held with three members of staff at Wellside. The three staff were selected to illustrate the range of staff's experience: one is a man with a considerable length of service in the Approved School system, who has a wealth of experience but has never received any formal training. Another is a man who left a career in industry in search of something more personally satisfying and has received training whilst in post. The third is a man who after graduating entered the child care profession, went on to complete his residential social work training and then entered the Approved School service.

Although the staff were not selected to illustrate any particular hypothesis it soon became obvious that their backgrounds and early experiences were not that far removed from the boys with whom they deal. The interviews also clearly illustrate the haphazard way in which each of them 'drifted' into child care, in most cases with very little knowledge of what the work was really about. As they talk they vividly portray the depth of their personal commitment to their work and their confusion over the mammoth task which faces them as to how to 'care for', 'control', 'cure' the children with whom they work.

MR. A.

I was born in a little village near Stoke-on-Trent, but we moved when I was about five years old and so the best part of my life was spent on a council estate just outside Newcastle-under-Lyme. My father was a clerical worker and rising very slowly through the grades until now he has got a pretty good job. We were never very desperately poor but we always had to wait for things,

101

like we had new clothes once a year, you know the normal sort of thing, not really poor but never having too much of everything. We always had good food and that's the only thing we had a lot of. We didn't have a television until quite late on, didn't get one until about 1960, most families in the road had got one by then, we never had a car. So we were sort of living comfortably but within our means and not getting much extra.

I had a very peculiar adolescence, actually I was one of the very few boys on the council estate to go to grammar school, and it was very difficult to keep up friendships. Really because I suppose I am a bit like my father, the family had got the education ethos and it was instilled into me almost from the beginning that you worked very hard at school in order to be able to get a good job, and it wasn't till later that I realised there were other things in life, and so really I feel it wasn't until I was about sixteen that my life began and I realised that you can flog yourself to death to no avail. But for the four or five years between eleven and sixteen while I was at grammar school the communication between me and the boys in the vicinity was negligible, just nothing there at all. I was staying in doing my homework and they were out and there seemed a lot of enmity grew up, fostered by families and the usual sort of 'You go to Grammar school and we don't, let's shun you.' It was quite a classic situation really. At school I accepted the major part of the ethos for the first few years because I was struggling to do better and get into the 'A' form and get the better chances there, because it was obvious from the start that the 'A' boys were going to make it and the people lower down were not. I used to get into minor scrapes and fool about with the rest of the lads, but the general ethos of our class was that you had to work hard. I don't think I am being fanciful, I think it's true especially as you got towards sixteen and 'O' levels started coming up. I think the teachers were there just to teach, simply that and nothing else.

My life at school was split off, I enjoyed life at school but there was little or no contact with boys at school once I came home. When I came home I was into my own little fairly isolated world, as regards the local vicinity anyway. I had a lot of friends but they lived farther away and I had to travel to see them, but the trouble was I couldn't match the money spending ability of my mates. My parents provided me with a fair amount of pocket money but it wasn't anything like as much as my mates had. But I don't know, it was probably less that and more me feeling embarrased when I went into a middle-class or upper-class home, I think my parents had fostered this idea, since they weren't quite at ease when a lad from one of the posher areas came over to our house and it took a few years to realise and accustom myself to interchange between our house, a council house, and a private house which was better furnished and the people seemed much more at ease when visitors arrived. I think it took a few years for my parents to work through this as well.

Most of my deviant behaviour in adolescence was channelled through, it sounds insipid really, the Church youth club and the types of deviant behaviour I got up to down there were ideological. I delighted in shocking people in almost any way I could and then try to get them to justify their own actions and ideas. After I was sixteen it was channelled through rock climbing and mountaineering, not only for the climbing but that meant I had a legitimate reason for travelling all over the country and indulging in fairly dangerous things with my mates rather than hanging about in the streets and smashing windows. It gave me a good excuse for hitching down to Wales and sleeping rough in a barn and cooking our own food and then doing some dangerous things, almost in fact getting killed two or three times. I stayed on an extra year on top of the sixth form year because when I was in the sixth I promised myself a year off. I'd worked so hard up to 'O' levels I decided I could afford to waste a year. At the same time, by chance, I had started rock climbing, so then when I was in the sixth form I worked it out. Once I spent at least a fifth of the year in the mountains, which is a hell of a lot, about ninety days in a year and a lot of that wasn't holiday times, it was weekends and I even used to scrounge the odd Friday off to have a long weekend. I suppose technically it was playing truant, but it was the end of the term when most people had finished their exams and I refused to go in for nothing. I just went off climbing. In the sixth form I did German, History, English and General Studies. The first year I took them I got English and General Studies, so I stayed on and got German and History.

So I left school at nineteen and went to a big north-eastern Technical College. I found the transition period very difficult indeed. Because being nineteen at a grammar school you only have to walk around looking sage and you are the old man of the school, anyway as far as the boys are concerned, so really it was a very protected atmosphere, which I had rebelled against verbally, but was really fairly satisfying in terms of personal security. You knew everybody and were involved with all sorts of things. Drama clubs, mountaineering clubs and it was a nice little world. Then when I got to college it took me about two years to

103

form any lasting and satisfying friendships because I didn't know where I was for the first year. It's indicative really of the sort of insecurity I felt, I suppose but I used to go to the pub quite a lot and to the pictures three times a week, just to escape – that's quite a lot, we were running out of films at one point!

At college I did a B.A. in Sociology, I can't remember why I chose that but as I said before quite a lot of my deviant behaviour was verbal and ideological, I hadn't got much idea of what sociology itself was and I could have done philosophy, but I knew even less about that as a subject. But what we were doing, like a lot of other people, was talking at great lengths on social problems. At college I had a fear of belonging to any formal social volunteer group but I got involved in social problems informally. The one that sticks in my mind because it lasted a year was my next door neighbour. You see I was in a flat in the slum area of town and next door lived a lady of about thirty-two who suffered from acute depression at times, that's only my layman's diagnosis but I should think that is what it was because she used to lay in bed all day. If she was going to get a job she would always fail to turn up. She would be delighted beforehand that she had finally found a job, and then suddenly she'd get sick. This didn't just happen once, it must have happened about twenty-five times during the year.

She had been separated from her husband for about a year and she'd got two kids, the husband had got them and she was trying to get them back, but one of the problems was that they couldn't possibly live with her because she was only living in one room, one bed. So she was at her wit's end, she didn't know how she was going to move, or get a job. The Social Security people were watching her night and day because she would sort of live at night and sleep all day, go to the nightclub, associate with some of the criminal elements, although she herself was not overtly criminal. She delighted in these associations and talked about them; some of them were quite big criminals. Also she'd bring her boyfriends back to her room. A crisis was reached when she became pregnant, ironically really because it was a week before she was due to start taking the Pill. My wife and I had persuaded her to take the Pill and she felt it was a good idea, but she got pregnant before she started on it. This really knocked the bottom out of her world. She went to the doctor but unfortunately the doctor was a Catholic and refused to give her an abortion, and by the time we had found a doctor who understood and would give her an abortion it was too late and she was pregnant and going to stay that way unless she had a miscarriage.

104

So she had the baby, didn't know what to do, completely con-fused and up and down like a yo-yo, happy, depressed, happy, depressed, that went on for weeks. She couldn't decide whether to have it adopted or what and we were ringing up the welfare and arranging interviews and when they arrived she would be out, and so it went on.

My wife and I met at college, we knew each other from the beginning, we were doing the same course, we knew each other the whole three years and got married the following October after we'd left. When I left college I went back home and was at a loss as to what sort of job I wanted and I was in limbo then for a while. All the friends I had built up over the past three years had gone to all ends of the bloody country. So I was at home but I didn't much like it, my mother and father had moved house and at the time I was a raving Communist and I couldn't stand living in a private house. It seems incredible now thinking back on it. The fact that my parents had moved up to the lower middle-class strata meant that my parents' attitudes were in a state of flux as well, they were trying to move from the council estate to the standards of the new area. Look-ing back on it it seems very funny but it was very real at the time.

Then I went to work in the reception centre in town, I rang up the Children's Officer there and she said there was a post of temporary housefather going in the reception centre so I went down there and I worked there for five months and found I thoroughly enjoyed it, I liked the boss there and he is still a good friend of mine. But then my wife had failed her degree, so she had to go back for a resit, she was working in the south at the time doing some interviewing, but after Christmas she had to go back to college but she couldn't get a grant so I went up there. We arrived on spec and slept at the neighbour's I told you about for about a week while I was looking for work up there. I got a job in a children's home, near the city; there were about twenty children there. I stayed there six or seven months and I think it was about the worst experience I ever had, but at the same time it might have done more good than I think, but at the time it used to drive me paranoiac. The woman in charge was an incredibly neurotic woman. She had been in hospital for three months the year before, and she was continually saying, literally screaming at the staff, that she wasn't getting control of the kids again because she had been in hospital last year and she felt the kids were getting on top of the whole place, and that she didn't know what was going on any more, whereas previously she had her finger on every button. I suppose really what it meant was the kids had got a bit of freedom while she was away and didn't want to lose it again. But I didn't see her before she went into hospital so I can't really say. From there I went to the reception centre in a north-eastern county and after about two months' struggling I have never enjoyed working anywhere so much. It was the first reception centre in the county and so we were getting it off the ground and I found it a very exciting year, altogether. I spent a year there, there was a constant interchanging of ideas and personalities, it was really rewarding when we finally got things fairly straight and then really gave the kids a good time and some really decent care.

From there I went to college again and did the year's course for the Certificate in Residential Child Care and then came to Wellside. Here? Well the formal duties which everybody sees, I suppose I could talk about them first, they are to take a certain amount of the breaktimes, dinner times, tea times every week. Within that framework what you have got to do with ninety boys at a time is to ensure that they line up properly, are fairly quiet in the dining room and also take a check of any possible absconders. That happens on every line-up which is about six times a day. Then you report absconders, first of all to the Headmaster and then to the social worker or police, usually the police if they have absconded from the school direct. If they don't return from leave you report the kid to the social worker and see what is going on first at home for a couple of days. In this formal bit of the job control is very important and when I first came I found it really difficult because I had never dealt with ninety boys, such a large number, before, and it was quite frightening. I found myself on many occasions just not knowing what to do. I'd ask for the boys to be quiet or keep still and they'd just carry on milling about and talking, playing about, shouting and even kicking a ball, when I'd asked them to stop. This had just not happened at the reception centre and I became quite insecure and just didn't know what to do, so I'd try all sorts of things and just keep struggling along at it.

I believe quite firmly, or believed quite firmly, that to give a boy a clip round the ear-hole when he needs it is good child care as long as you know what you are doing and within the limits of a relationship. Now the mistake I made was that it is quite easy to control twenty-four kids with the very occasional slap when it is needed, but if you employ that method with ninety boys then very soon you find yourself, especially if you are feeling insecure, as I was at the time, relying upon the hand

and you find yourself clipping more boys more often than ever you had thought you would, and this doesn't really do any good at all. It is very funny really, I don't know whether one is the product of the other but I feel as though I have got more control now that I am not clipping them, or not clipping them half as much. I think I have clipped three lads in five weeks, and two of those it wasn't a clip anyway, it was physically restraining boys from going mad and smashing things up and just doing themselves and everybody else harm.

The informal side is very difficult really because I suppose as yet I haven't worked anything out, I've only been here three months and I had great difficulties here when I came; one of the difficulties is inherent in the position, since I felt very strongly, and it has influenced my work very much, that housemasters are caring staff, although everybody should be called caring staff, and are separated from the teaching staff. This was a situation which I had not met before where the housemasters were very much looked down upon. There was a rift between teachers and instructors, but a greater rift between both of those and housemasters, a very large rift built upon such things as: the housemasters are not doing the job properly; they don't know the boys enough; they don't work as hard; they are not doing as many hours; they are not being seen to be working with, for the boys and everybody else; they are not seen to be co-operating with teaching staff, I think those are the main elements of one of the difficulties of the job. So that's one point influencing me, it may influence me too much, it's beginning to drop off now but in the beginning it was a major consideration. I think you also have to admit that most of the people who said these things are probably right.

Now when I come onto what exactly I should do, and what exactly the job consists of you go in for all sorts of idealogical pronouncements, but what I am concerned with is trying to put my ideas into the existing framework and if they won't fit forget them, or if it will take too long to change, forget it. I'm not going to be here in seven years. I'll support radical change but the important thing for me is change in the short term, gradual change towards the ultimate ideology. If I have an idea that won't fit in at present I can't see the point of creating a furore in the school and getting the reputation as a dreamer all for nothing. All you get is minute changes, often unimportant changes, but all these build up to change the overall ethos of the establishment. But this is the quandary, what is the next step, what do you change towards the ultimate goal? Immediately I'd like to see this as a unit school, I say that with some feeling because I'd like to be here when the units were going but I shall not be here seven years and that's about how long it will take, but I don't think we can impose therapeutic ideas on a block school with the amount of staff we have got at the moment, and the type of routine we have with line-ups and block dining. You've got ninety boys in the dining room with one fellow walking around trying to cope not only trying to control but trying to talk as well, discuss things with boys and so on. Dinner times are very important so there are great anomalies within the system at the moment, we are only really playing at caring in the way it ought to be done. I think smaller units, I may be saying this as a panacea for all the ills of the school, but I am used to smaller units and there you can put boys to bed, you can get them up and talk with them at these times, talk to them at meal times, you can get to know the boys you are supposed to be responsible for. I'm responsible for forty class boys here and it's just about impossible to get to know them. I think I'm beginning to preach but there you are. You see no matter how I try, and I try by taking different groups of boys to different places, there's a different group of boys I take to the scrapyard to get scrap for their trolleys, a different group I take home on home visits, and another group I do folk singing with Tuesday nights, and one or two others who come to our Friday meeting. No matter how I try there is always some fringe members, they would be there whatever the group but in a small unit the fringe is closer, here the fringe is way way away.

With the staff personal relationships are only just beginning to grow, and they will grow very slowly. Perhaps that is me because I don't form friendships very quickly, but the ones that I do tend to be purely on a pragmatic basis, consequently I'll form limited relationships with field workers quickly but they are for a limited purpose. But between staff members, getting to know each other and being able to work together then I think there is a long way to go, so far I have only just scratched the surface with one or two, I'm holding one or two off. Those that are a threat to me, I feel insecure beside, I am holding away, but those who could help me in very many ways and I feel it would be useful to get together with I am beginning to establish relationships with.

My political views have always been on the philosophical level and I don't honestly think they are relevant here except where they touch the school at a practical level. You know what the people in London are saying about what places like this should be doing. I certainly don't, as I used to see red at the name of Tory. I am just so busy here I don't think about much apart from work and sleep. You see I think the boys get into trouble for very many reasons. I wouldn't use my political views like some left wing sociologists do, and say it's all a matter of poor housing, or it's because the Tories are ill treating the workers. I don't think there is any point in working yourself up over that unless you are a committed revolutionary and I'm afraid that's not for me. I'm not working for any revolution, I feel I'm here now and there is so much of a job to be done here that there is a great chance, or danger really, that you will become isolated, or you become institutionalised. If I stay here more than three or four years I think I may well become insular because there is so much to be done here and so much to be thought about that if you start thinking about wider issues you are wasting your time going on in this work. If I start thinking about the wider issues of social policy everything becomes so depressing, I just wonder why I am here and what the hell I am doing and I may as well just pack up and go and work in a factory.

In very simple terms I suppose the school is trying to enable lads . . . well I don't know it depends very much on the kid, if the kid is primarily delinquent then the major aim for that kid would be to try to create a situation where he no longer needs to be delinquent, this is very difficult because of the wider social things. It's very difficult in the short term because you are very lucky if you change a family's attitude in anything but small ways. A difficult family, one with real problems, well it's just never done, you never change their attitudes, but you have got to work with that member of the family who is able to change and if that's the kid then you are on a safe wicket. The aim broadly speaking is to try to enable the kid to overcome his problems, or as many problems as are necessary for him to live a free life. Because most of our kids, or a fair number anyway, will go to other institutions and their freedom will be taken away from them. So you have to create a situation within the kid and within the family to enable them to overcome their problems and lead just an everyday life.

My future? Well sometimes I think I am not cut out for this work at all! I don't know really, if I go from here I would probably follow two or three channels. One is a very high falutin' one – that's becoming a Director of Social Services but that's about forty years away and then when I get there I probably won't be able to do anything anyway. The other

109

is that when we start a family I will have to go into field work, do another course and work in field services. I don't think I'd want to be in residential work with my own family. I've seen too many problems especially in small establishments. I've seen Wardens and Superintendents' children at the two extremes, one where the boss's kids have been encouraged to mix in with the kids in the establishment and one of these kids burnt down a shed one week and I think he is very disturbed, real peculiar because he is mixing in with these kids and his mum and dad just don't get enough time to see him and care for him because all their time is dissipated among twenty-four other kids. The other extreme I've seen is where the boss's kids are isolated from the community, the parents didn't get enough time with them like in a normal family, they work all hours day and night and the kids would go up to the flat like shadows, you'd never see them walking around the grounds or playing football.

I'm not sure that I see myself staying in the formal national network of social services. Another thought for the future when I've got a lot more experience, say in fifteen years' time, is to start a small unit of my own, but that's a dream all residential workers have and I don't know if it would ever come off. Just now though I couldn't tell you where I'd be in two years' time.

For me there's such a lack of knowledge about child care, it seems a lot when you are learning it but comparatively there are no rules, regulations or natural laws of social work, so you have got to treat kids and institutions on an individual basis. There is always going to have to be institutions whether there should be or not, because even if you get to the stage, which is highly unlikely, where you put a social worker in each problem family, even if it was desirable there will still be families who reject their children and refuse to accept anything to do with social services. There will always be children who either have to be removed for their own safety or removed for society's safety from their homes.

MR. B
Well I came from a similar sort of family to these boys, in fact I could go so far as to say that our home was equally as broken as theirs, in that there was always trouble between mother and father. His business went for a burton and my mother had to go out to work because he went blind. This led to all sorts of scraps, he never took any part in the upbringing of the family, he never showed any affection of any sort, he was out every night, we all knew where he was, drinking. He used to take us walks, that's as far as he ever went in showing interest in the kids. I had two

110

brothers and a third, the eldest, who died when he was about twelve, and two sisters.

I started my education at an elementary school which was attended by the boys of this type. I didn't live in the slums, but the school was in the slum area and most of the boys who attended it were from the slums. I went on from there to a secondary school run by the Jesuits, took school certificate and left when I was sixteen. At first after leaving school I couldn't get a job, it was in 1931, the big slump. Finally I got a job in a wholesale druggist at ten bob a week, I worked there for six months when I got the chance of a move to twelve and sixpence a week into a shipping office.

Actually the move was set up by my mother because it was very clear she was the one interested in us. She pushed for my education and sometimes I wished I hadn't had it, because the rest of my brothers didn't go to grammar school and they both learnt trades and are a sight better off now than I am. One of them was a difficult fellow, comparable to most of the lads in this school in his inability to learn anything and his violence. So that part of my background is very similar to these boys, in fact one incident sticks in my mind. I was very young, it was before I was twelve, we went to a school camp in North Wales and were on a day visit to one of the towns, when one of the lads turned up with a scythe sharpener. I saw him take it from the shop and it really made a big impression on me because right through school and when I was out of work I never got into any trouble. When I was out of work all my pals were the same nobody could get jobs, we used to play marbles all day on a field opposite the house, or we might play football or cricket but none of us got into any trouble, I think because honesty and our religion was instilled into us. It's funny but our dad never physically punished us at all, or at least not that I can recollect.

When I got to work in the shipping office it meant that I got to know my city well, I used to cycle to work and back everyday and home for lunch. I worked mostly in the office and around the town, mixing with dockers for three years. From there I went to the Middle East and from then until 1948 I was in the police there, except for a couple of years back in this country with the police here. In that job of course I mixed considerably with the criminal element. The police force in the Middle East was a bit different because we did the normal sort of police work in the town but in the rural areas it consisted of mounted police patrols mostly. I went up the ranks out there and spent a lot of time in the C.I.D. Later of course we were disbanded and when I

111

came home I didn't know what to turn to so I got myself a temporary job in the Food Control Offices because food rationing was still on after the war. I spent a few months there and then moved to a new job that was being set up in hospital records, it was set up as the new National Health Service came in. It was a really fierce interview with about twenty odd people. Anyway I got the job and a few months later I was approached with a view to going abroad again. I accepted this and I was to have gone with a commission to Africa. So I resigned with the Health Service and had the sailing date arranged. Just then my only son, twelve months old, died and an ulcer I had flared up. So we had to delay the departure and eventually pull out altogether.

We had a friend who was headmaster at an Approved School and I had seen a lot of him, and I also had a relation who worked in the Approved School system. Both of them said to me 'why not have a go' and after a couple of interviews I got a job in a school as a housemaster. That was how I started. I had three years there, it was quite a good staff with usual problems though, some people being too tired to work. They were going to build staff houses there and I was promised a house, and then when they did build I was told I couldn't have one. The salary at that time was low and the cost of living rising so I had to look for another job with accommodation, so I came down here. At that time there was a complete brothers' staff except for one layman who was the woodwork instructor, but almost at the same time as I started two other laymen started, as art teacher and a general teacher, that was twenty years ago because I came in 1952.

The régime then was entirely different; there was one housemaster, a brother when I came as the second housemaster. The brother had originally been the prefect of discipline, this was a post amongst the brothers, for brothers who were not teachers whose job was to establish and maintain standards throughout the school for boys outside of class time. They renamed him a housemaster and I was told just to start by following him so that was how I learnt the job. The régime was then very strict, I wouldn't like to see us go back to that, it was too strict. The headmaster then was a bit of a dictator and tended to be rather cruel. Anyway the régime meant that discipline was maintained to a high degree and the boys seemed to enjoy it, they never complained and we never had half the trouble we have now. You could start in the morning by going into the dormitories, and click your fingers and that was enough to get them out of bed, every bed was stripped and the boys up. There were

112

two men on every morning and the school of a hundred and four boys was divided up into four houses, four groups. One man went down to the showers and took one house with him, everything was done to the click of fingers so the procedure was, the boys would march in and stand in front of their basin, they always had to use the same basin every time, then (click fingers) wash (click fingers) soap up (click fingers) wash off (click fingers) clean teeth (click fingers) stand back. Then a bell was rung and the first group was held there while the next group went through the same procedure. When all the groups had been through they marched upstairs again.

There was never any bother, there were no privileges, every boy had the same. Saturday afternoons the whole school was changed into best uniform and marched in crocodile three miles to the cinema, accompanied by two members of staff, then marched back again. Hail, rain, snow, it didn't matter. I objected once or twice to it but the Head just said, 'The best thing they could have, I wouldn't stop that for all the money in the world,' and so they went. There was no 'tuck shop', they got a twopenny bar on a Wednesday and a fourpenny bar on a Sunday, each boy got the same. There was no television, no wireless, in the evenings each member of staff took a particular activity and each member of staff was responsible for his group for the whole of that period. There were usually three men on and you just divided the school up into three, one group to each man. As a member of staff you were expected to account for every boy in your group every single minute. The activities consisted of a choir, woodwork, library, stamp club or football, generally the mass of boys, remember there were a hundred and four, were in the hall all evening and in there was one table tennis table, a wreck of a thing, one half-sized billiards table also in bits, and three or four card tables at which the boys played small games, and this was all. They weren't allowed inside that hall at all during the day until half past six at night, no matter what the weather was they had to be outside. Certainly fresh air and exercise seemed to keep them healthy, you hardly ever had boys up the surgery.

Despite the spartan existence they led and lack of privileges you could count the number of abscondings over my first five years on two hands, which is some indication that they were quite prepared to accept it. For example, at dinner times and tea times every boy had to go out on the field and every boy had to be organised into some game or other. So you would have one man on the field supervising at least four games of football at once. The idea was they had to be occupied not only outside but

113

in inclement weather they would go under the covered yard and I had to organise activities, we had wrestling, boxing matches, pushing peas with straws, marbles, all sorts of things to keep them occupied and this I think is why they were so happy, they didn't have time to get bored. They were under constant supervision, they weren't allowed to go to the toilet other than in groups of ten with one boy in charge and he had to take them up and bring them back.

They went to bed at 8.30 p.m. every night under the same kind of system as they were got up in the morning. They were showered and teeth cleaned then straight to bed, no talking in the dormitories and all asleep by nine o'clock. At weekends again it was a question of every boy being under control and being organised, they didn't dream of objecting. If they didn't want to play football then it was a walk, because there were only two men on Saturday and Sunday, so one man would take half on to the field and organise games and the others would be taken for a walk. If you went for a walk you weren't allowed to stop anywhere, I was 'choked off' once for allowing them to stop on the common, I was told you never know what they will get up to so just keep them walking.

In those days boys went home only at the end of terms, so they went home by train with a member of staff to their destination and the member of staff was there to pick them up and bring them back, and you were never any short, every boy turned up.

Every boy then had to stay here three years or until they were fifteen years and four months whichever was the longer, and only a very small number ever left in less than three years. When they left they were under the supervision of a Welfare Officer specifically appointed by the Home Office as Care Agents for ex-Approved School boys. The country was divided up into areas and covered by these Welfare Officers who operated from their own homes. There were very few Catholic Welfare Officers, and of course at that time we never had anything but Catholic boys in the school, and our boys were placed with these Welfare Officers, who had to report on the boys every month for the first year after release, every two months for the second year and every three months for the third year.

The major change I have seen over the past twenty years is quite simply the relaxation of discipline and control of the boys. You see in those days with the Welfare Officers' reports you had a lot of follow-up material available and once I made out a pillar-graph which I took over the ten year period 1940-1950, working out how many court appearances, if any, these boys had during their three-year supervision following release. This graph worked out that an average of fifty per cent of boys who left at that time never got into trouble during their three year period. Of the rest twenty-five per cent were recommitted and twenty-five per cent had further court appearances. This seems to me to be a pretty good indication that although we didn't try to use their brains they learnt something from being at the school compared with the present-day set up.

Then there was a change of Headmaster and it was like taking a cork off a champagne bottle. The new Head wasn't nearly so severe as the old one, the cane wasn't used to quite such an extent, the important thing was that it was there as a deterrent, not so much to the boy who received it but to those who didn't receive it who were afraid to receive it. The possibility of getting it seemed to be the deterrent, because if you look at the punishment book it was the same boys who got it all the time, so obviously it wasn't a deterrent to them but for the others the fear was there. We had a system of rewards and punishment based pretty much on competitions between the houses, every-thing we did was organised on competitive lines, even to the extent of cleaning up the grass off the field after the Headmaster had cut it. You would organise a competition so that the biggest heap of grass cuttings collected got a prize. You see the boys had so little privileges then that a few extra sweets was a wonderful prize. They were happy then, they never bore any grudges or anything, you never got any backchat then because they just seemed to acknowledge it. When they left more boys used to correspond with staff or come back and visit than ever they have done in recent years. Boys then would often come back to see the place and the staff and say thank you.

With the new Headmaster back in the fifties things began to change because he didn't have the same control over the staff. The old one kept staff on their toes to the extent that if he saw any of us talking together during the time we were on duty he would choke us off; he would say that wasn't supervision. Super-vision was supervision then and you had to watch the boys at all times, and by heck if you lost a boy or couldn't account for a boy you were in it. Things began to relax and more new brothers came in who didn't appear to like the old régime and they began to relax things. At that time too, remember, the brothers were in the majority and they didn't really accept lay staff and there was a lot of conflict between the brothers and lay staff. In fact about that time I got really fed up because some of these were running the school and as far as I am concerned this was when

115

it began going down-hill, the young brothers came in and more lay staff because then the trade departments were opening up and all the instructors were lay staff.

As far as I am concerned things began to slide and I wanted to get out, and I tried to get out but I couldn't. I was considered as too old; at forty-five I was too old. I couldn't get a job in a Children's Department anywhere. I was working very hard at this time for two periods of twelve months. I was the only housemaster in the school and took all the supervision periods during the day on my own, I got my day and a half off each week, but apart from supervision I had all the office work to do for a hundred and four boys—their pocket money, home leaves, buying things in town for them, all that sort of stuff – all on my own. Then another housemaster was appointed and he seemed to get well in at the time and eventually went on the Senior Child Care course. When he came back he was made up to third-in-charge.

At that time he and I ran an Air Training Corps in the school, it was looked upon by the boys as really something and they thoroughly enjoyed it, it was something to work for. They were proud of their appearance, buffing up their boots and webbing and uniform. We had a band and for two years in succession we were the best squadron in the Area Wing and then for some reason or another best known to the Headmaster he declared it out-of-date, useless and redundant and had it disbanded, he just wouldn't let me carry on. Since then I've had many requests to start it again, and I think a training corps of some sort, preferably the Army, would be an advantage to the school. I'm still debating whether to try it, only this time taking a group of boys out and joining a local Army Training Corp.

I think the job of the school is clearly explained in this booklet laid down by the Home Office at that time and it still applies: 'The school should provide care and training and give classroom education, but its primary object is the readjustment and social re-education of children in order that they may be returned to the community. The aim is to base this process of rehabilitation on an understanding of the personality, history, abilities and aptitudes of each child and knowledge of their family situation, and promote it by a stable environment in the school, enabling remedial influences to be brought to bear and progressive training to be given.' I think this still prevails but so much of it isn't really done, we have never had the staff nor the set up to really do it. In fact I don't think you can work to those lines in a block school without the staff.

I think provided that we can get the boys to keep out of

116

trouble when they leave, no matter what the method is, then that's what we are here for. The most effective method is quite simply a strict, fair discipline. I don't think it is possible to get this type of boy, the delinquent type, to reason things out. Here again I think there are two general types, the delinquent type and the child that needs care, and I don't think it is possible to mix the two types. I don't think it is right either to mix them and attempt to use the same principles. But there is no doubt in my mind that the delinquent type, because of his very home and social background, responds better to a strict, fair discipline because this is what they see in the way they live, rather than to try and make them think things out for themselves. I don't think they are capable in the first place to think things out, very few of them have anything like normal intelligence, most of them are well below normal, also they are considerably retarded through having not gone to school, so they don't know how to use their minds. The very areas from which they come are a jungle. Who do they look up to there? the boss, the big cheese, the biggest bully. I'm not suggesting that we should bully them but they do appreciate, and I have heard them say this, strict, fair discipline. You see they are not capable of thinking for themselves and those who are capable don't want to.

It seems to me that they get into trouble because of their environment, the areas from which they come, it is some sort of subculture and this is produced by a lack of parental discipline from the day they were born. The reason why they get into trouble is because their parents have been permissive, because they just have not wanted the kids, and the kids are on their own from the day they are born. In 99 out of 100 of our boys there is no real family life, there's trouble between parents, or there is no father or no mother, step-parents, something like that and inevitably the child has missed not only the love and care they should have but also the discipline from a male parent. I think a child's character is formed by the time he is five years old, they start from the cradle, consequently most of the training comes from the mothers. The mothers are either too lazy or too tied up with the problems, or for some other reason are unable to look after the kids and give them what they need. You see once you have got discipline you can afford to give them some affection. If they respect authority you can give them the love and care they are missing. If they are not disciplined they just cannot take anything else in. Although of course in a normal child the two things go together, but by the time they get to us they must be controlled before you can give them any other

117

sort of freedom. I've proved this in the past, I've been very strict with boys and yet they often will bring me presents.

It is different when you have got all the boys together en masse then you must have firm and rigid control, but when you are in smaller groups the atmosphere is entirely different. This is how we built the club up, the group got together and made something of the club; we were a happy group, so much so that even though they were under strict severe discipline they would buy me presents. The problem of being a housemaster here is that you have to supervise the school en masse, this means that we are the main disciplinary figures in the school and this is contrary to all the principles of the sort of child care housemasters should do. I think we might get somewhere with this permissive approach if we had small groups and each group leader was allowed to do things the way he wanted to do them and sort of act as father and sanction the boys according to his precepts. You could divide the boys according to which housemaster they responded to so you get complementary characters working together. If this permissive attitude is allowed to carry on I think it might work better in small groups. I can't possibly see how it can operate when at times you have got one man trying to control ninety-five boys. They have got to the stage now when they can turn round and do turn round and say 'F . . . off, I'm going to see the Headmaster.'

There is just no discipline and you cannot train anything unless you have them under control. Start with plants or animals, you get them under control first and then you train them. I see the same thing with children, after all we do it with the British Army: the forces are disciplined, during the first three months they get severe training to sort the chaff from the wheat and when they get to the stage of being under control you can then train them and they turn out to be excellent men, excellent characters mostly. What we should be doing with the boys is getting them to see that they have to respect the written and unwritten laws of society. They have got to conform, they are all non-conformist and must learn that the laws of the land apply to them as well as everyone else. If everyone was allowed to do as he liked nobody could live in peace and freedom. It may sound simple but that's what our job is basically.

My future? I think I'll have to stay here until I retire, I can't afford to pack in. The salary has never been enough to save anything and keep a family reasonably comfortable, I can't afford to buy a house now. This is the big problem; I see a lot of people coming into residential work simply because they can't afford to buy a house. They see, in residential work, they have got somewhere to live for a few years to get them on their feet and then move on. This has been proved on lots of occasions with staff I've talked to. Take the teachers: they get £295 extra on top of the Burnham Scale as an inducement to compensate for having to live in a residential situation and yet they have a smaller class than any school outside, and I don't believe any of these boys are any more difficult than those in schools outside. They also get £540 extraneous duties allowance for doing an extra fifteen hours, minimum per week. So that's £850 a year more than anyone else and they only do the same hours as the housemasters and yet the primary object, as it says in the Home Office booklet I·quoted, is not classroom or vocational education, it is the readjustment and social education, but classrooms only have a part to play in this. But they come here attracted by the salary and a house. The turnover of staff here shows that. Just look at the trade instructors, anyone of those men could work outside in industry the same number of hours they do here and earn a damn sight more money, if they wanted. Why are they still here? They moan and complain. They don't have to stay apart from the fact that they can't afford to buy a house. Like me, I don't have to stay here but I've got a family to consider and I just can't afford to chuck the job in.

How would I improve the treatment of delinquents? Well I've thought about this a lot. I've always thought that if the aftercare of the boys was handled by a member of the staff from the school things would improve because I think the boys have established some sort of relationship with the staff. I wouldn't like to say how much now, but previously the staff had a relationship with the boys but the Welfare Officer hardly knew the boys.

I think basically though the whole social set up has to be attacked, the parents have to be re-educated. It would probably cause a revolution if the Government took the kind of steps I think are necessary but I can't see any other way of doing it. Parents have got to be educated into looking after their children from birth. I read of an experiment in America where they took twenty-five delinquent families and a control group of twenty-five non-delinquent families. They were all volunteers, the delinquent mothers were taken with their children and educated in how to look after them from the day they were born. After five years the two groups were tested and they discovered that the delinquent ones brought up under this supervision were far in advance of those children brought up under natural parental means. Something on these lines is the only possible way we could overcome it, but if the Government laid down laws about it you would get the old cry of imposing on people's individual freedom. However, I do think something voluntary could be tried, and supply a full care staff to educate the families how to bring up their children. It would grow from there if some sort of proof could be demonstrated to the general public, they would accept Government regulations. I can see no other possible way of overcoming the problem; it's a subculture that has got to be removed somehow. They have tried rehousing them but it's ineffective, they have just taken the delinquent areas with them into the new areas. The only way is to re-educate the families.

MR. C.

Well my father, and I only found this out later, was illegitimate, or I think he was because his name and my name are the same but his mother's name is different and all his sisters' names are the same as grannie's but different from his. I never discussed this with him. He lived with his mother and he was the only boy in a large family of girls. He left school about thirteen and went straight into the mines. He met my mother on holiday at a seaside resort. My mother was from Glasgow; I don't know very much about her background. I'm one of seven living children. I think my mother had a child born dead before I was born. There was also another baby later on who died after only a matter of days. I am the eldest child. There are four boys and three girls.

I had a happy upbringing, never a lot of money, but happy. I suppose I was rather narrowly brought up in many ways, because there wasn't the same broadmindedness then as there is today, so you tend to think of your own upbringing as narrow, and I suppose it was according to present-day standards. I don't think it has twisted me emotionally. I think I'm pretty emotionally stable because we were all loved and well cared for, despite not having a lot of money. My mother used to depend a lot on her mother, she was very good to us; so were my mother's sisters, you know in little ways, knitting jerseys, socks, that sort of thing. They would give us clothes at Christmas and leave the toys to my father, who would make things – he was very good with his hands. We all grew up in the mining community and it was very much a mining community. All the families were much the same as we were. There wasn't a lot of obvious poverty but it certainly wasn't anywhere near middle class, just a typical mining village.

I went to primary school and then moved up to junior secondary. It was all the same school as a matter of fact, it took both primary and secondary children. At that particular stage it was just after the war and me being a Catholic there were less opportunities for Catholic secondary education and if I had the opportunities that exist now I think I would have got on more.

I left school at fifteen, but in fact I passed my 11 plus, but then nine of us went to the high school where we had to sit another examination to get into the high school. There was only one place and us nine, it was that competitive. It's just not like that today – if you pass the 11 plus you go to grammar school. You see the facilities are there, the opportunities exist. Anyway I just wasn't as bright as the other fellow who got the place and so I went to secondary school and left at fifteen. My brother and I left together and we went down the local Labour Exchange and they put us on to a job in the steelworks, where we started as boy labourers, because you couldn't start an apprenticeship until you were sixteen. Anyway I finished up on a welders' bench. I enjoyed it, it was good. The chap I worked with was a nice fellow and he made you very much his mate, although you were only fifteen and apprehensive about work. He put you at your ease straight away so I guess I was quite lucky really. After a year there my mother wangled an apprenticeship with the local painter and decorator. She used to do cleaning for them at the odd times and she spoke to him about me, and he took me in as an apprentice, and that was the beginning of my career as a painter. I went through my apprenticeship. I went to night school for the first three years, decided I was wasting my time, night school seemed so futile, I just didn't seem to be getting anywhere so I gave it up. At that time as well I was playing a lot of football, training evenings and that.

Within weeks of finishing my apprenticeship I got my call-up papers. I went for my medical and I chose the Navy but they only had vacancies as cooks and stokers and I didn't fancy that so I went into the army. I passed my medical, joined the R.A.O.C. and went down to Portsmouth to do my basic training, then I did some trade training, when I finished that I was put down for jungle training for the Far East. That was one day. The following day Standing Orders came out and my name had been withdrawn from the draft, which rather annoyed me because I was quite keen to go abroad and see the bright lights of Hong Kong! I was really annoyed. I thought I'd get to see the world.

Anyway the following day I was up on Standing Orders with another fellow. We were told we were going to the Regimental depot, and it turned out we were being sent because they needed footballers. I couldn't believe it at the time but that was what the other fellow reckoned, and he was an old sweat been in three months longer than me! When we got to the depot and reported to the guard house, they sent us to the pay office and a major in there welcomed us with open arms. The same afternoon we arrived they fitted us out with football strip, tracksuits, the lot. I was in a bit of a daze, it all seemed so unreal, in the army and this is how you are treated. We were put in a special billet with sergeants downstairs, and upstairs on one side was the football team and the other side the tug-of-war team. That was it, nobody else was allowed in that block, it was quite incredible. I had a job in the company stores, but I only did that nine to five. In the morning we didn't have to muster like all the others, just got up at 7.30, down to the field for half an hour's training – we had our own civilian trainer – back up, have a shower. We had our own corner in the dining room, with different meals from everyone else. Oh, I thoroughly enjoyed my army time.

When I came out I got a job with a small painters, I was only there a couple of weeks when my father-in-law, he wasn't then, but he was a foreman painter with a furnishers in a city in Scotland and he got me a job in there. I was with them three or four years, during which I got married, and we got a small house, we were looking for a bigger one.

Then I started with the Development Corporation of a new town – at that time I was playing a lot of professional football in the junior league, not making a lot of money. So I decided it was time I pulled my socks up and so started going back to night school again. The outcome of this was that I met one of the teachers at night school and he wanted to know if I would like to go and work with him. He was a foreman with a brewing company, who were a good firm to work for. So when I'd been with the Development Corporation and got a house through that I packed it in and went to the brewers. I was there two or three years. It was good experience because you got a tremendous variety of work. I moved from the brewers to a shop fitting firm, with a foreman I had worked with in another job. It was a good job with possibility of promotion from charge-hand to foreman, which I got eventually. So I left the brewers which was unknown since people usually stayed with them until they got the sack because they paid well and it was a good job.

During this period I finished at night school and had got my basic City and Guilds, Higher City and Guilds, Finals City and Guilds and my full Tech. I had got a notion I'd like to do a bit of teaching and get out of the rut of pure painting. So I started looking around in the papers for jobs, and I saw this advert for a painter and decorator at a school. So I wrote to the school and got a reply asking me to go and see them. No application forms, just a letter from the Headmaster, so I went along and he told me it wasn't the job for me since I was equally as well qualified as the Instructor there at the time, who had been promoted to third-in-charge and they were looking for a painter as an assistant for him. Anyway I sat and talked to him because he wanted to explain the position, and that is one of the strange things that happen to you in life and changes your life because that is what it did for me. Because he asked me how I felt about going down to a job in England, I said I wouldn't mind as long as the job and place were suitable my wife would be happy about it. So he told me of this job at Wellside, which he reckoned was a nice place. Although the job wasn't ready at that time, he knew the painting and decorating instructor was leaving and if I was interested I was to get in touch with the Head, and he would also write to him. He gave me his address so I wrote and in due course I got an application form which I filled in and got called for an interview.

When I came down for the interview there were another seven or eight people for interview, we all sat in the room and talked about everything but what we were there for, you know, the usual interview situation. Most of these fellows seemed to know each other from other interviews and I thought, 'Well here we go Peter, this is the first one, how many of these do I go through before I get the job.' I was the last to be interviewed which didn't help my nerves very much, but when I went in the Head said, 'Well you are the guy the others have got to beat,' so I thought that's something, it is not all in vain, if I fluff it it's my fault no-one else's. So I went through the usual formal interview, what did I do, what did I like to do, what would I do in a job like this. I was quite blunt and frank and in fact ended up losing my temper with him. At that stage the deputy head came in and the Head got up and said, 'Look this guy's losing his temper, may be you can cool him down a bit.' It was very jocular in a sense and I'm not sure to this day whether or not it was a put up job. Anyway I finished and he showed me where to get a meal, I came back up and he offered me the job and I accepted, that's how I finished up at Wellside.

When I started I didn't feel as though I needed any training, because I was doing my own thing, doing my own job. This was really why I lost my temper at the interview. You see the Head was trying to tell me what I should do and should not do and so I told him he couldn't tell me that. No more than I could

123

tell him how to do his job. If he was going to employ me as a painting and decorating instructor then he had to accept that and leave the painting and decorating to me. If he just wanted somebody to come in and paint the place then O.K., but if I am the painter and decorator then I must have the opportunity of doing things my way. And this is how it turned out.

My duties in the school? Well have you got all night! Basically I suppose I am here to teach my craft to the boys put into my charge, but you can only teach them the basics. For one thing they are very young and an awful lot is expected of them. The one thing expected is that I keep the school up to standard, at a reasonable level of cleanliness, hygiene and decoration. When I first came I thought the place was terribly drab, lifeless, and it was a challenge. I looked on it as such and I suppose some of my fervour or enthusiasm rubbed off on the boys. This must happen. The only way to work with these boys is to encourage them in the best way you can, to give them some sense of achievement in what they are doing; that's essential because they are not getting paid for it. If you are going to put boys in a drab situation they are going to be drab, think drab and act drab. You have got to give boys a standard to work to and you can never have too high a standard. There are limitations in what you can do with them, but they amaze me, they make me think about myself and my training as a painter, when you see them turning out good jobs, jobs to be proud of, jobs I could be proud of and jobs the boys are proud of themselves. The place began to come alive. This is what painting should do to a place, it should bring it alive, brighten up the atmosphere and brighten up their thinking, their way of life. It is very special in schools, the decoration.

As well as my job as painting and decorating instructor I do extraneous duties, which involves meeting the boys in a different sphere, you get to know them that much better, and they get to know you better, because you are more relaxed and can afford to be, you don't have to be so disciplined in your procedures. I was always keen on art and at that time there was no art being done in the school, so I decided I'd run an art club, and it turned out very successful and they enjoyed it. I am a keen fisherman so I started a fishing club, and I think this is important – that you do an activity which you yourself enjoy. It all boils down to enthusiasm. I don't think you should choose an activity which you feel you ought to do but instead choose activities you want to do because then if you are enthusiastic the boys will be. You have got to get the boys involved and interested, and the big word there is 'involved', to do that you have to be enthusiastic yourself. You see I enjoyed doing art and I enjoyed showing the boys how easy it was; anybody can draw, it is just people's interpretations that makes an artist a good or bad one, more so now with some of this modern stuff people are getting away with.

The extraneous duties affect your family life but I think more so because you are living in the school. Again I feel strongly about this, I don't think it is a good idea having staff living in the school. If you live in the school you become so much part of the school, part of the environment, everything revolves around the school including your own family. If my family are out playing they are playing with children of staff, nobody else, it becomes terribly involved. It's bound to affect your family because of the involvement. It's not as though you are just on extraneous duties two nights a week. At other times you might have a boy coming up, or being sent up asking for the keys for this or that. Or boys who have been to the school and now left, they might come up with their girl friends or with their mates. There is always this involvement and I suppose it is very necessary up to a point, because I think my relationship with the boys is very good. I think I am quite strict with them in many ways, but I think I am honest and this is what it all boils down to, if you are honest and sincere and, what can I say, reliable, this is what these fellows need; consistency, if you are consistent and honest in your approach to these boys you can't go very far wrong.

At this particular stage I think this school is in a dilemma; I don't think anybody knows exactly what they are doing. Because there is no strong structure staff and boys are unsettled. At times I am not sure what it is we are supposed to do with these boys, I think what we should do is make them aware of the situation. Make them responsible, give them a sense of responsibility and just show them how worthwhile things can be, and how important it is for the future to have this sense of responsibility, this pride in themselves. And make them aware of other people too, and aware of other things going on about them. You find that most of these boys are not really aware, they are very sensitive and emotional but not really aware of what is going on. They are aware of a very small minority group, their parents and their own particular peers in their own small society which is, I suppose, opposed to the total society which is why they end up in places like this. Most of them get into trouble because they haven't been shown any other way, they haven't been shown how to steer

125

clear of trouble. They haven't got the same fear of being found out as any other child. Sometimes I am not sure whether it is respect for the law or fear of the consequences of the law that keeps most people out of trouble. These boys don't know what it is to fear the law. I was always brought up to believe that you don't go breaking windows, because they are not your property to break, and if you do it you are going to have the police on you, and then you know you will be prosecuted in some way or other. So I guess it was always fear, fear of being found out. I suppose I could be accused of conforming, but that is the only way you can live a rational life.

I think in schools like this their daily life should be much more structured; there's too much expected of them. They are asked to do too much of their own thinking. Take my own department for an example, if we go to do a job, supposing we are going to do Dormitory I, I say: Right you John, Gary and Colin, you three are going to decorate Dorm I. Now we go up and discuss colour schemes and so on. Before going up there I know in a sense how I think the dormitory should be decorated. This is something you do automatically from experience. You go up with these three boys and we take pattern books and colour cards. So we sit down and discuss how we should do it. In a way it is 'conning' them but if I left decorating purely and simply to their imagination it would be like nothing on earth simply because they haven't been trained, they can only think how they would like it to be. They can't see beyond a certain range because of their youth, their age, their mentality if you like. They have no sense of colours. Eventually they will come up with various schemes and throughout I will have been suggesting this and that, just suggestions, not saying we will do the ceiling this colour and that wall that colour, nothing like that, just suggestions. Eventually they will come around to my way of thinking. Now this is 'conning' but they still think that they are the ones who produced this colour scheme, and they are proud of it. They will take people in and say we chose the colours, we did this, we did that.

Now I think the same applies to how you should treat these boys in general. You con them into believing what you believe in a sense, into what society demands. Our way of thinking may not necessarily be the right way of thinking but the only way you can exist in society is to conform to a certain extent. I conform to a certain extent. I don't particularly believe in all the laws of the land but you can manipulate them without stepping beyond them and into trouble, and I think this is what these guys

126

have got to know as well. These guys have a total disregard for people's property, they can't see beyond themselves, any more than I could at that age. But I was fortunate in having my mother and father guiding me if you like. These fellows just don't conform in the same way as what you and I would call normal children, and I think they live in a different society to us, a different world. They are brought up differently, some of them purely out of neglect, others purely and simply because their parents went through the same problems as they are going through. An awful lot of their fathers have been in trouble or their mothers in trouble. It must be their environment, it must play a tremendous part in their finishing up in here.

I am not sure I know any solution to the problem, but I think once the children have got to this stage of development and into schools like this it is a bit late in the day. It is asking a lot of a school to undo in a couple of years what has taken thirteen or fourteen years to build up. So the place to start is right at the beginning, start from scratch, right from when they go into school. It is important to make society aware at a much earlier stage of the problems that are in society as a result of many things – poverty, neglect. Then you must do something right there and then, I don't know how you would go about it, counselling may be one way. Have counsellors in schools, but there again it very much depends on people. In schools there is such a tremendous emphasis placed on the children, like: 'The boys make the school, the boys are everything in the school.' The boys are not everything in the school, the staff are everything in the school because a school is only as good as the staff who run it. This all boils down to the selection of staff, and if you are going to select people as counsellors as I suggested earlier you have got to be very careful about the type of people who are doing the counselling and their awareness of the situation. I see no benefit in selecting counsellors straight from university with a degree in counselling and all the theory without having gone through life, the processes of ordinary life. People like myself score in schools like this, people who have come into teaching not by accident but who have gone through the process of apprenticeship, industry, met all sorts of different people. Probably the army had something to do with it as well. That way you get the opportunity of seeing life at so many different levels, you are bound to gain more experience of life than most teachers, who are institutionalised in a sense. They go from primary school to high school, high school to university, from there to training college and then bang they are teaching. Now I am not slating teachers, all I am saying is that if they have other experiences they would make much better teachers.

Plans for the future? I don't want to stay a painting and decorating instructor because I think I have got too much to offer for that. Probably because I feel very committed to this type of work, I feel it is my thing, I don't think these schools work at all at the moment and I would like to get into a position where I could make my own rules and regulations to some extent, and the only way I can do that is to get into a position of authority. My present plans for the future are to get on the Advanced Child Care Course at Newcastle or Bristol. Having done that – if I get on it! – I will have a much better chance of promotion and getting into a position of authority where I can have some say in how schools like this are operated.

As I said before I think staffing is tremendously important because in schools like this there are no external pressures on staff, there is nobody saying you have a certain syllabus to follow, so you are very much depending on your staff being thinking people, who can act and act sincerely without this kick up the arse that syllabuses impose on them. And this is where it is so important, there are all sorts of changes needed in places like this and one of them is staff living out, because living in they become institutionalised, they become too much a part of the institution, they become dead in a sense. If you get too much of anything it is like cigarette smoking, you get addicted to it and then you do things without thinking about it. I smoke cigarettes without thinking about it. Its the same with this institutionalisation of your spirit if you like. That's one thing, no teaching staff on the premises. Staff I think should be experienced staff. I know it is always difficult to get experienced staff and I am not saying that I would be the perfect guy to choose staff. I just think I would be able to choose staff to fill the particular post of responsibility, because it is a tremendous responsibility because you have not just got the boys from nine to five, you have got them all the clock round, and it is terribly important for them that they should enjoy this place.

I would also do my utmost to keep boys who are purely in for Care and Protection out of establishments like this because I don't think it does them one little bit of good at all. I think schools like this are in many ways breeding grounds for criminals, and an awareness of that is essential because it is no use kidding yourself on with all these bright ideas about 'we are doing this for them' and kidding yourself that you are going to turn out perfect citizens in two or three years, you are not. I would

128

insist on reducing the size of schools to a minimum, boys more spaced out. I don't think I would have this unit-type school in the sense that all the units are separate, but units in a combined school. A block school but broken down into small units where boys could have privacy and sit and feel at home. Make them feel at home and make it a home for them, proud of themselves and the school. I know it is an Approved School but why the hell shouldn't they be proud of it, proud of their achievements and what they are doing and happy too? Schools should be happy and staff should be happy; feel as though they are doing something. They should be praised up to the eyeballs, 'conned', by all means con anybody as long as you've got a happy situation because only in a happy situation can anything work.

Case Studies of Boys

The boys selected for interview were chosen at random from the boys of the school. Each of them proved to be cooperative and articulate and described in the most moving fashion the deprivation, and indeed degradation, which they have suffered in their lives already. They also give clear insights into the ways in which authority, in the guise of school and the courts, acts in what they perceive as irrational and confusing ways. The lack of understanding of how the 'system' operates causes them to blunder from one conflict to another.

Their alienation from adults and subsequent dependence on their peer group become obvious. They feel their parents neither understand nor show any interest in them. This lack of support, or inconsistent support, leads them into subterfuge against their parents and on to conflict with authority generally.

The most overwhelming impression created by the interviews is the emphasis the boys place on their search for happiness in the simple pleasures which are so important in childhood – the pleasure gained from parental warmth and affection; adventures involved in a den in the woods; and the family Christmas. The conventional image of the 'happiest days of our life' are shattered by the depressing memories these boys have of their childhoods.

X

Home? Quite a good house really, it has got about eight rooms in it altogether. It's like any other house, it's got a kitchen, one room where we watch the telly and one room where all the visitors come in to. It's got three bedrooms upstairs and an attic and a bathroom and toilet inside. Me Mum, Dad, three sisters and myself live there usually, but lately me Nan's been living with us. My three sisters are fourteen, nine and the young one's four. I'm the only boy in the family and the oldest. It's good because they look up to you in a way – you know, if they get into trouble they usually come and tell me before they tell me Mum, you know when they're fighting or when Marie comes in late she says, 'What shall I tell them?' and I just tell her things to say. I enjoy being the eldest. Me Mum and Dad are about thirty-four I think. Dad's a foreman with a civil engineering firm, only trouble is he is away from home a lot, he's always been away a lot. Like some home leaves I never see him because he don't know I'm home, but he has got to work away from home to get the money so I don't mind.

With me Dad I can talk to him about anything, he don't mind, but with me Mum if there is anything I want I ask me Dad and if he won't get it me Mum usually buys me it. I couldn't use her more, me Dad will buy me something if it costs a lot of money, but if it don't cost much and he don't reckon I should have it me Mum will buy it. I talk to them a lot about when they were kids, what they used to do when they were young. Dad usually talks about how he could run fast and that, he was known over in Ireland for running. He got into some trouble when he was a kid – the only thing I've been told about was when he was in a field where he shouldn't have been and then after that he got into a few more troubles and got put away when he was about twelve, he was in for about two years and then when he left at fourteen he came over to England. He says the school he was in was real hard, a hundred times harder than this place. They did mostly work there, not class work but learning a trade and that, and when he got hit they really got hit, and if you got into trouble they'd stop you going home for Christmas or something like that. He had it pretty hard.

I don't know much about me Mum. She was born in the Midlands where she's always lived, and when me Dad moved over to England he moved into the same street as my Mum, that's how they met. Me Nan, that's my Dad's Mum, talks about all the family she had, all the children she had, sometimes she talks about my Dad, often we just sit talking for hours about them. She says he was a good runner and that the family used to look up to him because of it, even though he was one of the youngest. When she came over to England, because me Dad asked her to come over, she moved into the same street as me Dad and she had more money than him and so she bought a few houses in the street, and now she's given them to me Dad.

130

I used not to tell them when I was going out, and don't know why; it weren't that I was scared, I just couldn't tell them. You know, when I was going out with a girl I wouldn't tell them, but now I tell them everything. I don't know what they would have done if I had told them, probably not let me go out. I used to go to football matches and I didn't think they would want me to go to them, so I just never told them about going. I'd just say I was up the park or somewhere if they asked.

It's a pretty good area we live in, I know a lot of people there and get on well with them. Some I don't like. I don't like the next door neighbour, he's always hitting his children, it's wrong the way he does it. He will buy them anything they want but he won't let them go out and play with other kids, and he hits them a lot. There's a lot in the area really, there's four cinemas near us, two parks and a swimming bath not far away, that's about all, not much really. We could do with a few more youth clubs, there's none near us, they are all in the town. I reckon it's a fairly respectable area, me Dad doesn't like living around there much, he keeps saying we'll have to move away from here sometime, he don't like it there. He wants to buy his own house with a garage for himself. He wants to get on really.

The first school I went to was the infants school that was near us, just two roads away, then the junior school was at the top of the street, but the senior school was about two miles away. I didn't get on well at my senior school, they were a load of snobs, that's why I didn't get on with them. A load of kids were snobs, the way they act, the way they talk and everything. I used to get sick of them and mess about and everything. They even ate like a snob. It was a secondary modern school, mixed. The junior school was better although it was all boys, we had better fun there. The yard was bigger and we could play football on it, I enjoyed it better.

I didn't have any mates in my senior school, I used to go round with a load of kids from other schools. I knocked about with a coloured kid mostly. He lived in the next street from us. He was about three years older than me. I used to go with him all the time; me parents didn't mind, they knew him and liked him. Then there was two brothers, whose parents were handicapped. They went to the same school as the coloured kid, they were the same age as me. Then there was one other boy, Bill, he used to go to the high school. That's all we went with, we just went out together.

We'd plan our weekends mostly, like Saturdays we'd go to the pictures in the morning and the football match in the afternoons.

131

Like Sundays we'd go down town about one o'clock and just knock around till four, go to the pictures and then to a discotheque after; we would come home late on Sundays.

Our group didn't believe in nothing really. We was always talking about girls and that, but if we seen any of them messing about with old ladies, you know cheeking them, we didn't like it much and tell them to go on and let the old lady go. We didn't really have a leader, we just went where we pleased. Mostly we looked up to each other on the clothes we wore, if we were smart and clean you were looked up to. If you weren't clean they didn't like you much and didn't want you coming round with them. Dancing didn't matter much, most of us didn't dance at the disco, we'd just hang about messing around and that. The best dancer was Jim because he was coloured and knew more about dancing than the rest of us. The kids at school didn't know me real mates except sometimes we'd meet after school and spend the whole night out. I wouldn't tell me Mum that, I'd just say I'd been at me mate's house, had tea and stayed there. We'd usually go to a disco or something, go out to a big town where the disco was famous. We'd take our good clothes in a big bag, a football bag, take them to school and then change after school. Discos are great for kids, you get to know people better. When you first go all the kids look big to you and you are probably a bit scared, but when you get to know them they are just normal kids, aren't they?

If anyone had a fight it would be Dick. He had more fights than any of us. He was the second oldest in our group. He looked real hard the way he dressed up – the 'skins' were out then and he used to dress like one of them, but most of us wouldn't get our hair cut, we'd all have real long hair, so he looked different to us and other lads would pick on him. Jim, the coloured kid, was the best fighter out of all of us, he wasn't scared of anyone really. I don't get into fights, I just mind my own business. You know if Dick got into a fight we wouldn't help him, we'd just watch him and then if we thought he'd get beaten Jim would just stop it; he wouldn't hit the other kid, he'd just stop them. Most of the fights would be over girls, or where you were going to sit, or say if one kid goes up and asks the man to put on a certain record, then if another kid goes up and asks for another record if that other kid's record got put on first they'd just start a fight over it. Because the other kid asked first his record should go on first, so they'd start arguing over it. Or like lots of time when you go in all the kids are up dancing and you'd sit down where you saw an empty place, then some kid would

132

come up and say it's his seat, you wouldn't know you'd just walked in the door, and they'd start fighting over that. If there's a gang of them, a few of them, they are probably looking for trouble, but if there is just one of them, say the four of us are sitting together and he comes up and says, 'Hey that's my seat', well nine out of ten we'd give it to him because he ain't looking for trouble if there are four of us, is he? But if there's a gang of them Dick will usually start a fight. There's one disco, it's like a gambling place, had roulette and that. They stay open until about four at night. I heard there were drugs going around there but I never actually saw them. I've never had anything to do with them nor have any of my mates.

Usually I go out with girls who dress up and look smart. I don't like girls who just hang around you messing about. I like them looking tidy and smart. We usually go up their house. I usually test them out to start to see how far they will go; if they'd let me go all the way I'd just pack them up. I don't like them doing that, I hate that. They're no good if they let you knock them off, but if they stop you they're alright. I'd like a girl like my sister. She doesn't let any boy mess around with her. She looks about eighteen even though she's only fourteen and she's real strict with boys.

Some girls come and ask you to go out with them and if you say no they say they'll get some kids onto you. We usually beat that type up. If we go up to a girl and say can I go out with you we want them to take their time and think about it. If they say 'yeah' I don't want to go out with them. Snap answers like that means they are no good. When we beat them up, usually, well say she threatened me, well Dick would go up to her and say 'You threatened my mate' and just bang her one and walk off. They ask for it. Some of them reckon because they've been out with a load of boys they'll stick up for them; they find out they don't. Dick has been all the way with girls; he's sixteen; he always does, he's had it away with nearly every girl he's been out with. Jim don't, nor does Pete, Dick's brother, well I think he has sometimes.

I reckon if I was knocking a girl off I might take precautions, no, I don't know, not really, I don't know if I would. I know I could but I don't think I'd go to bed with her. I haven't had any sex education really, me Mum talks to me sometimes, but really it's just what you pick up. Me Mum always says to me, 'Are you going to get married?' and I says 'No' she always says to me 'Ah, you'll have to when you've been with a girl.' I tell her I won't have to, I won't do it with a girl from our

133

town. It'll be somewhere, like coming back here, where they won't know where to find me or anything. I think me Mum thinks I'll have to get married because I've been out with so many girls, I've been going out with them for ages now, since I was about twelve and I go out with a lot. Mind you I always bring them home to meet my parents – they usually reckon they're pretty smart and respectable – and I go up and meet the girl's parents.

School was hard, I found a lot of the lessons hard to cope with, I didn't like it much. It was alright but the teachers kept sending you out for stupid things. They'd see you messing about once and send you straight up to the office. I'd usually argue with them and get into more trouble. I didn't like it because you couldn't talk to them, try to explain things to them, they just wouldn't let you. This school's better than any I have been to, I reckon because you can talk to the staff easier. Teachers outside, especially the women teachers, because we are boys they ought to be a bit scared of us but they teach us as if they own us, as if they can do what they like with us, that's why the boys won't do what they're told because teachers think they own us, but they don't.

I got into a load of trouble, fights and that, I got the cane a lot. One time I can remember was when I was on probation at the time and I didn't go to school because I had a load of money and me Probation Officer picked me up and sent me back to school. When I got there the headmaster caned me. I couldn't understand why he caned me. I know I should have been at school but me Probation Officer sent me there and after all I went on my own and yet I still got caned, I thought he'd just talk to me about it. After he caned me I felt a bit mad and acted a bit mad and that's when I got into a fight, because I'd lose my temper and if someone said something to me I'd start and take it out on them. This time I went back to class and the teacher asked me a question. I knew the answer like, but just said something stupid and then the kids started laughing at me and I'd lose my temper because I was already mad at being caned.

Once I got mad with a teacher, geography teacher, a woman. I never got on with her, she always used to pick on me, keep me behind at school, that sort of thing. One day she kept me behind and I just walked out. I came back and she wanted me to apologise to her in front of the whole school, so I just swore at her and told her what I think of her. I used all the language I could think of on her, I was so mad, so she sent me back to the headmaster and I got caned again. That's when I stopped going to school. I used to miss a lot after that. I was alright the first year in senior school and half the second year, then I started missing for ages, weeks, days everything. My Mum would send me but I was always the last to leave the house in the morning. My Mum used to go to work before I left, so she wouldn't know if I didn't go.

Most days I skipped school I went round my mates because they all did it, especially Dick and Pete, because their parents were handicapped and worked over the road in the disabled factory. I used to go up their house, just play the records and that, walk round town. One time I did a job while I was off school, but only once. It wasn't that school was boring, I just didn't like any of the staff, didn't like a load of the kids who went there. It would have been alright if the kids didn't try to act different from what they are, just act normal. Loads of kids are scared to act normal. If they're snobs they're scared to act like it, they try to act normal but they can't act normal because they have been brought up different. I hate that. You can't help it if you have been brought up by rich people and you are a bit of a snob, it ain't your fault. I just act normal, act like I am. I'm not from a rich family so I don't try to act like I was. We ain't poor. I've always bought a load of clothes so people think I'm rich. Clothes are important because you're up to date with the fashions, you look smart. Like now the fashion's smart, Crombies and that, after Christmas I'll come back with a Crombie. Last holiday I came back with a new jacket that cost a lot, and the kids in here think you're rich just because you have got a few clothes. That's why there is all the pinching going on in here because a lot of the kids can't get the clothes other ways.

The first time I done a job, was the next door neighbour's, I think. I was just turned thirteen. I screwed his place. I only done it because I lost my temper. He used to be always hitting his children and I was watching him then when he went out I done his place, just screwed the meters. I got about two bob and a load of foreign coins. I just broke a window at the back, opened a lock and got in. I felt chuffed at the time. I'd got in and got at him, but when I finished I wished I hadn't done it. I didn't feel scared because I lost my temper and didn't really care at the time. Afterwards I felt like running away, like the time I scived school and the Probation Officer caught me. When I got home that day me Dad went mad at me so I ran away to London. I got to London and came back next morning. When I got back me Mum started talking to me, but me Dad he was going to kill me, but my Mum stopped him. That normally happens, me Mum says me Dad's a bit hard on me because he got

135

into trouble and he don't want me to do the same, so he is pretty hard you know. If I come in late, like if I had to be in by nine and I came in 9.30, he'd go mad at me and either stop me going out or hit me, sometimes with his hands, sometimes with his belt across my legs, you know he'd hit me about six times. Like one Sunday we went to Mass and then I said I was going up to a mate's house for dinner. I went up and should have come back after dinner, but I never, we went down town and met Dick and me mates and then we went to the pictures. I got home late and me Mum says, 'Where you been?' and I told her I'd been to the cinema like I usually do. She said that was alright but my Dad went mad, he said 'I didn't know where you were' and he half killed me.

[First job – the neighbours] I never got found out for that. He thought it was the boy next door on the other side because he was always getting into trouble. He phoned the police but they couldn't do anything; they didn't know who it was. I was pretty scared when the police came, in case they found out it was me. The next time I got done, it wasn't for doing a job but just receiving, I received some money off Dick and his brother Pete. I got done for it. They didn't tell me at the time and I didn't ask where they got it from, they just give it to me and then when the police found out about it I found they robbed their own house. At the time I didn't really think it funny them giving me the money because their Mum and Dad are handicapped and they get pretty good wages and they just spoil their children – they've got more clothes than most kids I know, they're just spoilt. They just give me ten quid and we went to one of those slot machine places and spent some of it there, bought a few shirts and it was all gone by then. When it was all gone I wanted some more so I just kept screwing places until I got caught. You see what happened was I got done for receiving about two weeks after it happened. Dick and Pete owned up that they had done their own house and gave me the money, so the police came round our house. Me Dad nearly killed me, he really belted me and told me not to get into any more trouble. Then I got caught shoplifting and got belted again, and then just carried on. The police took me to court for receiving but I had to wait a few months before the court and in that time I got into trouble again, so I got brought up for several offences. I got a conditional discharge.

The shoplifting I got done for was just sweets and that, we used to just go into one of the big stores and take a few things and fill our pockets, and usually I wouldn't get caught but this time I did and they brought both cases up together. It was daft, I was with my cousin when we did it, and we were stood outside the shop talking about it, arguing about we shouldn't have done it. One of us said 'We shouldn't have done that' and the other said, 'Why not, we got away with it didn't we?' We were stood there about five minutes and then a lady came out and grabbed us and said. 'I think you have some property you haven't paid for,' and she took us to the office and searched us, told us to empty our pockets and so we did, she said 'Is that all you have got?' and we said 'Yeah' and when she searched us we had a load more on us. She called the police and they took me home. It would have been alright if it hadn't been for my cousin arguing that we shouldn't have done it, we always got away with it before. I knew what he meant because when I received that money I knew I shouldn't have done it. I thought it at the time but they kept tempting me, saying 'Oh come on' because I hang around with them, and they'd go into cafes and that and I wouldn't be able to buy stuff and they'd offer me the money in a caff.

The court scared me stiff; it was my first time. I knew I wouldn't get done much being my first time but I was scared. Then when I got a conditional discharge it meant nothing to me, it meant I'd got off, it didn't mean nothing. From then I just carried on doing places, especially Sunday afternoons when we'd hang around town, we'd do a load then, the Co-op and those sort of places. I got caught screwing the Co-op. We always stole just the money, we wouldn't go for anything. The most I ever had was about £80 to £100, but I didn't steal it, one of me mates stole a cheque for £100 and I changed it, that's the most I ever had.

As I said I got done for the Co-op and took to court. That time I got probation. Again I reckoned I got let off, all I had to do was see a bloke once a week, but they aren't no good, all they do is ask you how you are getting on, you could tell him a load of lies if you wanted to, that's all he did. I only saw him once a week or every two weeks, they can't keep a check on you like that. Sometimes I told him about some of my problems but not much. He was alright, a good bloke really but he didn't do much. He was young, you know, just starting and I don't think he knew much about it, he mostly just asked me how I was getting on, I'd just tell him and he let me go.

Next time I got done for doing a warehouse. I got taken to court and put away for it. There was ten of us in court and about forty cases against the ten of us. I was involved in four or five of

137

them – all sorts of different things, receiving mostly and one job I'd done myself. Most of the time we spent the money on clothes. When I done that cheque I bought a load of football gear. Me Mum didn't say much, I told her I had them given me or I found them, something like that. My parents were suspicious about the clothes alright because I'd been in trouble before and they thought I might be knocking them, but I always dirty it up, if I bought a new kit like I bought a brand new bag one time I'd dirty it up, tell her I found it up the park, get it washed and it would be alright then, they never suspect anything. One time I found some swimming stuff and my Mum made me hand it in but she never told me to do that much.

The time I got put away, there was ten of us up and it took a whole day, a girl had to read out all the charges, and it took all day nearly. I was the only one who got put away, and I was scared. I thought the others were lucky. I just thought, 'Oh well, get sent away, I had to I kept getting into trouble.' The others weren't in as much trouble as me, they weren't on probation or anything and so they got off and I got put away. My Mum was in court, and she started crying. I started crying when I seen her crying because I didn't know what they were on about at first, that's why I wasn't crying, but when I saw my Mum crying I knew something bad must have happened, and then she told me.

From there I went to a Remand Home. It was a good place that, they don't lock the doors and you are four to a dormitory, and it's all carpeted. Your parents are allowed to visit as well. Two policemen took me to the Remand Home, and then I was there about six weeks. My Mum used to come up at weekends visiting me. I wasn't bothered about going to the Remand Home because I knew what it was like because my cousin was in there and I'd been up to visit him a load of times, and so I didn't mind. But I remember thinking in the police car with two coppers, 'If I was a bloke how many cars would they have around me,' because I was only a boy and thought it was a bit mad, two coppers. I was bored stiff at the Remand Home, because you couldn't go out, all the others were at school except me. I just had to wait there until there was a vacancy. Then one day my Probation Officer turned up to take me to Wellside. I didn't know where I was going, I just got into the car and he brought me here. I expected all bars on the windows, and didn't think it would be like it is now. You see my Dad had told me a lot about the ones in Ireland and I thought it would be similar to them. My first day here, though, I was scared, all the kids were looking at you when you first come, and I didn't know anyone, and I was scared stiff. There was a load of big kids here then and I was one of the smallest I reckon, but after a week I settled in and the weeks went quickly. I think Mr. Z. was the first member of staff I met, in the office, he seemed alright to me.

During the week in the school you mean? Well Monday I take three exam lessons and then the rest of the lessons are mostly easy lessons and I do what I like, I usually do homework, something like that. Then we have swimming on Mondays so it usually goes quick, and the Court in the afternoons as well, that takes the time away. Tuesdays another three exam lessons and two for homework and then games in the afternoon, so that goes dead fast. Wednesday mornings exam lessons again and then games all afternoon, so that goes pretty quick. Thursdays we usually have a table tennis match in the evening and all day you're looking forward to that so it goes quick, and Fridays it's meeting and showers. On Saturdays we have a football match or go skating, the same Sundays, so the time goes pretty fast really.

I didn't really decide to do C.S.E. they just chose boys to do them, so I said I'll do them if you want and I started doing them and then when I got told more about them, how they will help me and that, I just carried on doing them and stuck to it. So I'm going to carry on. The classrooms here are much easier than outside, outside in school you go from one class to another automatically and you have to walk on the left hand side all the time. Here you are in no rush to go to another class, you can just take your time and walk where you want. The Humanities in our other school was English, History Geography all in one, they said it was Humanities. When I come here it was all different, much easier, easier work. I don't think you learn much because most of the work you do here you have done in the other schools, that's why it is easier because here they find out what you know and what you don't. The teachers treat you alright here, I get on with all the staff really, because you can talk to them easier, they understand you, especially Mr. X, you can talk to him about anything, he understands. All the class boys nearly, if they are in any trouble, go to Mr. X. and he tells you what to do and that. Not many of the staff knock the boys about, anyway the boys ask for it. I don't think any of the staff bully the boys. I've been hit loads of times but I've asked for it. Anyway its right that they should hit boys sometimes, because we are here because we got sent here and staff only want you to behave so that you

139

can get out quicker. If a boy keeps misbehaving they just bang you one so you won't do it again.

I think I got into trouble because I was bored mostly. I get bored easily if I haven't got anything to do, and I lose my temper because I haven't got anything to do and just go mad. I think that's how I got into trouble. So I reckon the school can help me by giving me something to do all the time. I'm alright then if I've got something to do. Last home leave I had nothing to do so I went and got a job and kept out of trouble. The other kids in the school are alright, I trust most of them, there are some I would not trust. I know a lot of them still do jobs on leave but there is nothing I can do about it. I don't tell on them. I don't reckon the kids here are disturbed. I reckon they are all normal, but I think they think just because they are in here they are different somehow from the other kids outside. Outside nine out of ten boys don't know you've been in trouble, but I reckon that's what is wrong with them.

Although I say I got put away, I don't really think it's punishment in here. It helps me I think, since I've been here I've learnt a lot, like how much you miss your parents and that. How much you miss all the things you used to do at night and weekends, I miss all that. I realise if I hadn't got into trouble I could still be out enjoying myself more. That's the way it helps you, by stopping you doing the things you like. I reckon when I get out I'll keep out of trouble because I'll be with my Dad mostly, I'll get a job with him. It's a good school, no I don't know really, it's the first one I've been to so I can't really say, but it's a good school. You are not locked in, you are free, do what you like mostly, you get tons of home leave, weekends are coming now, it's getting better all the time. I think in a way it should be harder because lots of boys do jobs on home leave and they don't get caught but if it was harder they'd be scared to do jobs on home leave in case they got brought back. They'd go home and say, 'I don't want to go back there again', and so they would not do jobs. The discipline's alright, but it's a bit easy.

The Court was a good idea, but I reckon the boys on the Court are getting more unpopular every week, and I should know, I'm one of them. It's not a Court really, its a council and we listen to all the evidence and decide who is guilty and who is not. Yesterday we said six of them were guilty but only one was charged. All the boys went mad over it and G. lost two days leave, the headmaster said so, and G. now reckons it's our fault, but he wouldn't get punished if he didn't bully kids that gave

140

evidence against him. Although I'm in a position of authority in a way, I don't look on it as anything special, although I was dead chuffed to get chosen by the boys to be on the committee, it shows you are pretty popular. But now lots of the boys don't like you because you are on the committee. They think we are staff now, but all we do really is write the cases down, we don't charge boys, we write what other boys charge kids with, but they are taking it all out on us. I just ignore the fact that some kids don't like us and try to carry on as before. It don't bother me.

I enjoy it, like when Brother A. asked us to look after Nick, I enjoyed it, looking after him for the week and then telling the Head how he had been behaving. Well at the Friday meeting I knew he had to get a good mark or he might get done, so I sat where I would be asked first and said nine marks, and most of the kids copy the first one. Mr. Y. asked why I said nine marks, and I said, 'He's going to get done for all the trouble he had been in so I think we should only give him a mark on his class work' and I gave him nine. So he got a high mark and I went and told Br. A. he had been behaving good, so I think because of that partly he got brought back here. I try to help other kids, tell them to keep out of trouble, like M., my best mate. He knocked a load of clothes the last leave, not boy's clothes but from outside and he brought them back here and got away with it. Me and S. try to tell him he shouldn't do it, but he just says he ain't got caught, he tells the other boys and they reckon he is good at thieving and that makes M. proud of it, but I try to stop him. You see the three of us hang around together mostly and me and S. can get our clothes from home but he can't get them as easily as we can, so he knocks them just to be the same as us.

You know the Council started off good but the last two weeks have been terrible. That's why I didn't sit on it yesterday. I sat with the boys to watch and try and see what all the arguing was about. I thought it was alright. The boys think it's easy sitting on the Council; in the meeting last week I said why don't four of you boys who were complaining sit on the Council, they'd soon find it wasn't easy.

The groups with the psychologist? Well sometimes I think it's a waste of time; a lot of us just sit there and say nothing you know, it's always the same boys bringing up things to talk about. The other boys will only talk about things when somebody else has brought it up, they seem scared to bring it up themselves. A psychologist? Well I don't think you do anything to tell the truth. The way I see it you talk to boys mostly, mostly the new

141

boys. I don't see you doing much else, you try to find out what the boys think of the school and how they'd run it, and talk to new boys. I don't think you could help me because I'm carrying on good at school now and shouldn't be here much longer, when I first came you could, not now though.

Well when you first . . . when you are in court and they say you have got to see a psychiatrist you think I must be a bit mad then, but you find out you are not. I haven't been told to see a psychiatrist but one of my mates has and I thought he must be a bit mad, but he ain't really when you talk to him about it. He's not mad and the psychiatrist is only doing his job. They try to find out how you work, I reckon, how you think and your reactions to things, what you think about staff and that, then they have got a rough idea of how you work. I don't think they are much good, they can talk to you and help in ways but they couldn't help a boy get out of here really, get released, you might be able to help make him stay and behave, but you couldn't go up to the Head and say, 'that boy ought to be released' or anything like that. Mostly it is because of psychiatrists that boys stay in the school, you talk to him about his life and you know how he works, what he is going to do and that. You can read him, like you read a book so you know what is going to happen and can stop it.

If I was headmaster of this school I'd let girls come to it more because I reckon that is one of the main things the boys miss. I'd have girls come to it and have like a disco twice a week, then you'd find the boys would stay here, because it would be like being outside then, you'd look forward to it and so you wouldn't bunk it then. That is all that really needs doing to the school.

I reckon I'll get released next year sometime, next summer, perhaps before. I'll get a job with my Dad first and earn some money, save some, and then I might go in the Merchant Navy. I don't know yet, all depends how I get on working with my Dad. I think if I work like my Dad did and save up the money I think I should be alright. I just don't want to see my children in a place like this, that's when I've got married and had them, same as my Dad didn't want to see me in here, but I ended up here didn't I. I'll bring my kids up by talking to them, making out it is worse than it is so that they won't want to go to that sort of place and do their best to keep out of trouble. I don't expect them to be angels, they might get into trouble but I don't want them put away. I'll tell them about how much they will miss the family and that. I miss mine a lot especially my sister, I miss her a lot, because she is nearly the same age as me and I can talk to her about everything, clothes, records, everything. I suppose if I don't get married I'll stay with my Mum and Dad most of the time but the girls, they'll get married and have their own house somewhere.

There's not much you can do about kids like us. I don't see what you can do once they get into trouble because mostly what these schools do is just keep you away from home, I reckon, and you realise how much you miss everything outside. I don't see what else you can do. You can't keep beating them because that is no good. I reckon if I was running this place I'd take them to a Remand Centre, show them a few prisons let them see what it is like and that way they would be too scared to go there and would probably behave. If you show them a prison and they see what it is like they'd soon say 'I don't want to go there' because you are locked in and you feel as though you don't belong to anybody, that's the best way to do it. If you show them a place that is all comfortable and nice they'd think 'I wouldn't mind coming here', so in a way you need to scare them, I reckon that is the only way to stop them.

Y.

Home, well it is a very small garden at the front, path to the front door which is red, you go in and there is a big garden at the back, we just got a new three peice suite and a coffee bar in the kitchen. It's got a toilet inside. It's about seven years old now; it's got a bathroom as well. My Mum, Len, my step-dad, Marie and Dave live there. It's a bit crowded because there is only the two bedrooms. That's my home now but where I was brought was a place with a big rockery in the front garden with steps up to the door, number 40 that was, a three-bedroomed house with a toilet outside, and a big garden with two old cars in at the back. Me Mum and Dad lived there with me, Ken and Diane. You see then me Mum and Dad got a divorce. I was about seven. I'm thirteen now. All I really remember was that we were playing about putting water in the drawers, me Dad came up with his big leather belt and just started hitting us. Mum saw the marks and went mad and they started hitting each other and everything and me Mum got a divorce but before she got the new house and moved out. Me Mum and us kids lived on the top floor and my Dad lived downstairs.

He was always brutal, like one Christmas a friend of ours who lived down the road was going on holiday and they had a dog and they couldn't take it with them so they asked us to look after it. But my Dad didn't like it at all and he kept belting it with the poker every time it went near the Christmas tree. He used to use his leather belt on us kids for all sorts of things like nicking or swearing. Once when I was about seven I nicked his watch. All the other kids had watches and I found this one at home in a cupboard so I just put it on and my Dad went barmy and chased me all round the sofa and really belted me for that, he said I stole it but really I only borrowed it. Now it's alright, I never see him. I don't want to see him again ever. I hate his guts!

Me Mum's different. I like her. It was great when Len got the new house. She met him at the dairy and when he got the house and the divorce came through she went there to live. The house is O.K. It's in a cul-de-sac and there is a big green in front and woods at the back. It's a pretty good area; you never get bored because you can always go down to the woods and climb trees and play around in our tree house. Only trouble is I never have many friends because before I came here I had to live with me Dad because when Mum moved in with Len they didn't have enough room so they left me with me Dad and his new wife, and she never let me go out much. She used to make me wash up, do the potatoes, sweep out, all that sort of thing. It was rotten really because it was getting near to Christmas when me Mum said she couldn't keep me and went off and left me at Dad's. I didn't want to stay, it really made that Christmas miserable. I spent a bit of time in foster homes as well, you know, when my Mum was in hospital either having another baby or when she gets very miserable. One foster home was great, it was on a farm, really nice there because they didn't hit you.

Going back a bit when we were talking about friends, I had one friend, a really good friend. We used to muck about together a lot. We used to go round together nicking from shops, you know, going in and picking two things up and then showing the other one and asking how much it was then saying it was too dear and putting it back and walking out. We used to nick sweets, penknives, toy cars, that sort of thing. Mind you it wasn't fair because I got put away and he never got anything; he's still at home now. I've never been in much trouble, it's daft really, all silly things, like the time I gave my brother and sister some pills. I didn't know what they were but they had to go to hospital and were made to spew up to get rid of them. They were in hospital for about two days. Me Dad threatened me and said I'd be next into hospital, but I think in the end he forgave me because I didn't know any better.

First time I got into trouble with the police was when my Dad

144

was on a tree felling course. He used to collect old coins, old two bobs and that and while he was away I spent them round the shops and when he came back and found out he took me straight down the cop shop and I appeared in court. I was twelve then. I suppose he had just had enough. In the court you sat outside till they called you in, you went in and stood up, they kind of ask you what you have nicked and I told them, so they said I was beyond the control of my parents and sent me to a Remand Home; it was my only time in court. I was at the Remand Home for nine months. My brother went to court at the same time and he told them at court he didn't like me Dad and Step-Mum so they put him into a children's home.

It was alright at the Remand Home, I liked it, the staff were good. Mr. F. especially. He used to take me and another 'care boy' there everywhere, camping, to watch him play rugby, all over. He never used to shout at us if he caught us fighting or quarrelling. He'd take us down the boot-room and make us clean all the shoes. I was really glad I'd got away from my Dad and Step-Mum. I sent letters to me Mum telling her what it was like. Then from the Remand Home I went to another school. I was there six weeks for assessment and they said Wellside would be good for me, so I came here. When I arrived I thought it was great, really big, there was so much space and you were free.

A normal week? Well we have Humanities every day of the week first period, then you have Art and Maths and the Council, so on all week. Class is alright but a lot of people skive. I like a couple of the teachers here. At weekends I go skating, or the pictures, or if I feel like it I go home for the day. I don't stay the weekend because there's not enough beds. I hope I will stay at home for Christmas because I did last year. I hope me Mum will have me for ten days. The staff here are alright. I suppose I am about the weakest fighter here and they protect me sometimes. It's not a hard life here; the other kids will leave you alone if you don't provoke them or look for trouble. I suppose the aim of the school is to stop you stealing by showing you what its like being away from home, you know not quite a punishment but sort of showing you that if you don't behave at home you won't be able to live there. I've been away from home for two years now; it's not too bad, it's not too good. I'm always picked on by the big boys like B. The Council doesn't really stop bullying, in fact I reckon it's a waste of time, you could be learning something.

The school can't solve your problems, you have to solve them yourselves by going home and trying to solve them. Mind you Mr. U. solved one, he said he has got a spare bed, a good one, that me Mum can have at home so that I could stay the night, but Mum says she hasn't got enough room, she can't get it in. There's one small bedroom with a double bed in for Dave and Marie and the other room Mum and Len sleep in.

I've learned a lot here, I'm catching up on my Maths. If you look in my file you will see I used to be pretty backward in Maths, but I'm catching right up now and I'm getting better at Art. If I was headmaster if one of the boys nicked something from the other boys I would stop the pocket money until I got it back. If it wasn't returned next week I'd give them 5p. less in their pocket money. With all the damages, the broken windows and so on I'd take 5p. out of everybody's pocket money to pay for them. I'd give a few more outings in the week for the class boys. You know it is a school really. It's called a Community Home, but it ain't a home really, it's like any school outside except you don't do G.C.E. It's much better here though. I didn't like my school outside, it wasn't for me, like, I was always nicking, the teachers always acted tough. The school was too big and you couldn't do anything without getting the slipper. I used to get it for nicking or playing truant. The deputy headmaster was always getting at me, if anything went wrong I'd get blame, I didn't enjoy it at all.

When I leave school I want to be a long distance lorry driver because Len is and he used to take me on trips sometimes right up to Scotland, it was a real adventure. I suppose I'll get married, get a house and car, a Mini I hope. I'd bring my children up different, respectfully like. You know I wouldn't swear because they'd pick it up; I'd tell them off for swearing. I wouldn't hit them. I know what it's like to be hit. I suppose it's alright if you get hit when you have done something wrong but not as hard as some adults hit you. I don't reckon I'll be in trouble again, I learnt my lesson in the Remand Home; you couldn't go out there except with a member of staff. I want to stay here until I'm old enough to leave school, it doesn't bother me being here another three years, only sometimes when I feel I want to get out of this place. When I leave here I hope I can go home if my Mum can keep me and try and get a job down the trading estate. Life's alright, things will get better as I grow up, they normally do. It's alright when you are grown up.

z.

Home? well it's a terraced house, it ain't a very old house, it is pretty nice. There's no front garden, the door opens right onto the street. There are two bedrooms, one big one for me

146

Mum and Dad and one for us three kids. Downstairs there's a kitchen, bathroom and living room and then there's like a cellar – we call it the dark hole and we keep all odd bits in there. The area itself is rough really, there's always lots of fights, used to be a lot of skinheads around, in fact two brothers down the road got knifed in a fight once. You often get a gang of kids coming up the street throwing bricks and shouting out dirty slogans. Just lately the police have been having a big purge picking up all the drunks because they are always doing a lot of damage. It's terrible really, our back entry you often go down there of a morning to find some drunks spewed his ring there the night before. There's always a few prostitutes around as well, you can always tell them the way they dress, the way they walk and that sort of cold stare they have all the time. It's a fairly rough area.

The family consists of Mum and Dad, me and two younger brothers. Things haven't been too good at home lately, Mum and Dad have been arguing a lot and when they do it usually ends up in a fight, crockery gets thrown about and my Dad will put one on Mum. Like on one occasion my Nan gave me a watch and my Mum didn't believe me and started saying where did you steal it from. My Dad understands me a bit and he said give him a chance he might be telling the truth and then they started going at each other and Dad tried to strangle my Mum and the kids were screaming and furniture got broke and everything.

I hate it when the rows are over me. Usually it's over stupid little things like money, clothes and so on. Dad's quite a heavy drinker; he can probably knock back twelve or fifteen pints. Christmas is the worst time, then he starts on whisky and gin and that. Me Mum drinks fairly heavily as well. It's rotten when they come in drunk. You hear them banging about and then being sick in the sink, then they come upstairs and flop on the bed and then you hear them being sick again. You know, being such a small house you hear everything. Usually I stay in bed and I thinks to myself, 'Well you're setting a fine example ain't you.' But sometimes Dad will get a bit rough if he has a drink or two, especially if one of the kids is playing up, then he takes it out on me because they leave me to look after the kids. I still get on best with my Dad, he helps me in a kind of way. He believes, or he tries to believe, what I say but Mum just thinks I'm lying, she don't try to help at all.

I used to have one or two friends in the area, not many. I never used to go out much. Might go to the pictures if there's something good on but most nights I'd have to stay home and look after the kids. I've never had friends to the extent that you could call on them for help, but if I'd got money or sweets, well, then everybody's got friends. I used to stick on my own a lot and not mix with anybody. The first school I got booted out of. The reason was I got into trouble and the police came to the school to pick me up and they thought it was giving the school a bad name so they kicked me out. The next school I went to I got on O.K. I had a few friends there. Mind you I used to play a lot of truant, nearly every day I'd skive off for the afternoon. That went on for weeks and weeks. It was a big comprehensive and no one cared. Mum never knew until one day when the school board man came and she had a letter, then she went mad. I used to say I didn't like the school, all the teachers nagging at you. One, a man, used to grab me by the hair and bang my head against the wall. I hated him. But now looking back on it I don't think it was all the teachers, it was that I just couldn't stick school.

At about the same time I used to run away from home a lot, I don't know why, it's a mystery to me. It started when I was about seven, I used to run away to places like Birmingham, but this past four or five years I have been going further afield, you know, London, Manchester. That's because I used to be in trouble at school and had problems at home that I couldn't face, so I'd just go. I'd think, well, the easiest way out is to run off.

First time I got caught and in trouble was when I was on a roof pinching lead; this bloke seen me and the police came. I got cautioned for that but I kept going back to the same place and stealing so that I easily got caught again and was taken to court and put into care. First off I went to a Remand Home. I didn't like it but I knew I was there for punishment and had to stay there so I took it. I was there for about three months. Sometimes I wish I could be back there now, I didn't like the locked doors but the atmosphere was good. I liked that, people weren't watching over you all the time. You could do models and things like that and you were left alone, not tormented and tantalised. I like that. I've done burglary, theft of clothes, radios, money; stole metal, you know, lead, brass copper; in all I suppose I've committed about twenty offences, but I've only been in court once.

First off they sent me to child guidance. I used to see a psychologist there because when I was at school I used to steal for no reason at all, and running away from home, also I used to soil my clothes and bed sheets, you know with shit, and I guess everyone thought there was something wrong with me. This psychologist was O.K. I got on with him well but he could never

148

figure out why I was doing it and up to this date he still don't know. I was about eleven then and when I found out he was a headshrinker. You know at first nobody told me and I thought he was just a bloke to talk to, and then when I found out what he was I wondered why they should want to send me to a place like that. I ain't mad. And then I thought I suppose they want to know what's wrong with me.

Some of the offences I committed with me cousin and his mates, but about ten of them were entirely on my own. Like the time I broke into a house and got a load of money out, about seventeen pound and a load of clothes. I did a lot of damage there, really smashed the place up. I got out but got caught. I don't know why I always smash the places up. I've got no motive; it's just the fun of it, smashing things up. I've always been a destructive child, like breaking up toys and fetching them to pieces. Most of the stuff I stole, I'd sell them or keep it or play about with it or just get rid of it. A lot of what I stole I'd swap then with other kids for something I wanted. I'd spend the money, money burns a hole in my pocket. I'd buy a few sweets, matchbox cars, go to the pictures, enjoy myself, that sort of thing, then afterwards I'd have to face the consequences. I've committed more offences since I've been here, first few times I bunked I never did a thing but the last five or six times are the only times I've ever done any damage or broken in, this has been because there's been another kid with me. I knew I'd stolen before and I think if he is going to steal it is no good me saying no and showing I'm 'chicken' so I go in first to show how big I am. Most of the time kids get into trouble because they've got home problems or got no home so they steal, because they think to themselves 'Well I can't get no fun any other how so I'll get my kicks by breaking in.' I do it just for the pleasure of it. I think kids like me ought to be sent to a school like this, to punish them, to take them away from home because, some boys, their mothers and fathers are on their side shielding them.

I'm in class here at Wellside. We do normal lessons in the morning, we do Humanities first and then you have a kind of set timetable when you go to particular lessons, but if staff aren't here, like they weren't here today, you have a choice between certain subjects. On the whole the school's good. It gives the lads the right kind of lessons, and you understand it better. The staff express themselves more clearly here and explain things to you, in a normal school they don't. Evenings and weekends I might spend some time reading and writing. I go to drama

149

at the moment. We are rehearsing a play for Christmas. If I get really down I bunk it, you know, abscond, and then I do all sorts of daft things like smashing people's houses up, thieving and pinching stuff. Afterwards I always feel ashamed of it and you only come back here so it is hardly worth going.

The school's O.K. now I've settled down, but before I found it hard because there were new faces, people I didn't know, I'd never seen before. I didn't know if I could trust them so for the first two or three months it was hard for me to settle down because I never knew anybody. As time has gone on and I've got to know the staff and trust them I've got on O.K. I get on with most staff – there's one or two aren't too good, those I don't get on with I hate the sight of because everything I do they moan at and nag me about. Sometimes I deserve it, but I don't think I do all the time. The school's here to help you I suppose but so far it ain't helped me because I ain't been helping myself. It's here to stop you from pinching I think and help you bring out a better character for yourself. It teaches you right from wrong and tries to help you stand on your own two feet. It ain't what you would call punishment, and I don't think it should be. It is supposed to be here for a good cause to help kids in care so there's no reason why it should be a punishment.

I'm not really interested in the Council at all. I just think it is a lot of trash, everything that is brought up seems so petty and a bit of a waste sitting there for an hour. That hour could be used in some ways like an extra Maths period for the kids who are no good at Maths or an extra reading period for the kids who can't read. Sometimes the group sessions with the psychologist are O.K., some good things have been brought up; others, well, like last week we went from one thing to another and another and another and it all amounted to nothing. But often if we get good points brought up they are useful. The psychologist does a lot of work on the boys socially, trying to help them with their problems at home. Housemasters are for that purpose but you understand the boys more than what the housemaster can because you have got more access to the boys really. Sometimes you can get down to problems that would never come out. You help the boys around the school sort out problems, like if they are going to bunk it you try to stop them and try to find out why they want to bunk it and help them.

If I had to deal with absconders I wouldn't stop two weeks' privileges. When they came back off the bunk, I'd give them the cane and stop a week's pocket money. I'd let them have their outings but the cane and losing pocket money seems more to me

150

since when they went to the Tuck Shop they couldn't buy any fags. I'd like the school mixed, with separate sleeping quarters – one half for boys and one for girls. I think it would quieten a lot of the boys down. I'd also like more outings at the evenings, more swimming and pictures and that. If like windows got smashed I'd make them pay for it. Any damage around the school I'd find out who it was and see if it was accidental, if it was I might let them off with it, otherwise I'd make them pay.

The future? I don't really know, I've been thinking about it a bit but really it just slips past my mind. I been thinking about jobs and the kind of future I would like for myself. Not a future where you have a good job and something crops up from your past and ruins it all. I think the future holds quite a bit for me really. I read the papers, the Stargazer, I don't take a lot of notice of it but I take it in and I think it holds a good future for me. I think I'll be able to get on at home. They have got quite a bit of money going in each week with them both working, probably fifty, sixty quid a week and then with me working as well, bringing in a bit extra. But I shouldn't stay at home all my life. I'd get married later on, say when I'm twenty-two, twenty-five, and have a family. I shouldn't want my kids to grow up like me, I'd teach them what I thought was right from wrong and I'd help them the way people have helped me. I'd kind of pass it on to them. I'd be strict with them but not strict to the extent where they call you 'Sir' and the Mum 'Madam'. But I'd teach them right from wrong and not go on the way I did because it is a shame on me really, because people outside would be thinking, he'd been in places like this and look what his kids have grown up to be, just like him.

CHAPTER VII

The Staff Role

The Role of the Headmaster – 'Uneasy lies the head that wears a crown.'

The most important role in any Community Home is that of Headmaster, because not only is his function to attempt to balance the two major molecules of the institution, the staff and the boys, and to act as a bridge between the institution and the community, but he is also a major force in shaping the policy of the Home and is the embodiment of the norms of the institution.

Community Homes are controlled by a management committee, the structure of which is laid down in the instruments of management which have to be submitted to and approved by the Secretary of State. The composition and activity of the management committee varies widely; some committee members may be persons qualified in social work who take an active advisory and supportive role within the Home, others prominent citizens merely acquiring an additional feather in their civic hats, and the extent of their involvement is the occasional committee meeting. Whatever the composition of the committee, the task of the day to day running of the Home, and the ultimate responsibility for it, falls squarely on the shoulders of the headmaster. With this structure one of the most important tasks for the headmaster is to liaise between the staff and the managers. To do this effectively he needs to be continually receiving relevant information from the staff, collating it and submitting it to the managers. He will be concerned with assessing the needs of the various areas within the school and attempting to gain resources to meet these needs. This task produces the first and major problem for the headmaster; as has been illustrated. Community Homes carry out a wide range of activity, from farming to psychotherapy, building to intensive case work, and the headmaster is expected to be an expert in all of these fields. Since no one can be a specialist in all these areas the head must delegate some responsibilities. However, this in turn means that his performance is dependent on the feedback of information from his staff. Unfortunately the effectiveness of this interdependent relationship is often greatly reduced since the relationship between head and staff has traditionally been autocratic in nature. This does not mean to say that all heads are authoritarian – this is obviously not so – it is a description of the way in which power is distributed in the relationship between head and staff.

The head of a residential establishment has enormous power over his staff. He has the power to 'hire and fire' staff – although officially it is the managers who have this power, they would normally only act on the headmaster's advice and wishes. For example, few managers would be prepared to push for an appointee to whom the head was strongly opposed. This right is of great significance for residential work since the staff are normally accommodated in the school's property, consequently dismissal also means the loss of one's home. The head also has many other subtle powers: he decides who should attend short training courses, and advises the managers as to the suitability of staff for secondment to further their professional training.

The head is also normally responsible for timetabling, although this is a duty many seem only too willing to delegate to their deputies. Timetabling is of great importance in residential establishments since the extraneous duties affect staff's evenings, and weekends and bank holidays, and so can intrude deeply into their private lives. Timetabling is a continual source of staff grumbling and friction between them and the head, who must ensure that the burden of the extraneous duties are apportioned fairly.

In the relationship between the head and the staff the staff's powers are negligible compared with those of the head. This unbalanced, autocratic situation leads to a distortion in the feedback of information. For example, no classroom teacher is readily going to admit that the expensive teaching materials he has ordered have proved inappropriate for use with the children; nor is any trade department teacher going to say that the piece of machinery for which he has been clamouring for several years has proved too complex for the boys to handle. There is even greater reluctance amongst staff to admit that they are having difficulties in controlling the boys since this is the ultimate admission of failure. Consequently the headmaster is often trying to administer an organisation whilst in possession of only a modicum of the necessary information.

Therefore, in order to increase the effectiveness of the manage-

153

ment, the distribution of power between head and staff needs to be radically altered. Staff need to be given, and to accept, more responsibility, and the head needs to be able to relinquish some of his authority. However, achieving this state has proved to be fraught with difficulties because, although staff often loudly proclaim they are not given any responsibility, when it is placed on them they find it both difficult to accept and to cope with, as D. Wills has shown.[1] Wills described a school where the authority structure was changed radically and rapidly. At Wellside the process was more gradual. In an attempt to democratise decision making and increase feedback a staff meeting was held each week for one hour. The meeting was conducted as an unstructured group, having no chairman or formal procedures, i.e. agenda, minutes, votes. All staff attended, except domestic staff who were represented by the matron and her deputies. This was necessary since the domestic staff, many of whom were part-time, far outnumbered all other professional staff. The head and his deputy attended but were not given any formal status. The aim of the meetings was to increase communication and develop a concensus on policy. The former objective was to a certain extent achieved, with staff coming to a point where they were prepared to openly criticise the actions and behaviour of both the head and their fellow members of staff. This openness of communication was often difficult to maintain because of the staff changes since it was so dependent on the level of mutual trust within the group.

The attainment of a consensus policy was perhaps more difficult, mainly because of the scepticism developed by staff through their previous experience under autocratic heads. Staff would often arrive at a consensus of opinion on a matter of policy, and the policy would be implemented, but many staff were unwilling to accept that they had played an important part in the achievement of the consensus. They often declared that they had been required merely to 'rubber stamp' a decision previously made by the headmaster, or an influential caucus of staff. The converse of this situation arose when the staff attempted to define a policy for the head for which he would be personally responsible but against which he was personally opposed. The most outstanding example of this at Wellside was over the issue of corporal punishment. The majority of staff were in favour of the use of the cane, and saw it as a necessary and helpful means of caring for the boys. However the headmaster, who would have to administer the punishment, and had occasionally done so, in the past, was personally opposed to corporal punishment. This situation produced an impasse that remains unresolved, with neither party able to convince the other of the validity of their viewpoint.

For the headmaster in this position life becomes uneviable. It seemed that either staff rejected the responsibility for decision making and then complained if the head made unilateral decisions, or staff accepted the responsibility and came up with decisions which the head for personal reasons felt unable to accept.

The organisation and decision making processes in an institution are of vital importance since not only do they influence the effectiveness of management, they also influence the therapeutic value of the institution. One of the major objectives of residential treatment is to provide children with acceptable alternative models of human behaviour. It is important that this be done both at the level of individual staff and at the level of the total organisation. It is one of the strangest anomalies of our society that although it purports to be democratic our children are educated in institutions which are basically autocratic and in which the leader is appointed for life. Polsky[2] has clearly illustrated the importance of institutional organisation in residential establishments. He has shown that where an autocratic, authoritarian régime exists, the residents develop a subculture which mirrors the régime and is itself authoritarian, rigid, based on fear and anti-therapeutic.

The autocratic model in Community Homes must therefore be discarded and replaced by a democratic model where power is based on the recognition of skills and ability rather than prescribed status, and where co-operation rather than collusion is the binding factor. Another important facet of democratic organisations is that they allow the individual members to develop new or existing skills. Conversely, an autocratic régime must be basically repressive; initiative must be stifled since it may prove a threat to the leadership. One of the important functions of the head of a democratic régime is to encourage the development of staff and boys. To do this he must inform himself of the resources available in the community. In order to be able to help staff develop he must seek out professional advisers, academics, experts in a host of interrelated fields who are willing to come to the school to talk to the staff and help develop their thinking. He also needs to be aware of what courses and training opportunities exist so that he can advise staff. This is an important function because in the past Approved Schools have been isolationist and staff have had little opportunity for discussion

155

with experts or access to professional advice. The head also needs to look to the community for resources which will assist the children's development, here the range is enormous: from psychiatric facilities to holiday camps, and from remedial teaching assistance to reduced prices for fishing permits.

However, in order to assist both staff and boys the Head needs to be outward looking and this inevitably will involve him in spending a good deal of his time away from the school meeting relevant bodies. These absences from the school are the source of a good deal of oppositional feeling from both staff and boys, both of whom demand that the head be available when they want to see him. Indeed they often interpret his absence from school as not being work at all. But feelings engendered by the head's absence are mild compared with those engendered by his other important function, namely that of arbitrator.

In the field of personal relationships it is impossible to establish 'objectivity'. Two people interacting have entirely different perceptions of the interaction, the boy sees the member of staff as continually picking on him, the member of staff sees himself as the butt of an unprovoked abusive attack. Who is to say who is right? This judgment of Solomon falls inevitably to the headmaster. This being so it is important that the head be both accessible to and approachable by the boys. The boys have a right to an impartial adult, as far as is possible, to whom they can turn for judgment when they feel aggrieved. This is not to say that they are given 'carte blanche' to manipulate staff, and here it is important to stress that staff must also have this right of judgment since one of the most important causes of staff insecurity is the constant fear of dismissal through accusations of misconduct – an occupational hazard when dealing with damaged children. For both boys and staff it is crucial that they should be able to take cases to the head for impartial judgment, since it is through the head's action that the children will develop his view of authority as just or unjust. The child will accept that he was in the wrong if he has been given a fair hearing and feels that the head has been fair. However, inevitably occasions will arise when the child is in the 'right' and staff often find this very difficult to accept since, in return for the loyalty the head demands from them, they demand support, even if they recognise they have mishandled a situation, since they see cohesion amongst staff as essential to guarantee security for staff. By virtue of remaining impartial in his judgment the head's position is a lonely one, and he must guard against collusion with either boys or staff.

156

From Homans' studies of groups[3] it is known that high status members of groups hold the norms and standards of the group more strongly than any other member. This is particularly true of the headmaster, for within him is embodied the norms of the institution; he is its public face; when he lectures to groups in the community he represents the school, he becomes indistinguishable from the institution. It is the head who appears on lecture platforms, who welcomes visitors to the school and negotiates with central and local government departments. He may well have to adjust his public face according to his audience; if talking to members of the local community he may assume an air of quiet respectability, thereby allaying their fears of having a Community Home in the neighbourhood; however, in negotiations with social service departments, he may need to appear as a forward-thinking, liberal-minded social scientist; within the institution he must appear as totally identified with the establishment and convinced of the valuable work being performed in it; he must never display disillusionment or disinterest.

In reality, the institution is also very much a reflection of the attitudes and ideas of the head. The ethos of the school is established and maintained by the head who has had in the past almost unfettered control of the school with advice and not direction being offered by central government except in the form of the Approved School rules. Whether the school utilised corporal punishment or not; whether the boys went home every weekend or every three months; whether army cadets were encouraged, rugby or academic attainments; whether girl friends were allowed to visit; whether boys could smoke, wear their own clothes and call the staff by their christian names – all these decisions and many others, which influence both the staff and children's lives, were the prerogative of the headmaster. It is to be questioned whether one man should have such power without some form of accountability and, conversely, whether one man should be expected to bear such a heavy responsibility with little support. As Tosh has so aptly described the position, 'A Headmaster is a lonely figure and no man likes to be lonely. No matter what the temptation, however, he must never be too friendly with any member of his staff.'[4]

I would suggest that under the Community Homes system the role of head needs to be radically revised in order to improve the position of all concerned. In fact there is a lot of evidence to suggest that within the new system the powers of the head will be considerably curtailed. For example, the power to appoint or dismiss staff does not in law rest with the headmaster, however much influence he may have. In a local authority or controlled Community Home staff are appointed by the local authority. In an assisted Community Home they are appointed by the voluntary organisation, subject possibly to a measure of control by the local authority. Local authorities controlling Community Homes also appear to want much greater influence on the internal organisation of the Homes than has previously been possible. However, at this stage it is too early to say exactly what sort of relationships heads will develop with their controlling local authorities as represented by the Director of Social Services.

The Role of the Housemaster 'Control supersedes all else.'

Polsky

In Chapter V the official definition of residential social work is examined in some depth, and the reader may have noticed that there is a marked discrepancy between the official definition and the descriptions of their work given by the residential social work staff in their interviews.

The role of the residential social worker (housemaster) in a block school is a particularly uncomfortable and unsatisfying one. The position in a unit school is in many ways quite different, because here the housemaster has a clearly defined territory, the house unit. This territory is important because the other professional staff groups have their own territories which are often closely guarded: the teachers have the classrooms; the instructors have their departments; and the administrative staff have their offices. The possession of a territory is often the first stage of role definition – protection and maintenance of one's territory becomes a major component of the role. The housemaster responsible for a unit in a unit school will spend much of his time organising and maintaining his unit, i.e. rearranging the beds to break up troublesome pairings; altering the seating arrangements in the dining room; decorating the lounge with travel posters and clearing out the cupboards. In the block school this function of the housemaster is almost non-existent because he is not directly responsible for the boys' living areas – most of this responsibility falls to the matron. Also, in a block school it is much more difficult to form meaningful house-groups of boys. In the unit school the boys resident in any one unit are the responsibility of that particular housemaster. The group is clearly defined and, since the boys are living together, soon develops a group identity and solidarity of which the housemaster is part.

At Wellside the housemasters had long been understrength.

158

There were only three housemasters responsible for ninety boys, and one of the housemasters was also third-in-charge – a post of responsibility exclusive to the Community Homes system. This involved him in a good deal of administrative work – for example, timetabling the six-monthly statutory case reviews meant contacting and arranging meetings with fifteen social workers and fifteen parents a month. The third-in-charge was also responsible for the boys resident in the school but working in the local community (see Chapter IX). This was a comparatively small group of boys, normally about ten, and yet they made a good many demands on the housemaster, especially since he was also responsible for seeking out and arranging employment for the boys – not an easy task in times of high unemployment.

The remainder of the school – some eighty boys – was arbitrarily allocated between the remaining two housemasters. One was responsible for the classroom boys and the other for the department boys. However, this division was not made along any existing group boundaries and the two groups really had no group identity whatsoever. They never actually met as groups, lived as groups or in any way functioned as groups.

The allocation of housemasters to these arbitrary and, in reality, non-existent groups made their lack of role definition even worse. Social roles are inevitably defined and shaped by the social group within which the individual operates. The teacher's teaching role is in part defined by the very existence of a class to teach. If the class is willing they may also allow him to develop an informal counsellor/case-worker role with them. The class and the teacher enjoy a symbiotic relationship which allows each to develop some form of identity. The class may become known as 'Mr. Smith's class,' or the teacher, as 'class II's teacher'; in either case both parties develop a shared identity and each will gain some satisfaction from the other. A group loyalty develops which is as important to the staff as to the boys in the group. This was particularly noticeable with the department groups – significantly, groups which spent most of their time working together – between which a friendly rivalry existed. Boys were commonly heard to express the opinion that the painters, joiners, or whoever were the best department; the instructors from these departments expressed the same sentiments as frequently.

The housemaster, however, had no such group with which to identify and on whose loyalty he could depend. Instead, for the majority of his time, he was expected to supervise on his own eighty or more boys through their meals and recreation periods.

159

When the housemaster was involved in a small group it was inevitably somebody else's group. Every Friday each class and department met with their teacher for an assessment meeting lasting an hour, in which the boys' behaviour over the preceding week was evaluated and discussed. The housemaster was expected to attend these meetings and comment on the boys' social behaviour and development, for which he was responsible. The housemaster in this situation invariably felt excluded, and not surprisingly, for these groups worked together for approximately thirty-five hours a week, often consistently over a period of four or five months. Studies of small group behaviour clearly demonstrate the rapidity with which group loyalties develop, and along with these go suspicion, distrust and exclusion of 'outsiders' entering the group. This was the position forced on the housemaster.

However, the housemaster suffered further since, not only was he excluded from the boys' group but, in many ways he was also excluded from the staff group. The housemaster who was responsible for the boys during their recreation periods tended to be on duty when staff were having their 'breaks'. For morning and afternoon 'breaks' the housemaster would be on duty on the yard with the boys while the remainder of the staff were having a cup of tea in the staff room. These periods in the staff room are crucial since the chatter and discussion which goes on is not pointless, as might at first appear, but serves an important function in delineating and clarifying staff attitudes and group norms. Because the housemaster is not there he misses this extremely important process of social integration. His pattern of work further excludes him, because his task of counselling and social education is easily seen as non-functional, and having no obvious end product. It has been shown that the majority of Approved School staff view life in functional terms; the housemasters' activities accordingly are very often seen as 'non-work'. To take a boy home to sort out problems with his parents or to spend time discussing a boy's progress with his social worker is seen as a 'cushy' job by other members of staff busy with a group of boys in productive labour. All these attitudes placed constraints on the housemaster's effectiveness – an effectiveness that should have made itself felt in a variety of ways. This is how the job of housemaster was defined by the school:

The housemasters are responsible for the boys during their primary life periods, i.e. bed-time, meals, recreation, and this inevitably demands a certain amount of 'staff' work but also

160

allows the housemaster sufficient time to develop his own interests with the boys. Present house staff have developed projects such as a Youth Club, vocational guidance and Community Service Volunteer work.

The housemaster is seen as having an important case-work function involving interviews and individual counselling with the boys in his care and keeping comprehensive records of these. Time is available for home visiting in conjunction with the local Social Worker to establish some case-work with the family. The school has an on-going group counselling and assessment programme in which the housemaster participates and he will be supported in this by the school psychologist. Part of his responsibility will also be six monthly reviews of boys and for this he would be expected to complete a report on the boy in conjunction with other members of staff, and work with the boy's Social Worker in constructing and implementing treatment programmes.

This job definition is taken from the details sent out to applicants for the post of housemaster at Wellside. Although all the housemaster's duties are outlined here none of the conflicts which occur through the basic organisation of the school are alluded to – the most far reaching of these being the conflict between casework and control. The housemaster was expected to supervise some eighty boys at mealtimes. These are the most explosive situations in institutions – exacerbated by the close proximity of the tables and the poor acoustics of the dining room at Wellside. Apparently the only method of keeping the situation under control was to be overtly authoritarian and regimental.

However, the housemasters were expected to fulfil this dual role of authoritarian overseer of the large group – their 'sergeant-major' role as they dubbed it – and at the same time be the confidant of individual boys in a case-work situation. It is questionable whether it is possible to fill this dual role effectively, and if it is possible it can only be achieved at great personal cost. The housemasters recognised this problem and it was a continual point of discussion amongst them. The conflict was resolved by some by clearly opting out of their case-work role and having minimal contact with the boys at an individual level. For others, who attempted to fill both roles, it was the cause of much anguish and anxiety since they felt overwhelmed with the problems of individual boys and although they had some understanding and insight into the way these problems influenced the boys' behaviour, they were unable to accept that behaviour when it was manifested within the large group. This caused blocks to the development of any deep personal relationships between boys and housemasters.

This unsatisfactory situation was finally recognised by the Department of Health and Social Security. They accepted the need for a massive increase in staff for residential social work, and initially agreed to the appointment of an additional six child care staff. These staff are being advertised for as this book is being written but their role will remain unsatisfactory without radical organisational changes within the institution.

The roles of matron and the domestic staff '. . . they will turn and bite the hand that fed them.'

Wellside being a block school, in which the boys lived 'en bloc', i.e. sleeping in dormitories and with a centralised dining room, employed a matron and domestic staff whose function was to 'feed and clothe' the boys. In the more modern Community Homes in which the boys are accommodated in small units, a number of housemothers are employed for each unit. The housemothers whilst carrying out some of the same domestic duties also enjoy closer relationships with the boys and in many cases have a clearly defined therapeutic role. The situation at Wellside is still common throughout the Community Homes system. Indeed in many homes the matron is an extremely powerful figure since she is the wife of the headmaster, and thereby is privy to much information not generally available to other staff.

The matron's role is extremely important. She provides the tangible evidence of 'care' within the institution. Food and clothes are not only important to personal survival they are also a central aspect of social behaviour. Meals play a significant part in our lives. As well as ensuring the intake of nourishment, they are used to mark important personal events in life; parties for birthdays, weddings, etc. The practice of sharing food and drink as a means of symbolising friendly relations between strangers is universally accepted. The digestive system is disturbed by fear and anxiety, and meals are often used to allay anxiety and cement relationships, as in the reception procedure described in Chapter IV. Meals often become highly symbolic events central to a system of beliefs, as is the last supper to Christianity.

In the same way clothing has much greater social value than its merely protective one against the climate. Clothes often indicate social status; they most certainly represent part of our

162

social identity. This can be seen in the stress individuals put on choosing the right clothes for themselves; the size of the multi-million pound fashion industry, and the way in which institutions remove an individual's clothing on admission in order to speed his integration into the institution, e.g. admission to the army or prison.[5] The importance attached to the egalitarian aspect of school uniforms, and the way in which some headmasters provoke crises over a child who wears jeans or the wrong shaped pullover all testify to the social importance of clothes.

The matron, therefore, has responsibility over an area of the children's life that is extremely important. In fact food, and most certainly clothing, are probably of more significance in adolescence than in any other period of life. How often are the parents of adolescents heard to say about their offspring, 'They treat this house just like an hotel.' This statement recognises that adolescents are independent in many areas of life but for food and clothing they are still dependent upon their parents. However, the adolescent often resents this last vestige of dependency and reacts against it. This reaction is further intensified within an institution, because catering cannot be geared to the individual, any meal which is provided for the ninety boys is almost certain to provoke a reaction of dislike on the part of a fairly sizeable minority. Even if a choice is provided of two, or possibly three meals there will inevitably be some boys who do not like any of the three provided.

The same is true of clothes. Although attempts were made at Wellside to provide some choice it proved financially impossible to provide clothes individually. A selection of pullovers, six or seven different patterns, could be purchased in bulk but, allowing for variations in size, the choice for a boy might eventually be reduced to one of three, all of which he found unattractive. This problem was exacerbated as the speed of changes in fashion increased. For adolescent boys clothes which were in vogue six months ago are old fashioned today, but often there were stocks within the school which just had to be used up.

From the boys' viewpoint then, there were some legitimate complaints about the food and clothing. However, in any institution it is these tangible aspects of institutional life that become the focal point for resentment and hostility. In any hospital, boarding school or army barracks the inmates complain about the food, as a way of complaining about the institution. This makes the job of the matron and her staff particularly unsatisfying since they may have worked hard in the preparation and cooking of a meal only to have it rejected by the boys with abuse and insults – often accompanied by fantasies about the lack of care in the institution: 'The meat is dog's meat really'; 'We only get factory seconds shirts'; 'The shoes are all rejects, you never see them in the shops, do you?'

As well as this formal nurturing role, the matron and her staff had a vital informal role, i.e. that of 'the women' in the institution. It was recognised at Wellside that there were insufficient women on the staff to create a balanced community. Despite the presence of matron and her staff – who in fact formed a sizeable proportion of the staff – and a female teacher and some administrative staff, Wellside was predominantly a masculine culture. If you toured the school the lack of female influence was obvious; there were few ornaments or flower arrangements to be seen, interaction between boys and staff tended to be boisterous and robust, boys playfully wrestling or sparring with staff; the gentleness with which a woman approaches interpersonal relationships was absent. This was a great pity because the boys' background showed quite clearly that in the majority of 'broken homes' it was the father who had left the home. This means that for most of the boys their relationship with their mother was extremely intense and dependent. Even those boys whose relationships with their mothers had broken down, still felt intensely about them in an ambivalent way, sometimes loving sometimes rejecting. When boys entered Wellside they often transferred their feeling about their mothers to the female members of staff. This transference would at times be so intense that boys when talking to the staff would inadvertently, and quite unconsciously, call the staff 'Mum'. This is a phenomenon that has often been reported by female staff in residential establishments, both for boys and girls, and yet I have rarely heard the converse, i.e. male staff being called 'Dad'. This indentification of female staff in the maternal role is extremely demanding for the staff, since it often generates extremely intense feelings both of affection and rejection. Often the boy will recognise his affection for a female member of staff and will resent his own feelings towards her and test her out endlessly in order to try to force her to reject him. Alternatively female staff may receive a boy's antagonistic feelings towards his mother for having 'put him away' and be extremely abusive and aggressive towards her as a result. This ambivalence was most obvious amongst a small group of boys who clamoured for female attention, continually presenting themselves at surgery with minor or imagined illnesses which were soon 'cured' by the nurse's attention and some friendly female contact. Alternatively

164

the same small group would be hovering around the kitchens willing to do small jobs. However, when the female staff attempted to assert their authority over the boys they would become extremely abusive and often verbally violent.

These relationships are obviously important, not only because of their intensity, but because they are often vital therapeutic channels through which the child can be reached. However, the tragedy is that these relationships are often discounted because they are with domestic staff, not professional staff. This viewpoint is reinforced in that most of the professional staff are men and regard the intrusion of women into the work with suspicion; women inevitably pose a threat to them. Much of the control within the institution is based on physical force and prowess, as I hope I have shown in Chapter V, the women, therefore, who must inevitably base their control on some other premise pose a threat to the men since their control may prove more effective. Boys may actually respond to a softer, more gentle, non-physical approach. The male staff, therefore, have a vested interest in keeping the women in a clearly defined domestic role, for in that role they are fairly isolated from the boys and, therefore, have no opportunity to demonstrate whether or not their approach is effective.

Also many of the male staff have a much deeper personal motive for keeping the boys and female staff fairly isolated from each other and this is their own sexual jealousy. This is more obvious with young, attractive female staff; the male staff will often unconsciously compete with the boys for her attention. The male staff would get particularly annoyed when they felt that the female staff were showing favouritism to particular boys. Occasionally crises occurred in the dining room if the kitchen staff gave an individual boy an extra egg for breakfast or provided a boy who did not drink tea with a special pot of coffee. The paradox of this situation was that the same men also advocated individual treatment for the boys aimed at meeting their individual needs.

These difficulties over the integration of female staff are not specific to Wellside, but occur throughout the Community Homes system, and it is of interest to note that it has now become quite common to find that a girls' school has a headmaster and several other men in senior positions on the staff. This is regarded as progressive and as a normalisation of the sexual balance in girls' schools. However, it is unknown for there to be a headmistress in a boys' school – in fact I know of no boys' school where a woman holds a senior post – and yet this has never been questioned. I can think of no better illustration of how the men in the Community Homes are restricting women to a domestic role.

However, the domestic role *per se* has important ramifications. In many ways it is a bridging role between the two major forces in the institution; the boys and the professional staff. Neither of the two major groups view the domestic staff as really staff – the boys do not regard them as having the same authority as the professional staff and often, for reasons outlined earlier, have a much closer and more familiar relationship with them than with the professional staff. Boys will often share a more horizontal relationship with the domestic staff, calling them by their christian names and identifying with their social and occupational role.

The professional staff exclude the domestic staff from certain staff activities. They do not attend, although they are represented at, staff meetings, case conferences or staff inservice training schemes. This division within staff works against the development of a truly therapeutic community. It greatly reduces the effectiveness of the institution in dealing with the child, since it ignores whole segments of the child's life. In effect, the staff who often have the closest relationships with boys and the greatest knowledge of the boys' subculture are not allowed to assist in the therapeutic process. Their contribution was evidenced by the way in which some of the domestic staff 'adopted' boys in the school who had no recognised family. Often these boys would spend their weekends and part of their holidays in the homes of domestic staff. The strength of their relationships persisted after the boys' release – some boys returning to the area specifically to visit the members of the domestic staff.

Since the domestic staff also represent almost the total female membership of the institution, this means that the question of how the boys relate to women is virtually ignored. This is extremely important since, as would be expected, the way the boys relate and react to women is inevitably entirely different to the way in which they approach men. But it was common at Wellside to have a case review, discussing a boy's progress and future treatment in the school, without a single woman being present. In effect what was being reviewed was only half of the child's life, the half that involved men.

This process of exclusion was damaging to boys in care since, as has been stated, the aim of residential treatment is to provide the child with acceptable models of adult behaviour with which to identify. The model of relationships between the sexes he was offered showed women in a subservient domestic role.

166

Their opinions were usually ignored or denigrated and they were seen as having relatively little contribution to make to life in the institution. This model must closely mirror the maladaptive model offered to the boy by his parents within his own home.

The Role of the Psychologist 'A Classic Cry'

Within the Approved School system there existed two types of school; classifying schools and training schools. The function of the classifying school was to assess and allocate boys to appropriate training schools. There were in England and Wales four, latterly five, classifying schools and, in the London area, Stamford House Remand Home. Each of these took boys from the court and kept them for a limited period of between two and eight weeks for assessment. On completion of the assessment they allocated the boy to a training school appropriate to meet his needs.

Each of these classifying schools employed a small team of psychologists who operated as part of the overall assessment team, mainly concentrating on assessing boys' intelligence, academic attainments and personality with the aid of standardised tests. Kingswood Schools, a classifying school with a training school on the same campus, had also experimented with the use of psychologists in a more obviously therapeutic role within the training school. In 1969, after several years of negotiations, Wellside gained Home Office approval to appoint a residential psychologist. This, as far as I am aware, was the first time a full-time psychologist had been appointed to a training school in England and Wales. I was appointed to the post, and in this section would like to describe my role within Wellside.

Since the post was without precedent it would be wrong to think that I can give a definitive statement of the psychologist's role, because no doubt many other psychologists, had they been appointed, would have interpreted the role in an entirely different way.

The psychologist at Wellside has four main functions; therapeutic; training and development of staff; management; research. At Wellside it seemed important to avoid any form of formal assessment role; the boys had been thoroughly assessed at the classifying school, and it was necessary to demonstrate to both staff and boys that the psychologist was not merely the man who tests, but had a clear therapeutic role. To say that the psychologist had a therapeutic function is not to say that he was the therapist. In any residential institution the whole staff are the therapists. (I have already pointed out that the women in the domestic staff often have the closest relationship with the boys and are, therefore, therapists.) There is no doubt that the department instructors played a very important therapeutic role; so did the teachers. The psychologist's role was to assist in this therapeutic operation in three ways: sometimes supporting and guiding staff; sometimes helping them to develop specific techniques; and at yet other times accepting individual boys for specific treatment.

The psychologist was responsible for the programme of group counselling, involving all boys and staff. The actual process of group counselling has been discussed at length in Chapter IV. The psychologist's role in this programme was to assist the staff develop their existing skills in group work. Many of the staff had been working with groups of boys for many years and had well-developed skills in this area. However, these skills had never been recognised and articulated. It was the psychologist's job to bring out these skills and to try to get staff to understand, at the cognitive level, group mechanisms and experiences which they already understood intuitively. The secondary role within the group counselling programme was much more mundane, although important, and that was to provide a focal point for the group. The staff and boys knew there were times allotted in the school's programme for group counselling; by his attendance the psychologist ensured that the group met formally. In fact the groups rarely met in his absence. A similar phenomenon occurred with case conferences for which a consultant psychiatrist attended. His attendance guaranteed the staff's attendance, and although the case conferences could be held, and were held in his absence, staff inevitably felt cheated and that something was missing unless he attended.

In the case of individual treatment by the psychologist an eclectic approach was adopted. Although a non-directive psychotherapy approach was generally favoured, the treatment was designed to meet individual need. Consequently, for a boy who had a long list of sexual offences, and who had previously received behaviour therapy on an outpatient basis with some limited success, it was possible to continue this mode of treatment on his committal to Wellside. The psychologist was involved in the reception procedure developed at Wellside, described in Chapter IV, and this was important since it gave both the new boy and the psychologist the opportunity of meeting on an individual basis. The new boy could meet the psychologist outside any assessment /interview role and chat informally. Hopefully, through this, he could begin to grasp the fact that the psychologist was one of a team of people whom he could approach for help. This is important, because many of the boys treated individually by the psychologist were self-referrals. Boys would often come of their own volition to see the psychologist 'just to talk'. They were aware that he had no executive power within the school and no power to grant them extra leave or extend their weekends – for this they had to see the headmaster – and yet many came to discuss their problems. Obviously the psychologist was not alone in this; boys took their problems to all staff at different times. However, the important point is that often children and adults are unwilling to see the 'headshrinker', and yet at Wellside this sort of attitude was overcome by the psychologist being available and by allowing the boys to see that the psychologist was a complete human being – somebody who played football, had a family and got annoyed – rather than an aloof figure behind a desk.

Staff referrals to the psychologist took many forms. A teacher might be having difficulties with a particular boy; a housemaster might notice a boy deliberately cutting himself; or the nurse might be concerned about a boy who was obsessed with the belief that he had venereal disease. All staff could refer boys to the psychologist. This was very important as often in institutions formal referral for specialist advice is the prerogative of just one or two staff members, and often these staff members are those high in the staff hierarchy and consequently most removed from the clients. It is, therefore, important that the staff who are closest and in most direct contact with the client should have the right of referral. Often the psychologist was unable to help directly since the referral was not of a 'clinical' problem. But even by discussing the problem with the staff he may have given them greater understanding of the situation.

This function led on naturally to a supportive role with staff, most particularly new staff. Newly appointed staff, especially if they have had little or no experience of residential social work, need a great deal of support. Initially they are being tested out by the boys and their performance is scrutinised by established staff to see if they will 'make the grade'. All sorts of subtle group pressures will be put upon them by the staff group in order to force them to accept the staff group's norms. Often, if untrained, they will be entering the work with a variety of ill-informed and altruistic notions and they will be shocked to find the boys apparently unresponsive and openly hostile. If trained they will begin to question the value of their training in the practical situation. All new staff have to face these problems and they need support from someone who will respect their confidence. The psychologist is in a position to do this: he has no statutory power and no fixed status within the school hierarchy. New staff will be more willing to discuss their feelings of inadequacy and anxiety with him than with the head or deputy head.

This function in turn leads on to the training role of the psychologist. This was performed in many informal ways. First, by informal discussion with staff, often about particular individual boys. The psychologist would attempt to keep staff informed of developments in an individual's life and how these related to his treatment within the school. Again with individual staff specific incidences could be analysed in depth. Recent research findings could be informally discussed with staff, or books and articles recommended.

The training and development role could also be carried out within the staff meeting. The staff group met for an hour each week. In this unstructured group the psychologist attempted to play the role of participant/observer. Since the group met to discuss implementation of policy and staff and boy behaviour the psychologist, as a member of staff, inevitably became a participant wishing to express his view of the school and the behaviour of people within it. In the same way staff often wished to comment on his behaviour within the school. However, he also attempted to remain an objective observer, interpreting back to the group a certain amount of the ongoing behaviour. He attempted to alert staff to fantasies or personal relationships they had which were impeding their development. This role was particularly difficult to perform because, being residential, the psychologist was himself often caught up in the complex web of personal relationships which flourish in residential institutions. However, within the staff group he also attempted to supply relevant informational input, pointing out that the school's problems did not exist in isolation but that research throughout the Approved Schools system showed common trends.

There were two other aspects of the training and development role which were important. The psychologist was responsible for student supervision. He attempted to use students as an aid in staff training. Students who were involved in a wide range of training courses – social work, both residential and field, teachers' training and clinical psychology – were encouraged to interact closely with staff and to discuss developments in current literature and thinking to which they were being exposed at college. This, to some extent, helped keep staff abreast of thinking in social

170

work and education. Each year Wellside held a three-day in-service training course for staff. This took various forms, from formal lectures and discussion with relevant experts in the field, to experiential learning of small-group behaviour. The psychologist assisted the headmaster in the construction of a scheme to meet changing staff needs and in the staffing of such training. This was his formal training and development role.

The research and managerial roles were both informal and closely linked. The research carried out was what is popularly called action research and is basically a monitoring process. When a new policy or development is implemented its effects need to be monitored and the results fed-back to management. This is essential if management is to be effective. In Chapter IV an example of this is given where a new procedure for reception was established, evaluated, found to be effective, and therefore continued. The converse, however, also applied, when the psychologist was able to recognise certain institutional rituals which were long established but in outcome were anti-therapeutic. These he could bring to the attention of staff and they could be examined and, if found to be useless or damaging, removed. The psychologist was also heavily involved with staff selection, seeing and interviewing each applicant and reporting his opinion to the headmaster, thereby providing the headmaster with additional information on which to come to a decision.

Finally, as both the psychologist and the institution gained confidence in each other an interesting form of leadership developed. The headmaster was obviously the formal leader within the school. However, the psychologist, having no formal status within the school, was often able to observe the role of the head and monitor his performance as leader, at the same time observing and monitoring the impact of his leadership on the staff. Being in this unique position allowed him to feed-back information on the head's performance to the head himself who, if necessary, could readjust his performance in the light of the additional information. This informal co-leadership would seem to be relevant and valuable within the residential setting and eventually may be formalised and itself monitored in an institution.

There were inevitably many difficulties involved in the psychologist's role. Since the majority of the staff had never previously worked with a psychologist their reactions to one varied. Often he was seen by staff as the epitome of the liberal/progressive viewpoint which was undermining their traditional authoritarian role. At other times, I feel, he became so identified with the staff that he was unable to fulfil his objective, social scientist

171

role. Many of the staff did not see his contribution to the institution as 'work'. This was exacerbated by the fact that Wellside was only allowed to appoint a psychologist as long as they were prepared to forego a housemaster. Since the two performed entirely different functions it means that the housestaff were permanently understaffed and this inevitably provoked some initial antagonism. As the psychologist I often felt irresistible pressure to either collude with the staff, collude with the boys or opt out into research work and publications. I often found myself identifying with Goffman's comments about professionals within institutions:

The management of inmates is typically rationalised in terms of the ideal aims or functions of the establishment, which entail human technical services. Professionals are usually hired to perform these services, if only to save management the necessity of sending the inmates out of the institution for servicing. . . . Professionals joining the establishment on this basis are likely to become dissatisfied, feeling that they cannot here properly practise their calling and are being used as 'captives' to add professional sanction to the privilege system. This seems to be a classic cry. In many mental hospitals there is a record of disgruntled psychiatrists asserting they are leaving so that they can do psychotherapy. Often a special psychiatric service, such as group psychotherapy, psychodrama or art therapy, is introduced with great support from higher hospital management; then slowly interest is transferred elsewhere, and the professional in charge finds that gradually his job has been changed into a species of public relations work – his therapy given only token support except when visitors come to the institution and higher management is concerned to show how modern and complete the facilities are.[5]

CHAPTER VIII

The Role of Formal Education in Residential Treatment

To discuss the role of formal education in Community Homes is extremely difficult. Although education is probably the most widely discussed topic in present-day society, it is also exceptionally ill-defined. Today education is seen by many people as the key to social mobility. Parents feel that if their children get the right kind of education it will pay financial and social dividends in adult life. Yet others, probably the minority, see education as an important means of ridding the world of social evils in the next generation; they feel that, given the right kind of education, children will develop into adults who see the futility of war, the irrationality of racial prejudice, and the destructiveness of violence. The conflicting ideas, together with a wide range of other divergent views, give rise to heated public debates on education, and on the respective merits of selective or comprehensive, vocationally or culturally based, single sexed or co-educational education. The large percentage of the national budget now being spent on education has brought with it an increased demand from the educated middle class for more parental involvement in schools and greater integration of schools with the community.

Influences of schooling on children

All of these factors are based on the assumption that schooling actually influences children, an assumption which has only recently been challenged. For example, although in Britain evidence of any correlation between education and the level of adult occupation is limited, it was shown by a follow-up study to the 1966 sample census, that while the average earnings of forty-year-old men were in the region of £1,250 per annum, for men holding Higher National Certificates it rose significantly to £1,800 per annum, and for those with degrees to a surprising £3,000 per annum. Whether these differentials are the result of differences in educational background is questionable. As Little suggests,[1] the educational process may merely be reinforcing existing personality and attitudinal differences amongst pupils. He argues that the differences may simply be explained by the fact that clever people and/or hard workers may do well both at school and at work and that really the education process has very little significant influence on outcome. Little strengthens his argument by referring to a study by McQuail on the influence of public school and state grammar school education on young people's political attitudes. McQuail's conclusion was that neither school experience effectively influenced the children's attitudes and, furthermore, that any differences between school samples could as well be explained by differences in social background as in school experience.

Similar kinds of equivocal results also emerge from research into delinquency and schools. Power et al, in 1967,[2] produced an exciting and worrying thesis in which they stated that their studies of schools in Tower Hamlets indicated that some schools actually appeared to be turning children from delinquency-free neighbourhoods into delinquents. On the positive side, they also noted that some schools appeared to be successfully protecting delinquency-prone children from active delinquent behaviour. This was strongly supported by Hargreaves[3] in a participant observer study of a secondary modern school in which the organisational structure and the attitudes of teachers appeared to produce 'delinquescent' behaviour amongst a minority of the pupils. However, when the Cambridge Study in Delinquent Development published their research results they showed that differences in delinquency rates between schools were best explained by the differences in intake. They claimed that the 'delinquent' behaviour of boys before entering secondary school was a more important determinant of actual delinquency than the secondary school attended, thus they reaffirmed that 'delinquency begins at home'.[4]

Do schools then influence children's development? The answer is most probably yes, but not in the way that most people believe. First, education must be distinguished from schooling, since schools have many other functions apart from education. As suggested earlier in Chapter III, they have a custodial function. They are also important in transmitting society's customs and mores. They provide children with their first experience of

174

having to operate and co-operate with groups of peers and their first experience of having to accept an authority that is not based on a blood relationship, i.e. the authority of the teacher and not the parent. I believe that it is these informal functions of schools which have most influence on children since they effectively govern the child's peer group choices – most children have school-based, rather than home-based, friendship groups, the greater part of their life being spent at school. Also, the teachers' attitudes represent to them society's attitudes. They learn what behaviour is deemed socially acceptable and unacceptable. In this context it is interesting to note the rapid growth at present of behaviour modification techniques being used in the classroom. As Goodlet[5] says, 'Behaviour modification has been very useful in dealing with the mentally ill – particularly in treatment of phobias – and with the mentally retarded in toilet training and so on. The examples I shall be giving, however, apply to children in the classroom – particularly those whose behaviour interferes with the work of the class, or else with their own learning.' The implication in this quotation is quite clear; normal childhood behaviour becomes abnormal in the classroom; playing cowboys is alright but not between the hours of 9.00 a.m. and 4.00 p.m., it then becomes hyperactivity. Obviously the proponents of this school of thought would not have much time for A. S. Neill, who wrote, 'No teacher has the right to cure a child of making noises on a drum. The only curing that should be practised is the curing of unhappiness.'[6]

Obviously much of the controversy over education is not over 'learning' but over the informal functions of school. And it is these informal functions that influence the child; the way he relates to his peer group will affect his behaviour much more than the hours spent memorising geometry theorems, or declining Latin nouns. In this chapter, however, I want to focus attention on the learning component of education, since the informal influences of Community Homes, both from staff and peers, are discussed elsewhere in the book. If formal education is accepted as an important component in residential treatment, what form should it take and can its effectiveness be increased? These are the kinds of questions I hope to answer here. However, before examining the type of educational experience given to children in Community Homes it is important to examine, first, what type of educational provision they are in need of and, second, the ability of the teaching staff to meet that need.

Educational needs of the boys at Wellside

From the Appendix below, certain features of the boys at Wellside can be highlighted. (It should be remembered that there is little evidence to suggest that the intake to Wellside in any way differed significantly from the national intake of boys into Community Homes.) First, it is important to remember that 5–10 per cent of the boys admitted were classifiable as subnormal, i.e. had I.Q.s less than 70; also that a further 20 per cent were classifiable as educationally subnormal, i.e. had I.Q.s less than 80. However, this picture is even more depressing if the academic retardation of the boys is considered. This was not studied in detail at Wellside, but from Fields'[7] study of 123 boys in Approved Schools the levels of retardation are obvious:

> The average extent of retardation was about two years in reading and slightly more in arithmetic; and this retardation was greater the later the age committed. The most striking finding is how few of the boys' attainments reached the level indicated as possible by their intelligence quotients, and it is clear that about half of the boys needed some very intensive remedial education to alleviate this situation.

Certainly this picture was reflected at Wellside. It can be said with certainty that very few, if any, of the boys admitted had academic achievements commensurate with their intelligence levels. One of the main reasons for this was that the boys had rejected the conventional education system. This was illustrated by the high incidence of truancy amongst the boys and obviously had important implications for any form of compensatory educational experience that was to be offered. Apart from these general factors, there were specific variations among the boys which drastically affected the classes. These were age, intelligence and behaviour. The classrooms at Wellside had to cater for boys ranging from eleven to fifteen years of age and, in exceptional cases, beyond fifteen years, with I.Q.s ranging from approximately 60 to 130, and with behaviour ranging from the extremely withdrawn, depressed introvert to the violent, explosive extrovert. Obviously the educational needs of these boys were just as diverse.

Educational resources of Community Homes

When the manpower resources available to cope with this huge educational problem are examined there is a notable lack of evidence. I am therefore grateful to Sullivan,[8] who has briefly reported some basic research in which seventeen junior and intermediate boys' Approved Schools, as they were then, were surveyed to investigate the facilities provided in them for boys of school age. The findings of this survey related to both the professional qualifications and the teaching experience of Approved School teachers, and the educational advice and assistance available. Of the sixty-three teachers involved in the investigation, 8 per cent were found to have had additional qualification in special education; 19 per cent were junior school trained; 62 per cent were secondary school trained; 11 per cent had degrees; and 8 per cent comprised one-year trained, emergency trained during the War, or those holding a City and Guilds qualification. From these figures Sullivan concludes, 'With 92 per cent of teachers with ordinary teacher qualifications, support and guidance in treating their boys within the school from services which are near at hand would seem most necessary.' He continues by showing that of the seventeen schools investigated, 71 per cent had the advice of a psychiatrist; 51 per cent a psychologist and 23 per cent an adviser in remedial education. From these figures he states, 'The striking feature that emerges is the relative lack of educational guidance compared with psychological guidance.' The validity of this statement would appear to be questionable but the overall lesson from his survey is important: namely, that the vast majority of teachers attempting to deal with the educational problems of boys in Approved Schools have no specialist training for the task. Nor do they readily have access to specialist, consultative support services which may help them in their work. It certainly seems extraordinary, and yet it is quite common, that a teacher who may have previously been teaching the sixth form in a grammar school, or the nine-year-olds in a junior school, should be expected, without any additional training, to be able to teach a diverse group of deviant boys, many of whom are regarded as maladjusted, educationally subnormal, school phobics. On the limited evidence available I feel justified in saying that the teaching resources available to Community Homes are limited.

It is probably futile to attempt to give a definition of education which is acceptable to all but, for the purposes of this chapter, I want to suggest that the learning component of education should provide the child with certain formal skills which are prerequisites for independent adult life within a given cultural context. Certain aspects of this definition need expanding, especially the words 'should provide' since this no doubt will be interpreted by some as a return to the 'empty vessel' theory – a child is seen as an 'empty vessel' into which knowledge must be poured, rammed or

177

beaten. This is far removed from what I mean. Children are naturally inquisitive and eager to learn and the role of education is to stimulate this desire to learn by providing appropriate stimulii and direction. The direction is necessary to ensure that the child acquires the necessary formal skills for his own culture. Obviously in our present culture basic literacy and numeracy are crucial skills for adult independence. This definition, however, allows for changes in education to meet changing social needs, both through time and across cultures. The aim of education in industrially developed western society must be different from that of basically agrarian societies elsewhere. Similarly, with major advances in technology, one can foresee major changes being required in western education as mechanically mediated means of verbal communication, i.e. telephone, television, etc., become the accepted means of communication, and a decline in the need for literacy may well occur.

However, at present literacy and numeracy are important to adult independance. But so are other skills, which are often not recognised within the purview of general education. I will discuss these later, but first I should like to concentrate on the '3Rs'. As stated earlier, most of the boys in Community Homes are academically retarded and this poses a serious problem to teachers. However, on the positive side, there are certain features of the Homes which allow them to tackle this problem more effectively than would be possible in normal secondary schools. These features are: first, small classes. Although there are no definitive staff/pupil ratios laid down for Community Homes, as there are for schools for the maladjusted, it has been recognised that classes must be small in order to carry out the necessary remedial education. In keeping with this most Community Homes have enviable staff/pupil ratios. At Wellside, for example, there were four full-time classroom teachers and, although the number of boys in a class fluctuated, it was consistently between forty and fifty boys, thus the staff/pupil ratio was approximately 1:11. Second, the classrooms in Community Homes have always been well supplied with material resources: allowances for books, scientific apparatus, art materials, remedial reading schemes, etc. This is because the importance of compensatory education for children in care has long been recognised. Thirdly, the timetables for the classrooms have always been extremely flexible. Teachers have not been saddled with rigid syllabuses geared to examinations and have been able to abandon the time-table at a moment's notice if circumstances demanded it. Along with this factor, has been the generous provision of transport.

Most Community Homes have had their own mini-buses for taking the children out. These, with appropriate financial allowances, have been available to teaching staff who can therefore easily arrange and organise educational visits and, if they desire, base much of their classroom work on extra-mural activities. A further feature of Homes which may prove both advantageous and disadvantageous is that the classrooms have not in the past operated on a terminal basis, but have had to remain in operation continually throughout the year. This means that the child spends a much greater length of time in the classroom than he would in a normal secondary school. It also means, of course, that timetabling difficulties arise when teachers' holiday entitlements have to be met. However, generally teachers in Community Homes are in a position to initiate and develop teaching schemes based on the individual needs of the child. This is absolutely necessary if the educational process is to have any value because, as described earlier, there are wide variations in age, intelligence, motivation and ability within any class of a Community School.

Classroom organisation – streaming

Given that the educational process must be individually based, how should the classroom organisation be structured? This is an important question, since some schools, and at earlier stages in its development Wellside included, merely reconstruct the streaming system of the secondary schools which many of the boys had found so degrading and damaging. For example some schools which undertake examinations, normally Certificate of Secondary Education, will have an examination class, the top class. Within the same small classroom block will be the remedial class, the bottom or backward class, and between these two extremes will be perhaps two other classes graded on more suitable criteria. This streaming process is damaging because the boys are soon aware of their own positions within the hierarchy. For the boy who has already been branded by the school system as a failure, to be further identified as such is brutally damaging, not only to the child's self-image but to the educational process. It is now well established that the 'labelling' of children in such a way imposes on them self-fulfilling prophecies whereby they react by producing behaviour compatible with their 'labels'. Thus, immediately a child is placed into the remedial group his motivation to learn is further depressed. The streaming process in a Community Home can also have marked disadvantages for those in the 'top

179

stream'. Often if a boy is academically 'bright', working hard in class and achieving some success, it is assumed that he has no 'problems'. Yet this is patently not true since, almost by definition, the fact that the boy is in the Home means that he has come into conflict with society. Just because he has adjusted to institutional life, and appears to be grasping the opportunities it offers him, does not mean that he has resolved whatever produced his initial conflict with society.

Classroom organisation – the use of primary school techniques

Much has been written about the disadvantages of streaming in secondary schools and many of these are exacerbated within the situation of Community Homes. On the other hand, the small number of children and the high staff/pupil ratios make Community Homes the ideal places to experiment with techniques that have been successfully developed in primary education but never really attempted at secondary level. The three techniques which would seem to have particular relevance to the Home situation are those known as *family grouping, the integrated day* and *team teaching.*

FAMILY GROUPING

Family grouping is diametrically opposed to streaming. Classes or groups are of mixed abilities and mixed ages, the basic assumption being that the older and more able children will participate in the learning of their younger and less able class mates. The learning process is seen as a two-way system in which the 'teacher' is consolidating his own learning and advancing by helping his peers. This technique has already been adopted in many Community Homes – through force of circumstance rather than as a matter of policy. As has already been stressed, any one class will necessarily contain a diversity of abilities and ages, so that the family grouping in effect already exists. However, if the family grouping is not accepted as a formal technique, the boys' behaviour tends to be interpreted in a way more in keeping with streamed schooling. For example, if a barely literate child is struggling to write a simple essay and asks his more able friend for help, this may be interpreted as cheating, rather than as constructive co-operation which is helping the education of both participants. Family grouping is particularly important, too, to the problem of teaching reading in Community Homes. Most adolescent non-readers are acutely conscious of their disability but often attempt to conceal their concern behind a façade of aggression or feigned non-interest. This facade is often very difficult for the teacher to break down and yet it can easily be overcome if the 'teacher' is in fact one of the boy's own peers. In any residential school it is easy to find informal examples of this form of mutual assistance: the illiterate boy who receives a letter from home will readily turn to his best friend asking him to read it to him and if necessary write the reply. The child will much more readily turn to his peers for help than to the staff, perhaps because of his embarrassment but, whatever the reason, it is an important aspect of adolescent behaviour on which the teacher should capitalise.

The idea of family grouping should be extended beyond the school if possible. For example, at Wellside many of the boys were involved in a Community Service Volunteer scheme, in which they spent one afternoon per week at a local hospital for the mentally subnormal helping and playing with the mentally handicapped children. Some of the boys, themselves barely literate, spent hours designing and producing work-cards which could be used to help the subnormal children learn to read. This situation – which obviously benefited the boys as well as the handicapped children – could well be extended, using the boys as teachers to help immigrant children to learn to read.

THE INTEGRATED DAY

At secondary level education has been artificially and arbitrarily divided up into subjects by schools. Obviously disciplines overlap and interact: mathematics is as common to all science as English is in the reporting of experiments; history and english literature are inseparable and if artificially separated lose much of their worth. The introduction of the integrated day into teaching should abolish these artificial boundaries and allow the child to select and develop the information he needs. The child working under the integrated day system normally carries out individual or group projects, which may be on any topic but as an illustration a project on canals will be considered. In studying canals the child will need to refer to: history, for their development; geography, for the scope of the canal network; engineering, for their construction; art, for the decoration of the boats; social sciences, to understand how employment and redundancy among canal workers are linked with the economic changes of the industrial revolution. The child will also need to develop his reading for searching out and understanding references, and his writing, for recording and presenting the project. Obviously such a process destroys the artificial subject boundaries constructed by most schools, but it also destroys artificial time boundaries. The child cannot guarantee that he will find his references and produce data in the allotted period. The day must therefore be treated as a whole, with the child developing the topic throughout it, rather than being arbitrarily cut off when he may be most highly motivated.

TEAM TEACHING

The integrated day has important repercussions on the teaching staff. When formal divisions in subjects are broken down, teachers can obviously no longer remain as specialist subject teachers. Instead they must develop themselves as part of the resources available to the children. The child will need to circulate among the teachers as his project develops. On the canal project he might need the assistance and guidance of the history/geography teacher initially, but then might move rapidly to the art teacher, or the teacher best versed in social studies, and so on. This means that a teacher is now responsible with his colleagues, for part of an overall project. Teachers in this type of organisation must be prepared to co-operate more closely with one another than they do in the formal, subject-based school. The child will not be submitting work directly to them, but will be submitting a project, part of which has been done with them, to another teacher. Teacher co-operation is probably the biggest stumbling block in re-organising secondary level education because one of the basic 'professional' attitudes of teachers is that of classroom autonomy. This attitude assumes that what an individual teacher does in his own classroom is his own business. Here teaching methods used, the sort of discipline exerted, and the teacher's 'philosophy of education' are regarded as matters of personal choice.[9] This point of view becomes most obvious when a young teacher with 'progressive' ideas attempts to put them into practice within a fairly rigid school structure. He may not be criticised openly for his work by his older colleagues, but will often become the butt of staff-room comments about the noise level in his class, or his apparent lack of control. Team teaching if it is to be successful must overcome this attitude.

Project work

I said earlier that formal education should be based on individual project work, but this statement raises a further problem of how the projects are to be chosen and initiated. Obviously if the child is to be motivated to carry out the project he must choose his own area of study. This is essential, because if the project is imposed on him by the teacher, he will most probably react with boredom and obstruction. Project work will only be successful if it is self-motivated. This does not mean that the teacher plays no part in the selection of the project, but it does mean that he should not censor or discard the child's ideas. He should play an active part in helping the child decide what to do, and will need to react with enthusiasm once the choice has been made in order to maintain the child's interest.

At Wellside one of the basic sources of project work became the Humanities Project,[10] which soon became an indispensable part of the classroom programme. The Humanities Project was an experimental teaching scheme developed by the Schools Council, under the aegis of the Nuffield Foundation, and it was aimed at those children at secondary school who were affected by the raising of the school leaving age to sixteen years.

The Project was based on five major premises:

(1) That controversial issues should be handled in the classroom with adolescents.

(2) That the teacher accept the need to submit his teaching in controversial areas to the criterion of neutrality at this stage of education, i.e. that he regard it as part of his responsibility not to promote his own view.

(3) That the mode of enquiry in controversial areas should have discussion, rather than instruction, as its core.

(4) That the discussion should protect divergence of view among participants, rather than attempt to achieve consensus.

(5) That the teacher as chairman of the discussion should have responsibility for quality and standards of learning.

From these premises it is obvious that the role envisaged for the teacher is very different from that normally accepted. However, there is a close similarity between the teacher's role in the Humanities Project and the staff role envisaged at Wellside in the group counselling, as described in Chapter IV. The basic aim of the Humanities Project is to develop an understanding of social situations and human acts and of the controversial issues which they raise. It attempts to do this by providing discussion-based groups with material on basic social problems, viz. Law and Order, the Family, Relationship between the Sexes, War. The material is presented in the form of a multi-media pack containing poems, songs, extracts from drama, maps, cartoons, questionnaires, graphs and tables, advertisements, tape recordings and recommended films. Having read or seen a particular piece of material the group then discuss it. Discussion under the neutral chairman, the teacher, should be based on evidence.

The Humanities Project was particularly relevant to boys at Wellside. It not only served as a useful catalyst for further individual project work, for example, the pack on relationship between the sexes led to work on general sex education and biology, as well as to modelling of the human form. It also directed the attention of the boys into those areas of education which are vitally important and yet are not formally recognised.

Limitations of primary school techniques

I believe that the formal educational needs of the majority of boys in care in Community Homes could best be met by the systematic application of techniques developed at primary education level. However, I am *not* advocating the use of primary level material. Most children learn to read at primary school and so most reading schemes are aimed at this age group. It has been a long-standing complaint amongst remedial teachers of adolescents that little suitable reading material has been available. The position has now been rectified and there are a reasonable number of reading schemes aimed at adolescent non-readers. It is essential that these be utilised, because there can be nothing more degrading for a fifteen-year-old non-reader than to have to attempt to read books designed for six year olds. This only serves to strengthen his image of his own inadequacy.

At Wellside many primary level techniques were employed, not so much as part of a deliberate policy, but because many of the teachers who worked there were trained and experienced in teaching at primary level. The fact that primary techniques were only introduced at an informal level was in many ways unfortunate since, although it proved successful with most of the boys – many of whom commented on the differences between the classrooms at Wellside and those of their secondary schools – the techniques were often severely criticised by other staff, who saw the classes as lax, chaotic and failing to teach. This situation arose, in part, because of the failure of the teachers to specify and explain what they were attempting to do and how they hoped the boys would benefit.

There was also a group of boys at Wellside for whom primary techniques might have been beneficial in some ways, but were also socially handicapping. These were the boys of above average intelligence who were capable of sitting and passing state examinations. Wellside had a moral duty to help these boys pass examinations: whatever our personal opinions about examinations, they are obviously regarded as important by future employers. Consequently the teaching staff attempted to provide an examination syllabus for certain boys, leading to the Certificate of Secondary Education. Judging by the examination results, they were successful in these attempts. This aspect of classroom work was important, not only because it attempted to ensure that no boy was handicapped in his education by virtue of the fact that he was placed in residential care, but also because for some boys, who would normally not be regarded as examination material, it represented recognition that they were not complete social failures. This was most true in art, in which some boys who were virtually illiterate and regarded as educationally subnormal achieved examination successes at C.S.E. This success did untold good to the children's self-images, and this is what much of the education in Community Homes should be about – not just remedying academic retardation but repairing the damaged self-images of boys by allowing them to succeed, at no matter how low a level. This process has important implications for the boys' employment, as will be seen in the next chapter. However, it should be emphasised that if the boys are to be encouraged to attain academic success of any form, it does mean that teaching must be based on individual rather than group needs.

The functional aims of education

I have defined education as providing those formal skills which are prerequisite to independent adult life within a given cultural context. Our given cultural context is an extremely complex technological society governed by a representative democracy. Given this situation, formal education should try to provide children with the knowledge necessary for them to function within our society. This knowledge falls into three main areas, all of which overlap. These are: political education, legal education, and consumer education. If a society is to be truly democratic, and remain so, then it is essential that its children be given some understanding of the political structure of the society. It is also essential that this be done in a politically neutral fashion. But children need to know what political parties represent; how they are elected to government; government's responsibility to the electorate; what pressure groups are and how they function. This task is particularly essential with children in care, since the care order is in force until the child reaches the age of eighteen years, the age of majority. Residential education should, therefore, educate the child in order that he be able to exercise his democratic rights when he is discharged from care.

Similarly, with legal education, if our legal system is to be truly impartial and universal then individuals must be made aware of their legal rights and how they can exert those rights in law. The complex legal measures recently passed to protect tenants in privately owned property cannot do their job unless the tenants, and future tenants, are made aware of their rights. If society really wants to try to end the exploitation of the deprived sections of the community then it must inform the deprived of their legal rights. Where better can this be done than in schools for the deprived adults of the future?

Consumer education needs to be viewed in its widest sense. To be an independent adult one needs to be aware of the demands made on one by advertising, hire purchase, and the problems of planned obsolescence and pollution. The child in care today is likely to develop into the inadequate adult of tomorrow. Inadequacy tends to manifest itself in things like an inability to manage successfully personal finances; eviction for non-payment of rent; electricity and gas supplies being cut off because the bills have not been paid. It seems essential that if we are to break through the 'cycle of deprivation' then education should teach children about the problems of adult life and how to cope with them.

The therapeutic aims of education

It would be dangerous if education were seen only in functional terms. It should also cater for the expressive needs of the child. In doing this, it often has a very definite therapeutic value. Art, drama and music are not merely 'school' subjects but very basic and universal means of expression amongst children. Very young children, from eighteen months of age, find expression through rudimentary forms of art and drama and music. They will become engrossed and gain great satisfaction from 'drawing' and colouring; will beat out basic rhythms on improvised drums, usually to their parents' annoyance; will role-play: going shopping, tea parties, etc. These forms of expression are important because they are a means of expressing personal feelings and of understanding the feelings of others. Children and adolescents will paint 'angry' and 'violent' pictures, thereby utilising a socially legitimate outlet for their aggression. If the teaching staff are sensitive they should be able to take advantage of this non-verbal

186

attempt at communication as a means of coming to understand some of the children's difficulties. Drama or role-playing has a more overt therapeutic function because it can allow the individual to express his feelings openly in a controlled situation, but also, more importantly, it can allow him to act out the roles of others, thereby allowing himself some insight into their feelings and behaviour. It can be an extremely illuminating experience for adults to observe children acting out their roles. At Wellside the Drama teacher encouraged the boys to enact a Review Meeting, with boys taking the roles of staff, discussing the cases of individual boys and deciding their futures. It soon became obvious that the boys harboured all sorts of fantasies about staff's omnipotence and motivations in dealing with boys. This role-playing naturally led on to a discussion of the Review Meeting procedure in reality, and how it could be better organised in order to give the boys greater participation in the decision-making process which so radically affected their lives.

The arts have an important and essential role to play in education in Community Homes. But too often their contribution is based on the enthusiasm of one member of staff, who in turn feels alienated from the total institution. It has been mentioned elsewhere that the majority of staff in Community Homes have a strongly instrumental attitude to life. This being so, the expressive arts are regarded as irrelevant – being good at painting or drama is not going to help a boy get a job. As a result the arts are given very low priority by staff other than those directly committed to their teaching. As the boys share this instrumental attitude with staff, they also see the arts as irrelevant. But it is in this connection that the arts have the greatest contribution to make to education. The very fact that they are non-functional is important because it teaches that the self-satisfaction gained from having achieved something is an end in itself. To create a model in clay or paint a picture to one's own satisfaction are extremely important experiences for children to have, particularly deprived children. In the realm of art no-one can question their judgments; their opinions of their own work are what matter, no authority can come along and mark them right or wrong. The creator also has the power to dispose of his own work – it can be very distressing to see a deprived boy spend hours working on a model or a painting and then, when it is finished, destroy it within seconds, saying glibly, 'It wasn't any good anyway.' In that act can be seen the damage society has done to the child – anything he makes is useless; he knows because he has been told so often.

CHAPTER IX

'The Devil makes work for idle hands'

The moral value of work

Most of the Victorian philanthropists and idealists who initiated the great social reforms of the nineteenth century – in areas like child care, mental health and the penal services – were devout Christians. They brought to their work a moral point of view which could be described as a kind of puritan ethic. In general terms this preached that salvation was not to be gained by monastic withdrawal from the world, or by the performance of 'good deeds', but by following one's calling – whatever that might be – industriously: *working* for the glory of God.

This view – that work has some intrinsic moral value – has permeated the British penal system since the nineteenth century. From here is was transferred to the reform school system when that was first set up. As West[1] points out, writing about the development of approved schools:

> The number of juveniles incarcerated in prisons with adults gradually decreased, until the Children's Act of 1908 finally abolished imprisonment for those under fourteen, and placed restrictions on the imprisonment of those in the fourteen to sixteen age groups. The reform schools in England and the houses of refuge in the U.S.A. served to rescue young people from the adult gaols, and to give young paupers and criminals (at that time these categories were scarcely distinguishable) *a chance to learn a job and earn their bread* [author's italics]. These schools long preceded the establishment of compulsory school. They were the precursors of the present day approved schools, which are institutions run by local authorities or voluntary bodies, 'approved' and inspected by the Home Office.

He continues by pointing out the present-day situation:

188

In general Borstals lay great emphasis on training in habits of steady work and on trying to arouse interest in a job. The aims are of course particularly appropriate to the large number of incompetent and work shy youngsters with whom they have to deal. Everyone puts in a full day's work and the tasks provided are useful and constructive such as building, farming, carpentry and mechanics. Trade training courses, utilising skilled instructors and impressive workshops are given to those sufficiently able and conscientious to follow them.

West's comments are equally appropriate to what were the intermediate (aged between thirteen and fifteen years) and senior (fifteen to eighteen years) Approved Schools – as witnessed by the impressive array of trade departments, the high quality of their output and the widespread staff attitude of teaching boys a pride in their job, and that nobody gets 'aught for nought'.

The trade departments at Wellside

Wellside was obviously infected by this school of thought, like all its fellow schools. It had four well-established trade departments: painting and decorating, joinery, gardening and building. Each department had approximately ten boys, but this number was fluctuated according to the total number of boys in the school at any one time, and the ages of those boys. The fairly ill-defined and consequently flexible procedure of placing boys in the departments was as follows: boys aged approximately fourteen and a half to fifteen years, with reasonable academic attainments – basic literacy and numeracy – and with sufficient self-control to be able to benefit from the comparatively loosely supervised department setting, were selected for entry into a department. The boys were then asked for their own first and second choice of department and then allocated as far as possibe to the department of their choice. Occasionally this was not possible because of an absence of instructors. The boys inevitably put the instructor before the job, and chose to work in the department alongside the instructor they liked most. This was acceptable because the instructors no longer saw their job as that of masters training apprentices – the original concept implied in the name 'trade training departments' – but as child care workers with specialists technical skills which they could utilise to establish a close relationship with the boys. The boys viewed the move into the departments as a significant step in their lives. They regarded it as a marked change of status from that of 'class boy' to 'working man'.

189

The work carried out by the departments was impressive, and the instructors and their boys were responsible for the vast majority of maintenance work throughout the school. This created tremendous conflict as to whether the departments were in fact serving the interests of the school or the interests of the boys. However, let me first describe the work performed before returning to discuss this persistent and apparently insoluble conflict.

THE PAINTING AND DECORATING DEPARTMENT

The painting and decorating department was responsible for the decoration of the whole school. This was an unending task, rather like painting the Forth bridge. Every time the decoration of one dormitory was completed another required attention, or the assembly hall needed painting, or the classrooms, and so on, in one perpetual round. The boys learnt the basic skills of decorating, painting, care of brushes, paper hanging as well as choice of décor – the boys were responsible for choosing their own decorations whenever financially possible (they often had expensive taste in wallpaper!). Each department was important in its own right but perhaps the painters' importance was more easily seen, as the instructor, as shown in his interview, was aware of the importance of the physical environment in a treatment setting.

He was conscious that the décor of a room may be a factor which contributes to an individual's affective state. Consequently he and his boys worked unfailingly to produce an environment that broke down the 'feel' of an institution. Some of the painters took up apprenticeships in the trade after leaving the school, but they were few in number. However, many boys' homes took on a brighter and more exciting appearance after their experience in the painters' department, if the many reports of boys spending their holidays at home decorating are correct.

THE JOINERS

The joiners, like the painters, took on important maintenance tasks throughout the school. In the main house they renewed and relaid all the dormitory floors, and they made and replaced all the rotted sash windows. They constructed commercial-sized greenhouses and turkey sheds outside. They also found time to make coffee tables and other presents to take home. The equipment they used in their workshop was the kind to be found in any modern commercial joinery concern. One of the instructor's ideals was to produce boys who had a wide range of experience with modern joinery equipment, so that if necessary they could always call upon this knowledge to obtain work. The instructor extended this idea by arranging visits to engineering works, smelting factories, hotels, machine-tool manufacturers, and carpet works. These visits were aimed at giving the boys a wide range of ideas for occupations so that they could make a choice for themselves.

THE GARDENING DEPARTMENT

The gardening department was really a misnomer, it was in reality a combination of horticulture, agriculture and animal husbandry. The instructor, a man with considerable experience of teaching educationally subnormal children, as well as commercial experience as a farm manager, was convinced that the only way to interest boys in horticulture was to do it on a commercial scale. His experience had taught him that to give each boy a small plot and designate it his garden was disastrous. The end result was, in his words, 'a lot of graves with a row of peas at the top, a row of cabbages, a row of radishes, and so on, plus a group of uninterested boys.' So the gardening department worked on a commercial scale. They had eleven thousand chickens, with a full-time poultry man responsible for them and the boys assisting when and as they wished. There were about ten acres of vegetable and soft fruit grown on commercial lines. The produce was sold to the school kitchens as well as taken by the boys to the local market, thus they knew if they picked the strawberries they would be benefiting at lunch-time. They knew also that nobody was too concerned about how many they ate while they were picking, except the matron who found herself faced by an epidemic of diarrhoea. They boys also drove tractors, rotavators and other machinery, and learnt welding and some basic motor maintenance, all of which are now important aspects of farming.

The instructor was convinced of the importance of providing animals to assist in the treatment of disturbed children. He felt that boys who have difficulty in relating to adults can benefit from 'relating' to animals. He certainly shared this view with many others. Franklin,[2] stated for example, about Q Camp, a camp for maladjusted boys aged eleven to fifteen years:

> . . . animals, small ones as pets and large ones on the farm, are playing a very prominent part in the emotional lives of the boys. The boys can play with them, they can mother and protect them and they can learn to train and control animals bigger than themselves.

191

The instructor also claimed animals were a useful adjunct to sex education and that seeing a lamb born, if explained carefully, would teach any child more than all the lectures and films put together.

Apart from these factors there was one other important aspect of the farm. Most of the boys at Wellside, as at any Approved School, are from the large urban conurbations and, like most urban children, they have very little opportunity to see rural life. Consequently the farm would seem to provide invaluable learning experience for any child. He learns that chickens actually lay eggs, tomatoes grow on plants, potatoes grow underground, sheep are shorn, and so on. These experiences, with the correct tutelage, are in a direct line of descendance from Rousseau's educational philosophy.

THE BUILDING DEPARTMENT

The building department carried out maintenance and improvements throughout the school. Much of their work radically improved conditions for the boys. For example, one summer was spent digging out and enlarging the play area and establishing an adventure playground, working with an Army Youth Team who had volunteered to help. The boys' showers were refitted with attractive ceramic tiles and futuristic, free-standing wash basins. The building department by the nature of its trade was a 'man's world', this was reinforced by the instructor who was a tall, burly, Rugby League enthusiast. Yet being visibly so masculine it attracted immature boys who desperately wanted to prove their masculinity and adulthood, although unable to sustain this stance. So at any one time the builders had a sub-group of physically and emotionally immature fifteen and sixteen year olds – 'My Diddy-men', as the instructor affectionately called them. Consequently, whilst some members of the group were arduously constructing a brick wall others would be playing with the mortar, flicking it at each other or using it to make models. The instructor's strength was in his ability to deal with both groups equally, playing with the immature group and treating the mature group as adults.

From the description of the departments' activities the reader may sense the nature of the conflict alluded to earlier. The basic problem was – how do you provide meaningful work experience without sacrificing the needs of individual boys? For example, the decorating has to be done, but how can that be reconciled with the fact that the boy you have taught to paper-hang may be so depressed by news from home that he has no interest or desire to work. Alternatively what do you do, having taught a boy bricklaying, when a large project involving bricklaying arises at the same time as the possibility of the boy obtaining employment out of the school? This conflict is by no means found solely at Wellside and has been reported in other schools,[3] nor was a solution found at Wellside. However, an uneasy compromise was reached, with each instructor attemping to put the needs of the child first. In all cases the instructors were genuinely attempting to consider the child first, but from an objective standpoint they often failed.

THE 'WORKERS'

A similar conflict arose over the 'workers'. These were boys selected by the staff for work experience outside the school with local employers. The workers enjoyed a privileged status within the school, going to bed later, receiving £2.50 pocket money from their wages (as opposed to the 30 pence of boys in school. The remainder of their wages went in statutory accommodation charges and enforced savings. In the evenings they went to the local cinemas and discotheques, and their lives were much less supervised and restricted than the majority of boys. There were normally eight or ten workers at any one time although this varied with the employment vacancies available in the vicinity.

The selection of boys who were ready to go to work was interesting, because the staff's criteria for selection varied. Some staff chose boys because they were stable and reliable and would do a good day's work; others chose boys whom they were 'unsure of', in order to put them in a comparatively unsupervised situation where they could be 'tested out'. And others used concrete criteria, choosing boys from exceptionally materially deprived backgrounds who would benefit from the extra money available.

This wide range of selection criteria makes it difficult to assess the success of the scheme. However, in the vast majority of cases the boys worked without complaint from their employers until released from the school. A minority of boys were dismissed for bad time keeping and, occasionally, petty pilfering. In material terms boys benefited, at times being released with up to £100 in savings, and having stamps on their insurance cards – an important consideration in a time of high unemployment.

The workers posed a problem to the school. They were obviously young men, physically mature, with girl friends, and earnings of up to £20 per week, and yet they were living in a school, i.e. an institution which dealt with boys in a pupil (dependent) role. The workers often demonstrated their independence by staying out late, spending hours in conversation on the telephone with the latest girl friend and buying scooters. All this is normal acceptable adolescent behaviour in society, and yet it was deviant from the norms of the school society, and was often perceived by staff as being a further 'symptom' of the boys' delinquency. This situation needed continual examination in order that staff's judgments about the workers could be kept in perspective.

The major conflict over the workers was, once again, the problem of whose needs were really being met. Were the boys gaining useful work experience or were they merely being used by employers as cheap labour? If an employer had a vacancy and no boy was ready to go to work should the instructors recommend a boy they felt inappropriate or should the employer be told nobody was available at the risk of losing that vacancy at a future date? These problems continually worried staff and occupied a good deal of discussion at staff meetings, but, inevitably, they were never resolved.

The functions of the trade department

In Chapter II it was shown that a sample of delinquents – the total population of an Home Office Approved School – had significantly lower levels of achievement motivation than their controls from a secondary modern school, when matched for age, intelligence, social class and religion. This finding has important implications for the role of departments in the residential treatment of delinquents. Having described the situation at Wellside in some detail it is important to consider the function of trade departments generally in residential treatment. The trade departments have two clearly defined functions: the primary one is that of social education; the secondary one is the teaching of skills.

SOCIAL EDUCATION
Social education is aimed at teaching boys behaviour appropriate to the work situation. A boy needs to be taught basic work procedures; to arrive at work on time; to get changed into overalls before starting work; to follow instructions, since failure to do so may prove disastrous, especially if working with machinery; to work in co-operation with others; to take care of an employer's property, tools, protective clothing, etc.

194

THE TEACHING OF SKILLS

Teaching of skills works in conjunction with social education and is aimed at teaching the boys the skills appropriate to their particular trades. The teaching of skills often starts as an extension of class-room teaching, particularly if the boys are academically retarded. For example, boys may be taught how to measure and perform simple calculations concerned with area, mass and volume. From this, skills pertaining to the trade itself will be taught; the correct usage of tools and materials; specific skills such as bricklaying, glazing, paper hanging, floor-laying, ploughing, etc. Many of these specific skills are not designed solely to be useful in the boys' future occupations, but also aimed at making them more independent so that on release they will be able to carry out simple maintenance on their own accommodation.

These two specific functions of the trade departments were well recognised and provide the overt 'raison d'être' of the departments. However, there are many more important, covert reasons for the existence of the departments. The first of these is that trade departments are the essential core of many institutions dealing with delinquents. The range of institutional treatment available for delinquents is wide, ranging from the authoritarian 'short, sharp, shock' régime of the Detention Centres, through the more moderate, quasi-public school system of some Community Schools, to the liberal, therapeutic community approach of others. In all of these varying approaches the trade departments play a prominent role, not merely by keeping the boys occupied throughout the day, but also by providing a focus of commitment for the boys. When asked what they get out of the school the boys frequently reply that they are given a chance to learn a trade. The following is a quotation from interviews:

> 'What do you think the school has taught you?' 'I've learnt a lot I wouldn't have learnt outside; in the departments you learn how to get on with people and how to work with them.'
> 'What do you think you have learnt here?' 'Apart from a bit of gardening, nothing.'

The departments offer a concrete service which the boys see as relevant to their lives outside the institution. For this reason they are prepared to commit themselves to the institution and accordingly accept all the other, to them, irrelevant aspects of treatment, whether it be two hours' physical training or two hours' groups counselling a day.

Throughout this book it has been stressed that an important

aspect of treatment is the boys' identification with adult models. In this respect department instructors are in a unique position. They play the role of a 'working man'; they wear overalls and perform tasks such as building and gardening; this is within the boys' sphere of experience and one with which they can readily identify. Similarly, the boys have much greater opportunity for identification with the instructor who is often not doing things *to* the boys but *with* them. For example, the instructor is likely to be building a wall with the boys rather than trying to teach them formally.

This position of working with the boys is extremely important since the possibility of communication between the boys and the instructor is greatly increased. The formal interview situation is very difficult for most boys to cope with – previously they have probably been approached in this way only when in trouble, for example when they have been summoned into a police interviewing room. However, in the work situation the boys have the opportunity to communicate with the instructor and, more important, the opportunity to control the communication. When working with the instructor the boys can begin talking on whatever subject they like and when they feel they have said enough can terminate the conversation, either by turning back and concentrating on their work, or by asking a question about the work in hand.

The 'failure' of the trade departments

The trade departments therefore serve not only the important overt functions of education and training, but also the covert functions of providing both a core for the institution and a vital therapeutic channel. However, the concept of trade departments is under attack throughout the Community School system because it appears from the results of the boys' behaviour on release that the trade departments are failing in their job. One of the most common reasons given for a boy's reconviction after release is his failure to find and retain suitable employment. This is seen as a failure of the part of the trade departments. Consequently it is argued that trade departments which employ highly skilled instructors and are extremely expensive in both plant and materials, are not economically justified. Similarly, research has shown that very few boys take up apprenticeships in the trades in which they have been trained and of these only a small minority complete their apprenticeships.[4]

Thus, although there are opportunities for identification with a successful achievement model – the instructor – there are factors which hamper this identification process. One of these factors is that the trade departments are geared to dealing with a group rather than with individuals. Consequently if a group is working on a project certain individuals within the group may be unable to cope and this may reinforce their self-concept of failure. Also, in some schools it is questionable how much the boys participate in the trade departments. They may have been detailed to a trade department in which they have no interest, and the projects which are chosen for them may appear to be irrelevant, for example, maintaining lawns on which they are not allowed to play.

The trade departments at present are concerned with the teaching of skills and yet the research mentioned previously suggests that the boys' problems do not arise from lack of skills but from lack of motivation to apply these skills. The boys often have the intelligence, academic attainments and basic skills required to obtain an apprenticeship. But, if they lack the motivation to achieve they have very little interest in completing apprenticeships. The departments, therefore, need to concentrate as much on motivation as on skills. McClelland[5] has described a teaching programme aimed at raising adults' levels of achievement motivation. The four main aims of this programme are quoted below and are followed by suggestions as to how the techniques may be applied to the treatment of Community School boys.

McClelland's training programme in achievement motivation

In broad outline the courses had four main goals:

1. They were designed to teach the participants how to think, talk, and act like a person with high Achievement Motivation.
2. The courses stimulated the participants to set higher but carefully planned and realistic work goals for themselves over the next two years.
3. The courses also used techniques for giving the participants knowledge about themselves.
4. The courses also usually created an 'esprit de corps' from learning about one another's hopes and fears, successes and failures, and from going through an emotional experience together, away from everyday life, in a retreat setting.

Application of the Training Programme

This training programme could be applied to departments in Community schools in the following way.

1. TO TEACH A PERSON HOW TO THINK AND ACT LIKE A PERSON WITH
HIGH ACHIEVEMENT MOTIVATION

This would seem the essential starting point with young offenders, the majority of whom consider themselves failures and have had this view reinforced for them by society. This part of the programme could be implemented through two approaches, the indirect and the direct.

The indirect approach would entail offering the boys information about high achievers through literature, the importance of which has been demonstrated by McClelland's[6] analysis of folk tales. Here he shows that folk tales reflect the economic achievements of a society and apparently guarantee its continuance by the indoctrination of future generations. The school library, therefore, should have novels, biographies and autobiographies of high achievers and the classroom current affairs lessons should pay particular attention to contemporary high achievers. The boys should also be shown films, both fact and fiction, portraying high achievers and their lives, and be encouraged to write essays and stories which centre on achievement.

The indirect approach should be extended to role-playing, and the boys should have to act achievement roles. This can be carried out in three possible ways; first the boy can be given an achievement role to act in an otherwise unstructured dramatic situation, as suggested by Moreno.[7] Second, he can be instructed to perform an achievement role in a face to face situation with a therapist in the way suggested by Kelly's[8] Fixed Role Therapy. Thirdly, the boy can be given the task of arguing for, and elaborating on, high achievement in a group situation and, as Janis and King[9] have shown, this can have a profound effect on the individual's attitudes and behaviour following the group situation.

The direct approach entails demonstrating to the boys their ability to achieve, and emphasising the fact that they need not be failures in all fields. The teachers and instructors should select tasks individually for each boy in the knowledge that the boy, with some limited effort, will be able to succeed. This could be adopted in all fields – for example, plant growing, simple furniture making, reading, model building, physical education, etc. This would lead to individual programmes for each boy. The programmes would consist of graduated stages through which the boys worked, the stages increasing in difficulty as the boys' confidence in their ability to succeed increased. In the work situation the boy should be involved in a position of shared responsibility with the instructor, enjoying an equal status with him rather than a subordinate status. If the boy is involved in a specific job he should, with the advice of the instructor, cost the job himself and order his own materials. If growing vegetables he should take them to market himself, see how much he is paid in return for his labour and compare his produce with those of other concerns. In this way he would be accepting the responsibilities of high achievers as well as gaining personal satisfaction and some financial reward.

2. THE ESTABLISHMENT OF PLANNED AND REALISTIC WORK GOALS
In the trade departments this would seem an essential therapeutic approach. Initially, because delinquents appear to be psychologically tied to the present and are unable to think in long-term goals,[10] the work goals should be established on a daily basis in simple numerical terms. For example, the number of bricks to be laid or feet in a cabbage field to be hoed, or floor boards to be sawn and prepared in a day would be possible goals. At the end of each day the boy's performance could be measured against this level of aspiration. Initially the instructor would have to guide the boy so that he was not continually overestimating his possible performance and consequently failing. The instructor would then encourage the boy to progressively raise his work goals over a longer period of time so that the boy would be setting his own work goals for the week, and then for the month. It is essential that the boy's performance be compared with his levels of aspiration so that he may receive 'feed-back' and experience the satisfaction of achieving his established goals. As the boy gains greater confidence and motivation it is important that he occasionally fails to achieve his goals so that he experiences the dissatisfaction of failure. As the boy approaches his release he should be encouraged to visit building sites, farms, factories, offices, etc., to observe a variety of occupations in order that he can establish work goals for when he is released.

3. THE PARTICIPANT GAINS KNOWLEDGE ABOUT HIMSELF
The continuous assessment of performance against work goals would be more effective if carried out in groups than if merely carried out with the instructor and the individual boy. Lewin[11] has shown that participation in group discussion is more effective in bringing about attitude change than traditional 'lecturing'. The instructor should meet with his group of boys to discuss their performance, why they have succeeded, why they have failed, why they have persistently over-estimated or under-estimated their ability. In the group situation the boy would receive support and encouragement from his peers, and would be able to assess his

performance and progress with them. These discussions could then be allowed to range over a wider sphere, incorporating not only work goals but life goals. When they are interviewed most boys stated that their aim in life was to 'have a good time'. Criticism of this attitude by staff would be ineffectual since the boys might feel that staff were failing to understand his point of view because of differences in age, background, etc. However, in a group situation, where the boy's peers may voice criticism of this life goal, the criticism would be much more effective.

4. AN 'ESPRIT DE CORPS' CREATED IN A RETREAT SITUATION
Community schools are very much a retreat situation. Indeed they are often geographically isolated from society. The institution is not only physically isolated from the boys' homes but also isolates them from their family background through the attitudes and experiences it presents. This retreat situation can be both destructive and constructive. It is destructive if an 'esprit de corps' arises that does not represent the total institution but a subculture within it. It is possible for the boys to build up their own culture which is totally opposed to that of the staff and society. This 'inmate' culture possesses its own jargon and rituals. It is extremely easy for this situation to develop in Community Schools since the boys are not there voluntarily and so see no reason to support or identify with the total institution.

To provide a constructive 'esprit de corps' within a school it is essential that the boys and staff feel they share responsibility for the institution. This can be brought about by the boys and staff being made aware of each others' feelings, hopes, failures and successes. The most efficient way of doing this would appear to be for staff to participate actively with boys in the assessment meetings discussed above. If the boys know the staff's work goals and how they interact with their own work goals, and learn how each is dependent upon the other, it would seem that a constructive 'esprit de corps' might be a viable proposition.

Whether these ideas would be effective in reducing the reconviction rates of institutionalised delinquents is purely speculation. This could only be established with certainty after an extensive period of experimentation.

Summary: The drawbacks of vocational training

Although I believe the departments have a useful role to play in residential treatment I would like to conclude by expressing my reservations about the whole concept of vocational training. The subject is of special interest at present. With the raising of the school leaving age much discussion is being given by the headmasters of state secondary schools to the idea of making the final school year one of vocational training.

My first reservation would be that vocational training is often aimed at teaching out-dated trades. In recent years society has changed very rapidly, and some of these changes have led to the collapse of traditional trades and the development of new trades. The wages demanded by tradesmen have often limited their market – the classic example being the once flourishing trade of painting and decorating, which is now in decline since all but a select few householders carry out their own decorating. At the same time the increase in the number of car owners has led to the expansion of the motor industry. A danger arises when an institution establishes a vocational training programme for once and all time, and persists in training boys for trades that are no longer appropriate. This time lag problem is likely to increase in the years to come, as adaptability on the part of semi-skilled labour becomes more and more important. It is estimated that the present school generation will change not only their job but their whole career at least three times in their life, as industries become redundant in the future. This being so, surely the need is to educate our children to be adaptable and to think for themselves, rather than attempt to lay down at fifteen how they will use the next fifty years of their working life.

My second reservation arises from the work of Everett Reimer,[12] a 'de-schooler', who has attempted to outline radical alternatives in education. He argues that education today is essentially an instrument for transmitting the ideology of a technological society. He says,

> Different schools do different things, of course, but increasingly schools in all nations, of all kinds, at all levels, combine four distinct social functions; custodial care, social-role selection, indoctrination, and education as usually defined in terms of the development of skills and knowledge.

If Reimer's analysis is valid, and it would appear especially so for Community Schools, then what better means is there of social-role selection than vocational training? On these grounds, trade departments in Community Schools are 'sorting' boys for unskilled work. This is in fact confirmed by the official statistics[13] which show that, of the boys entering employment on release from Approved Schools in 1969, over 75 per cent entered unskilled jobs; less than 2 per cent entered professional and

201

technical employment; and less than 1 per cent higher clerical and less than 2 per cent any routine clerical post. It can be easily argued that this is to be expected from the population entering the schools. But the fact still remains that underprivileged children enter Community Schools where they are offered an education which is aimed at perpetuating their underprivilege, despite the fact that their intelligence is of almost normal distribution.

CHAPTER X

What Needs to be Done?

It must be obvious to all that something needs to be done about the residential treatment of young offenders in this country. At present institutional treatment fails to alter the behaviour of the majority of offenders. There are also signs that the impact the institution has on the individual during treatment is declining rapidly, as shown by the growing figures for absconding and consequent offences. This failure of institutional treatment is achieved at considerable financial cost – there would be cause for concern if it was only a matter of the taxpayer not getting value for his money. But this failure more importantly reflects the irreparable damage done to children by the state. This damage is poignantly expressed in the reported words of John Williams, a man with a considerable prison record, describing the causes of recidivism:

> It starts when they're kids, you take an eight year old, stick him in an institution or children's home and he adapts to living by other people's rules. If he drifts through approved schools, into petty crime and to Borstal, he's well on his way to his first prison sentence. Nobody likes doing bird, but if you have no friends and no family the inside is more attractive than a cold bed-sitter.

The first thing that must be done is for society to decide whether it wants to treat or punish its deprived children. This is essential, because staff in Approved Schools are uncertain about which function they are expected to carry out. Schools are openly criticised by the media at one moment for being excessively punitive, and the next for being too permissive. Staff react to this uncertainty by ineffectually maintaining the status quo, and rejecting experimentation and innovation in case it leads to undesirable publicity. They abide by the rules and collude with

203

society by trying to keep their charges 'out of sight and out of mind'. Society must be made to accept it's responsibility and have its attention focused on the plight of its outcasts. The horrified reaction of the public to the facts about the treatment of the mentally subnormal patients within the admired National Health Service was overwhelming. This public reaction precipitated political action, and freed resources for the improvement of hospitals for the subnormal. In the same way the community must be made aware of the conditions provided for many of our children in care, and must decide whether it wishes to continue to treat fifteen-year-old boys in the way described by a young boy of my acquaintance sent for Borstal training:

Well apart from ten months here I spent a month in the Green [Winston Green Prison] and six weeks in the Scrubs [Wormwood Scrubs] awaiting allocation. The Scrubs was murder. You were three to a peter [cell] in there, you had to eat in your cell as well. You had association two nights a week that's all, the rest of the time you was banged up [locked up]. What a doss, six weeks in a cell. Do you know at weekends you were locked in Friday at six o'clock in the evening and then let out Monday morning. You couldn't sleep in that place for bloody cockroaches all over your bunks. I done all these tattoos in there, nothing else to do. This geezer in my cell got some ink and I split a match, because we couldn't get a pin, and I did all these. I'm keeping out of trouble now, I can tell you that. I know I've said that to you before, but I mean it this time. I couldn't face those bloody cockroaches in the Scrubs again.

This boy was released after ten months' Borstal training; three days after his release he was arrested for 'mugging' a fifty-year-old man.

Society must recognise that in heavily industrialised urban cultures delinquency is for many a normal part of adolescent development. Consequently, the vast majority of young offenders should be cared for within the community, since the very process of labelling and institutionalising a child weights the odds against the child achieving normal adulthood. The community will have to bear the cost of minor delinquency. In most cases this cost would be considerably lower than the cost of placing the child in an institution. One hopes that the deterrent effect of punishment on children has now been sufficiently discredited.

The Approved Schools should become an additional resource available for the community care of the child. Consequently they should be based in the child's neighbourhood so that initially the child could remain at home and attend the school daily. If this proved ineffectual, either because the child failed to respond, or because he continued to be abused by his family, then there would need to be adequate accommodation provided for the child to move in and live in the school. There should also be adequate accommodation for his family to move in with him if they desired, or if they needed to in times of crises – like the threat of eviction. This would necessitate a major re-siting of Approved Schools, the majority of which are sited in relatively remote rural areas.

It is at this point that the central Government and local authorities would need to reappraise their management procedures. A cost benefit analysis approach should be adopted which would provide resources to meet needs in a realistic fashion. At present many of the Approved Schools are sited many miles from the areas from which their boys are drawn. This means that vast transport costs are incurred. Also since many of the schools are housed in totally unsuitable houses, a good deal of money is spent in attempting to repair, maintain and heat inappropriate accommodation, the capital assets of which could be realised and used to purchase appropriate accommodation in the areas of need. Appropriate accommodation may prove not to be the purpose-built, hygienically clinical house unit with every available space designed and allocated for a specific purpose. It may prove to be terraced houses scattered throughout the twilight areas of the inner city ring. Perhaps every 'delinquent' street should have its own 'corner shop' Approved School, which could become a community resource offering advice to parents, organising tenants' associations, adventure playgrounds, youth clubs, etc., and thereby prevent delinquency as well as treat it 'in situ'. It is well recognised and accepted that removing the problem child from his environment does not solve any of his problems. Treatment, therefore, should be offered to the child in his own environment. In that event the treatment can be two sided: operating on both the child and his adverse environmental conditions.

If local Approved Schools were developed, with specialist teaching provision, then there is no reason why they should be reserved only for delinquent children. They could be available for all the children in the area manifesting learning difficulties; the slow learners in secondary schools, the educationally subnormal, the partially hearing and sighted could all attend the specialist school within their area. This would avoid the removal from home of additional groups of children and create a more normal culture within the school. Similarly, some of the delinquent children who were not having any schooling problems could live in the Approved School and yet continue to attend their secondary schools. This would need close liaison between education and social services departments at local and central Government level. At present no such liaison exists and this makes for inefficiency in the care of children, by causing inappropriate divisions within the service. Schools for the maladjusted are under control of the education authorities; Approved Schools are now under local authority social service departments; and adolescent psychiatric provision is the responsibility of the National Health Service. Each of these services attempts to cope with the same population of deviant children; each branch has much it could learn from its colleagues if liaison only existed to allow it. An integrated service would undoubtedly serve the children more effectively.

Local approved schools of this kind would naturally be mixed, because with certain families both brothers and sisters would need to be taken into care. Mixed Approved Schools would obviate the necessity of splitting families. An approved school of this type, firmly based within the community, offering a service to the child's family, friends and school, and with close links with the neighbourhood, could really begin to call itself a Community Home. The representative nature of the Community Home could be increased by providing accommodation for the elderly and chronically disabled. This would combat the isolation normally suffered by these two groups, and the children in the Home would be able to offer them service, help and compassion – important ingredients in the experience of developing childhood.

The Community Home based in the boys' locality would resolve many of the problems now facing Approved Schools; absconding, for example, would no longer be perceived as a problem; truancy might occur but this would be greatly reduced if the boy's social worker and family were closely integrated in the same community. The children's anxieties about home – the source of much absconding and truancy – would be greatly reduced if, for example, their mothers could drop into the school on their way to the shops. This situation would be radically different from the one which prevails in many Approved Schools at present, where visiting by parents is restricted to certain days in the month and often involves journeys of fifty miles or more. Absconding would also no longer be a problem since the Community Home would not see custody as one of its major functions. Instead its primary

206

function would be to encourage the child's development within the family and community.

However, before such a situation could be achieved a great deal of change is required in other areas. The first area which would need to change radically is that of the leadership and support offered to Approved Schools. Since April 1973 Community Homes have been the responsibility of the local authorities. Prior to that Approved Schools were, for an interim period, the responsibility of the Department of Health and Social Security, who succeeded the Home Office. Consequently, within four years, Approved Schools have been the responsibility of three different authorities. This has unfortunately meant that many schools have been in limbo, working from day to day unguided and undirected. Thus first of all, if approved schools are to change they must be given unequivocal support and guidance from the authority responsible for them. Insecurity amongst staff hampers development. This insecurity is not without foundation; one of the problems of working with deprived children is that they have profound anti-authority feelings, coupled with disturbingly worldly knowledge for ones so young. These factors often combine to manifest themselves in particularly unpleasant and distressing allegations against staff. Sometimes these allegations are not without foundation. But on other occasions they are completely baseless and yet can often only be proven to be so after lengthy investigations which are particularly disturbing to staff's families – especially if the allegations involve sexual deviancy. And even if the allegations are proved to be false, the staff member's credibility is often lost because many of his colleagues will work on the assumption that, 'there's no smoke without fire'. Consequently staff see themselves in a particularly vulnerable position. Much of the anxiety generated by this position could be alleviated if the authority responsible for the schools were in close contact with the institution and supported the staff in their difficult task.

The other important change that is needed in the management of Approved Schools is a particularly thorny one. Approved Schools are involved in the 'law and order' issue; a politically sensitive issue upon which reputations can be made or broken. The Home Secretary's position has always been viewed as one of the most unstable of ministerial posts for this very reason. In the same way the authorities responsible for Approved Schools have had a vested interest in maintaining the status quo. At best they have followed a gradualist policy, allowing small progressive steps to be taken with little publicity. The authorities have rarely initiated or supported radical innovations in the treatment of young offenders. The most influential and progressive work has been carried out by independently financed bodies outside the Approved School system. This situation is equally true of education generally – witness Summerhill and the Liverpool Free School. The central authorities must alter this position even at the risk of political embarrassment. Decision-making in this sphere should be firmly based on research findings and not political expediency.

On this point, it is interesting to note that many decisions made about the treatment of offenders run counter to the findings of research carried out by the same Government department. A recent example of this can be seen in the announcement by the Secretary of State for Social Services of a rapid increase in the amount of secure accommodation to be provided for young offenders. On 15 January 1973 he announced that a large increase was planned in the number of secure places for the long-term treatment of persistent young offenders, some of whom were said to be beyond the control of the Approved Schools where they had already been placed. At that time 127 such places were available within the Approved School system, and the Secretary of State envisaged an additional 200 places being made available. This announcement was made in response to pressure from the Magistrates' Association who were concerned about what they called, 'the failure of the Children and Young Persons Act, 1969 to deal with young offenders'. However, in 1971 the Home Office Research Unit had issued their research findings on absconding and from them it was concluded that in-school environmental factors seem to predominate in the causation of absconding and that, at present, the best hope of reducing absconding would seem to be in the manipulation of factors in the school environment. The Secretary of State's announcement, therefore, appears to run counter to findings of research commissioned and carried out by a complementary department.

Instead of providing finance for the building of more 'cells' perhaps the same end result could be achieved by increasing staffing and resources in open schools, severely hampered in their work by lack of both. Such a decision however, would probably not have had the same political impact. Whilst approved schools remain at the mercy of politicians no significant progress will occur. What is required is a commitment on the part of the responsible authorities to support and encourage new models of treatment. At present the range of treatment within the Approved School system is in fact very restricted. There are minor differences within the régimes of various schools, but if closely examined these differences are often in inconsequential areas. The overall ethos is the same. As there is no such thing at present as the successful treatment of delinquency all approaches should be encouraged and carefully monitored to measure their effectiveness. Truly therapeutic communities need to be developed alongside 'token economies', traditionally-based schools offering naval training, and progressive child-centred schools, all need to be evaluated. Unfortunately there is now little opportunity for this to occur since, with the passing of the Children and Young Persons Act 1969, central Government has handed over responsibility for Approved Schools to local authorities, and very few local authorities have the kind of complex research unit or the resources necessary to carry out this type of comparative study.

The other major area of change needs to be in the assessment procedures used with children in care. At present the procedure within the Approved Schools system is that a child is placed first in a classifying school for assessment, which is carried out by a team of residential and field social workers, psychologists, psychiatrists and teachers. After the assessment period the child is then allocated to the school offering a régime which will best meet his needs. This procedure is theoretically sound but it is hopelessly optimistic to expect it to work in practice: Allocation according to need is an unrealistic precept since it is just not possible at present to truly evaluate a child's needs and I suspect it will continue to be impossible for a long time. Intelligence tests and tests of academic attainment do not demonstrate a child's educational needs, even if the assumption, which is in reality a value judgment, that educational needs are important to the child's development is valid. However, more importantly, there is no sufficiently sophisticated means of assessing and evaluating institutions to tell whether that institution will meet the child's needs. As I hope I have shown, institutions are organic structures which are constantly changing; staff and children pass through altering the ecology of the individuals in such a situation. How can it possibly be ascertained what an institution has to offer a child? This approach also fails to take into account the influence the child brings to bear on the institution; immediately he enters a school, that school is no longer the same place, his presence there alters the situation.

Another major criticism that can be made of the current assessment procedure is that it is the labelling game 'writ large'. The implication of the procedure is the child is abnormal on admission. He then passes through a screening process which ensures that his 'abnormality' will be confirmed. For example, the majority of boys will be seen by a psychiatrist, who will discover that very few of the boys passing before him are psychiatrically disturbed. It would be interesting, if such a screening process were applied across the total child population, to see whether the minority found to be psychiatrically disturbed in the total population is comparable with the minority from the carefully selected group in a classifying school. However, the problem of base rates is irrelevant, what is important is the underlying attitude which assumes that careful assessment is essential because the children are abnormal. Since there is no agreed cut-off point for normality, any behaviour can eventually be conceived of as abnormal. Consequently the assessment reports tend to become chronicles of the children's unsavoury features since these are seen as aspects of behaviour worthy of comment. A child might comply with staff's wishes on nine out of ten occasions, and these pass without comment; on the tenth occasion when he refuses to do what is required of him he identifies himself as anti-authority, and this is noted. However, since the 'normal' child's reaction is unknown in this situation, the delinquent's behaviour, because he has already been branded delinquent, is noted as further evidence of his deviancy, and he becomes an anti-authoritarian delinquent. The ultimate effect on the child is to fulfil the expectations of the role thrust upon him.

Assessment, therefore, should highlight the child's positive attributes as forcefully as the negative ones, so that those who are treating him know on what foundations they have to build. Assessment should also concentrate on the situational variables surrounding the child during assessment. Blanket terms such as 'he has difficulty in making relationships' are meaningless unless the person or persons with whom he is unable to relate are specified. Assessment as it is presently conceived is doomed to failure. In the same way that you cannot abstract a child from his environment and hope to treat him for a condition which arises at least in part from environmental factors, how can it be possible to remove a boy from his usual situation and assess his needs, many of which will be specific to the situation? Assessment should be of the child in his home situation, within his day school and within his peer group; only then will we begin to understand the dynamics of his deviant behaviour.

Another major area where change is needed is in the training of residential social workers. For many years Approved Schools have depended for staffing upon men and women, often of very high principles and with genuine concern for young people, but who are, in the majority of cases, willing amateurs with little or no training. As we saw in Chapter V, the percentage of trained residential social workers amongst staff in child care is very small. This situation is scandalous. The workers in this area are dealing with society's most difficult problem children and are expected to do this with little or no formal training. Obviously training is not the complete answer: there is little doubt that the ideal residential social worker is the product of the interplay between personality, experience and training. However, the argument that held sway until comparatively recently – that if you were the 'right type' of person to deal with children, then training was irrelevant – is nonsense. Even the 'right type' of person needs to be given formal skills with which to operate.

Training, however, should not be seen merely as providing formal skills; it also needs to be experientially based in order to give the individual greater personal insight and awareness and greater understanding of the situation of the client. The most glaring example of how training is often deficient in these respects occurred at Wellside, where psychology graduates, working for their masters' degree in clinical psychology, were accepted for placement. These people were extremely intelligent and able and had acquired many of the formal psychological skills. They could carry out a detailed assessment or clinical interview with a boy very efficiently. However, many of them found themselves unable to relate personally to the boys outside the formal, clearly-defined interview role. They were able to interview boys but unable just to talk to them. Moreover, they somehow felt that this was outside their professional purview and, indeed, often saw personal relationships with the boys as unprofessional. This is a crucial point particularly now that residential social work is beginning to emerge and define itself as a profession. It is essential that the correct meaning of 'professional' be established. Too often it is taken to mean strictly observed hours of work and clearly defined duties. This should not be so. By professional should be meant a personal commitment to the client, acceptance of him as a person, and acceptance of the demands he will make on one, both within one's formal role and as an individual person. Professionalism should also include the understanding and acceptance of one's responsibility in the caring process; the understanding of what responsibilities are involved in influencing a client's life style, family relationships, peer relationships and behaviour.

Professionalism in child care is extremely difficult – every one, and especially parents, has firmly held views on how to bring up children. Residential social workers are no exception and some of the most frequently heard phrases amongst staff in residential child care establishments are: 'I would never expect more of them than my own children', or 'I treat them no differently from my own children'. The fact that they are not our own children somehow gets forgotten. However, the important fact is that residential social workers often have their own deeply felt personal views on the discipline and control of children. To question these views is to hit at a very fundamental aspect of the individual's personality. This must be overcome, for a truly professional approach staff must be able to be questioned by their colleagues about how they have dealt with particular situations and treated specific children and, one hopes, if necessary they must be able to modify their subsequent behaviour. It is extremely difficult to accept criticism. Not only does it call into question staff's job performance but it attacks very basic personal attitudes. But it is necessary if a truly professional approach is to be devleoped.

Finally, a professional approach involves a commitment to the client. Approved Schools will have come of age when they clearly demonstrate their commitment to the child, and not to the concept of social control. Approved Schools deal with society's failures – failures who are often inarticulate and consequently unheard. Approved Schools have a responsibility to rectify this situation and they should become the spokesmen for the deprived. They are continually in contact with the most appalling suffering produced by an exploitative society. Few people are in a better position than they to force society to examine these less pleasant facets of itself, and to compel society to question whether or not it is prepared to break the vicious circle of deprivation by caring for the children of the deprived.

APPENDIX

The Boys of Wellside: Training and Experience

In the same way as I have given some of the background training and experience of the staff at Wellside, I now hope to continue the analysis at the molecular level by examining the training and experience of the boys. In Chapter II a general explanation for delinquency was offered, now a detailed analysis of the intake into Wellside will be undertaken. This will be done by examining in detail the social and personal backgrounds of fifty boys who have been discharged from the school in the past five years. These fifty boys were chosen from a possible two hundred and six boys. They were chosen at random from the total number of discharges. In order to check whether they were representative of the total population the figures for the parental relationship, the boys' ages and I.Q.s were collected for the total population. Comparison of these figures with those for the small sample (50) showed the small sample to be representative.

Of the fifty boys, thirty-nine (78 per cent) came from the Greater Birmingham conurbation, including Coventry, four boys (8 per cent) from the East Midlands urban complex, Notts – Derby – Leicester, and seven boys (14 per cent) from further afield, South Wales, Northants, etc. None of the present sample came from rural areas.

In Table I the parental relationships are given for the small sample (50), the total population (206) and for one hundred and twenty-three boys in twenty-three intermediate schools as given in *Thirteen-year-old Approved School boys in 1962*.[1] The results from this study will be quoted throughout this section since it allows a comparison to be made between the situation in Wellside and that found nationally.

213

TABLE I

Percentage of boys coming from homes with parents married and both present, one or both parents, step-parents, or a single parent or 'In Care'

	Both parents present	Step-parent(s)	Single parent	'In Care'
Small sample (50)	62	10	24	4
Total Population (206)	68	5	26	1
13 Year Old (123)	70·7	4·9	15·5	5·7

N.B. Figures do not make 100% since study had additional categories

These figures show the position at Wellside differed from the national situation in that a higher percentage of boys came from single parent families, although fewer boys were 'in care'. There is no readily obvious explanation of this. Although 62 per cent of boys in the sample had both parents at home this is not necessarily an indication that the majority came from stable homes. The parents might not be married, might come and go, or in other ways provide an abnormal situation.

The sizes of the boys' families were significantly larger than the general population. In the sample, the average number of children was a little over six per family, whereas the figure for the general population is a little over three children per family. The increased family size cannot solely be attributed to a Roman Catholic population since Trenaman[2] in a religiously undifferentiated group of delinquents, found an average family size of 6·3 children.

It was impossible to ascertain the social class of all members of the sample. However, there is little reason to believe that it would differ significantly from the results of Field's study[3] which is quoted below.

TABLE II

Occupation of Boys' Fathers

Occupational Level	Boys' Fathers %	1961 Census Figures %
Professional, Managerial	6·4	19
Skilled (Non-manual and Manual)	43·5	51
Semi-skilled	22·3	21
Unskilled	26·1	9

The excessive contribution of the unskilled class to the figures for delinquency should be noted. This finding is one continually reported in studies of delinquency, and again suggests, when considered in conjunction with increased family size, that many of the boys' families would be under financial strain, with the attendant problems of poor housing, diet, clothing and inadequate schooling.

Table III shows the offences for which the boys were admitted to Wellside. The percentages exceed one hundred since the groups are not mutually exclusive, i.e. a boy could be admitted for a collection of offences drawn from more than one group. Also shown in the table, for comparison, are the National Criminal Statistics for fourteen-year-old boys. As shown in Chapter I, there are many difficulties inherent in using the National Criminal Statistics. The figures should be treated with caution, but they clearly show that the boys at Wellside were not the collection of violent thugs of popular imagination.

TABLE III

Showing the Admission Offences for boys at Wellside, and the National Criminal Statistics for Fourteen-year-old Boys

Offences	No. of Boys	Wellside Sample (50) %	National Criminal Statistics (1965) %
Violence	1	2	1·5
Sex	2	4	0·8
Theft Act*	43	86	90
Malicious damage	2	4	Not quoted
Driving & taking away	1	2	Not quoted
Trespass	1	2	Not quoted
Truancy or transfer from Children's Home**	4	8	Not quoted

*Theft Act: Included in this group are larceny, breaking and entering, fraud, receiving.
**These do not in fact constitute offences as usually defined.

It is obvious that the vast majority of boys are admitted for theft of some form. The higher incidence of sexual offenders is to be expected since criminal statistics are based on court appearances, and it is generally accepted that magistrates are more likely to institutionalise sexual offenders than to attempt treatment in the community. This gives a raised incidence of sexual offenders in any institutionalised sample. It must also be remembered that only two boys are involved here and, as with all the low numbers on the table, it is not really valid to turn such low numbers into percentages since it distorts the picture that emerges.

Eleven boys of the fifty (22 per cent) had a previous history predominantly of larceny. (Predominantly being defined as more than three-quarters of his previous convictions. Twenty-six boys (52 per cent) committed predominantly breaking and entering. Nine boys (18 per cent) had a history of wilful damage, violence or possession of weapon. Four boys (8 per cent) had a history of other offences – boys in this category had fairly trivial or insubstantial history. These figures are important since they put the boys' admission offence into perspective. For example, although only one boy was admitted for an offence of violence, nine boys had 'violent' offences in their history. Truancy from school was common to almost all the boys in Wellside, but was not necessarily one of the factors leading to their appearance in court. Many boys had a history of mixed offences and truancy.

The records were examined to determine whether a boy committed the majority of his crimes on his own or with others. The results showed that thirty-eight boys (76 per cent) committed the majority of their offences on their own whereas twelve boys (24 per cent) committed the majority of their offences with others. The validity of this finding is questionable since the records did not always state whether the boy was charged individually or with others. However, if these results are accurate they are important, because many explanations of delinquency are based on the fact that it is a group activity. For example, Cohen[4] argues that working-class adolescents, who are deprived of legitimate means of acquiring status, turn to delinquent gangs to provide status. This may go some way towards explaining 'normal' delinquency – delinquency can be regarded as normal adolescent behaviour. Gibson has shown this in a study in which grammar, secondary modern and Approved School boys were asked to 'self-report' their delinquent behaviour. He states:

> The rate of admission in this study was high, but not altogether unexpected in view of the high level of undetected crime. Even in the best behaved group, the Grammar School boys, half of them admitted to one or more serious acts which would have landed them in serious trouble had they been detected, in which case they would have been officially classified as 'delinquents'.[5]

Thus the 'normal' delinquent may commit his offences in a group in order to achieve status amongst his peer group, whilst the 'abnormal' (persistent) delinquent commits his offences individually and eventually requires residential treatment.

Many of the boys had received one or more forms of treatment before admission to Wellside. Eleven boys (22 per cent) had been to an Attendance Centre; six boys (12 per cent) had been in Children's Homes; five boys (10 per cent) had spent a previous period in an Approved School, and seven boys (14 per cent) had been in detention centres. Finally six boys (12 per cent) had spent an extended period (i.e. 1½ months) in a Remand Home. All this adds up to the fact that the boys entering Wellside have had a fairly extensive experience of a variety of institutional treatment. This previous experience will obviously affect the views they have of the school.

Table IV shows the ages of boys on admission, the numbers and approximate percentages are given for the small sample and the total population.

TABLE IV

Age on Admission

Age in Years	Small Sample (50)		Total Population (206)	
	Number of Boys	Percentage	Number of Boys	Percentage (approx.)
10–11	0	–	1	1
11–12	0	–	2	1
12–13	4	8	9	5
13–14	16	32	65	30
14–15	26	52	103	50
15–16	4	8	23	12
16+	0	–	1	1

These figures show a clear 'peak' at fourteen years of age, and this is reflected in the National Criminal Statistics. However, it is now expected that this 'peak' will move up to fifteen as the school leaving age is raised to sixteen, a similar move having been observed when the school leaving age was raised to fifteen years. Table V shows the range of intelligence for both the small sample and total population.

Table V illustrates several important points: first, the wide diversity of ability of boys entering the school; secondly, the mean I.Q. of 88 is lower than that found by Field, i.e. a mean I.Q. of 93·3. This difference may not be significant but may merely be a result of the use of different intelligence tests. But it may suggest that Wellside does take boys of slightly lower intelligence than

217

TABLE V

Intelligence Range

Intelligence in I.Q.	Small Sample (50)		Total Population (206)*	
	Number of Boys	Percentage	Number of Boys	Percentage (approx.)
–60	–	–	1	1
60– 69	5	10	10	5
70– 79	11	22	35	17
80– 89	11	22	45	22
90– 99	18	36	47	24
100–109	4	8	25	13
110–120	1	2	8	4
120+	–	–	1	1

Mean I.Q. = 88

*The numbers do not total to the size of the sample, nor the percentages to one hundred since I.Q.s were not available on all boys.

those admitted nationally. Thirdly, there is the fact that between 5 and 10 per cent of boys admitted to Wellside are classifiable as 'subnormal', and a further approximate 20 per cent are educationally subnormal. This obviously has important implications for both 'teaching' and 'training' in the school. It is also important to sound a note of warning. Difficulties inherent in the use of tests for defining intelligence must be recognised – lack of verbal facility, a characteristic of many underprivileged children, frequently affects results and may well have done so with the boys at Wellside.

Field found that only 38 per cent of the large sample of thirteen-year-old Approved School boys studied were classified as 'normal' on the Mulligan scale of maladjustment. In the present analysis, being a retrospective study, the means available for assessing maladjustment were limited. A very crude method was decided upon, i.e. whether psychiatric supervision was or was not recommended by the classifying school or in the case of a direct committal, in court reports. In fact eight boys, 16 per cent, were recommended for psychiatric supervision. This relatively low number may well be increased as psychiatric services in schools expand since in the social services diagnosis (demand) is often geared to provision (supply). It is important to note that of these eight boys, four were transferred – which in fact means they had no greater chance of being transferred than all boys in the sample. There was no relationship between need for psychiatric supervision and persistent absconding.

The frequency of absconding was examined rather than the number of abscondings. The number of abscondings was averaged over the total period when the boy was officially in the charge of the school, except where individual absences lasted *over* six months. Thirty-four boys (68 per cent) either did not abscond at all or did so less than once every six months. In other words absconding was relatively 'no problem' for 68 per cent of the boys. Eight boys (16 per cent) absconded on average once every three months; two boys (4 per cent) at least once per month; and six boys (12 per cent) more than once per month. These figures are important in view of the following factors.

The last three groups can be considered as 'persistent' absconders. In fact fourteen of these boys were transferred to other institutions, presumably as a result of their abscondings or their outcome, and the other two were not recovered after absconding. Nineteen boys (38 per cent) of the boys who absconded were charged with offences whilst absconding – eleven of these were from the persistent absconder group. 52 per cent of the boys were not charged – this, of course, is no guarantee they did not commit offences – and this figure also includes those boys who did not abscond at all. The importance of absconding has been discussed in greater detail elsewhere in this book but, as demonstrated below, it has radical implications for the 'success' of a boy's stay at Wellside.

Table VI shows the length of time boys stayed at Wellside. As a general rule any boy discharged in less than a year was transferred to another institution. Of course other boys were also transferred at a later stage in their career, and this is examined later. The average stay of boys released in the past five years (117) was twenty-three months ('released' here is defined as returned to the community).

TABLE VI

Length of Stay of Boys in School, Small Sample (50)

	Number of Boys	Percentage
Less than 3 months	4	8
3– 6 months	5	10
6–12 months	4	8
12–18 months	11	22
More than 18 months	26	52

Twenty-two boys (44 per cent) were transferred to other institutions, of these fourteen were the persistent absconders. Twenty-six boys (52 per cent) were released, and two boys (4 per cent) were not recovered after absconding. These figures show that a boy entering the school has only a 50 per cent chance of remaining in the school until his release. This drastically affects any 'success' figures produced.

Four boys (8 per cent) were charged with offences within three months of their release. This figure (8 per cent) is for the total small sample admitted and these four boys are in fact 15 per cent of the boys actually *released* since, as shown above, only 50 per cent of boys admitted are released. Thus for these results both percentages are quoted. No boys were convicted between three and six months after release, but five boys (10 per cent) were in trouble between six and twelve months, and one further boy (2 or 4 per cent) between one and two years after release. The remaining sixteen cannot be said to be 'trouble free' since no data was available on the majority of them – either because they had not offended, or because they had only recently been released or transferred to another institution.

The question of transfer and release is important as illustrated by an examination of the last three years' figures given in Table VII.

TABLE VII

Outcome of Boys Career over Period 1969–1970

	1971	1970	1969
Total no. of discharges	70	37	56
No. of releases	43	18	29
No. of transfers	27	19	27
No. of releases reported in further trouble	Not applicable since insufficient follow-up period	7	20

These figures show a change in policy in 1971, when many more boys were released than in the two previous years. This may be the result of more frequent review meetings. More importantly, many more boys were released than transferred, and this was not true of the two previous years. Finally, the 'success' rates of 1969, the only year with sufficient follow-up period at present, give cause for concern. Of fifty-six boys discharged in 1969, only nine boys were still out of trouble two years later – this is a 'success' rate of only 16 per cent. Alternatively, nine boys out of twenty-nine released remained out of trouble, i.e. providing a 31 per cent 'success' rate. This figure is comparable with the national figures quoted in Chapter III.

220

NOTES

Chapter I

1 GIBSON, H. B. (1967). 'Self reported delinquency among school boys and their attitude to the police.' *British Journal of Social and Clinical Psychology,* 6, 168–173.

2 *Criminal Statistics, England and Wales,* 1971. London: H.M.S.O.

3 SHORT, J. F. & NYE, F. I. (1958). 'Extent of unrecorded juvenile delinquency'. *Journal of Criminal Law, Criminology and Police Science,* 49, 296–302.

4 FERGUSON, T. (1952). *The Young Delinquent in his Social Setting.* London: Oxford University Press.

5 NEWSON, J. & NEWSON, E. (1968). *Four Years Old in an Urban Community.* Middlesex: Penguin Books, Chicago: Aldine.

Chapter II

1 BURT, C. (1925). *The Young Delinquent.* London University Press, Mystic: Lawrence Verry, Inc.

2 WOODWARD, M. (1955). *Low intelligence and delinquency.* Institute for the study and treatment of delinquency.

3 McCORD, W. & McCORD, J. (1959). *Origins of Crime.* London: Columbia University Press, Montclair: Patterson Smith.

4 DOUGLAS, J. W. B. (1960). 'Premature children at primary school'. *British Medical Journal,* I, 1008–1113.

5 LOOMIS, S. D. (1965). 'E.E.G. Abnormalities as a correlate in behaviour in adolescent male delinquents'. *American Journal of Psychiatry,* 121, 1003–1006.

6 CASEY, M.D., SEGALL, L. J., STREET, D. R. & BLANK, C. E. (1966). 'Sex chromosome abnormalities in two state hospitals for patients requiring special security'. *Nature,* 209, 641–662.

7 BURNAND, G., HUNTER, H. & HOGGART, K. (1967). 'Some psychological test characteristics of Kleinfelter's syndrome'. *British Journal of Psychiatry,* 113, 1091–1096.

8 GLUECK, S. & GLUECK, E. (1962). *Physique and Delinquency,* London: Harper, Millwood: Kraus Reprint Co.

9 FERGUSON, T. (1952). *The Young Delinquent in his Social Setting.* Oxford University Press.

10 McCORD, W. & McCORD, J. (1959). *Psychopathy and Delinquency.* London and New York: Grune & Straton.

11 EYSENCK, H. J. (1964). *Crime and Personality.* London and Boston: Routledge and Kegan Paul.

12 WEST, D. J. (1963). *The Habitual Offender.* Macmillan.

13 GIBSON, H. B. (1967). 'Self reported delinquency among school boys and their attitude to the police'. *British Journal of Social and Clinical Psychology,* 6, 168–173.

14 SPROTT, W. J. H. (1954). *The Social Background of Delinquency.* Nottingham University Press.

15 MAYS, J. B. (1954). *Growing up in the City*. Liverpool University Press.

16 STOTT, D. H. (1960). 'Delinquency, maladjustment and unfavourable ecology'. *British Journal of Psychology*, 51, 157–170.

17 TUTT, N. S. (1971). Achievement motivation and the criminal personality. Unpublished doctoral thesis. Nottingham University.

18 McCLELLAND, D. C., BALDWIN, A. L., BRONFENBRENNER, U. & STRODTBECK, F. L. (1958). *Talent and Society*. London and New York: Van Nostrand.

19 WIRT, R. D. & BRIGGS, P. F. (1959). 'Personality and environmental factors in the development of delinquency'. *Psychological Monographs*, 73, 15.

20 COHEN, A. K. (1956). *Delinquent Boys*. London: Macmillan, New York: Free Press

21 CLOWARD, R. A. & OHLIN, L. E. (1961). *Delinquency and Opportunity*. London: Macmillan, New York: Free Press.

22 DOWNES, D. (1965). *The Delinquent Solution*. London: Routledge and Kegan Paul, New York: Free Press.

23 YABLONSKY, L. (1962). *The Violent Gang*. London: Macmillan, New York: Penguin

24 TUTT, N. S. (1973). 'Achievement motivation and delinquency'. *British Journal of Social and Clinical Psychology*, September 1973.

25 WINTERBOTTOM, M. R. (1958). 'The relation of need for achievement to learning experiences in independence and mastery'. In Atkinson, J. W. (Ed.) (1958). *Motives in Action, Fantasy and Society*. Van Nostrand.

26 ROSEN, B. C. & D'ANDRADE, R. G. (1959). 'The psychosocial origin of achievement motivation'. *Sociometry*, 22, 185–218.

27 SPROTT, W. J.H., *et al*.

28 NEWSON, J. & NEWSON, E. (1968). *Four Years Old in an Urban Community*. Middlesex: Penguin, Chicago: Aldine.

29 WILSON, H. C. (1962). *Delinquency and Child Neglect*. Allen and Unwin.

30 PLOWDEN, B. (1962). *Children and their primary schools: a report of the central advisory council for education*. H.M.S.O.

31 HARGREAVES, D. H. (1967). *Social Relations in a Secondary School*. London: Routledge and Kegan Paul, Highland: Fernhill.

32 STEPHENSON, G. M. & WHITE, J. H. (1968). 'An experimental study of some effects of injustice on children's moral behaviour' *Journal of Experimental Social Psychology*, 4, 460–469.

33 WORKING PARTY OF THE NATIONAL YOUTH EMPLOYMENT COUNCIL (1970). *At Odds*. Department of Employment.

Chapter III

1 H.M.S.O. *Statistics relating to approved schools, remand homes and attendance centres in England and Wales for the years 1963, 1965, 1967, 1970*.

2   *The Times*, 8 and 10 November, 1972.
3   FIELD, E., HAMMOND, W. H. & TIZARD, J. (1971). *Thirteen-year-old approved school boys in 1962.* H.M.S.O.
4   HAMMOND, W. H. (1964). *The sentence of the court.* H.M.S.O.
5   MELVILLE, J. (1972). 'Attendance Centres'. *New Society,* 26 Oct.
6   *Report on the work of the Prison Department.* 1969. Statistical tables.
7   *Children in Trouble* (1966). H.M.S.O.
8   GREENWOOD-WILSON, A. (1970). 'Punishment and therapy'. *Community Schools Gazette.* Vol. 64, No. 10, 572–579.
9   CLARKE, R. & MARTIN, D. (1971). *Abscondings from approved schools.* H.M.S.O.
10   MAPSTONE, E. (1969). *'Children in care'. Concern No. 3,* 23–28.
11   HART, T., NATION, R. & NOBLE, P. (1972). *Drug-taking girls.* Cumberlow Lodge.
12   BANKS, C., MALIPHANT, R., *et al.* (1971). Unpublished data reported to the British Psychological Society Working Party on the treatment of the young offender.
13   CLARKE & CORNISH (1972). *Controlled trials, paradigm or pitfalls.* H.M.S.O.
14   NEWTON, M. (1969). *Reconviction of borstal boys who receive treatment at H.M. Prison, Grendon.* Office of the Chief Psychologist, Home Office Prison Dept.
15   NEWTON, M. (1971). *Reconviction after treatment at Grendon.* Office of the Chief Psychologist, Home Office, Prison Dept.
16   SINCLAIR, I. A. C. (1971). *Hostels for probationers.* London: H.M.S.O.
17   GOFFMAN, E. (1961). *Asylums.* Middlesex: Penguin, Chicago: Aldine.

Chapter IV

1   H.M.S.O. (1970). *Statistics relating to approved schools, remand homes and attendance centres in England and Wales for the year 1969.* London: H.M.S.O.
2   HOME OFFICE (1969). *The Sentence of the Court.* London: H.M.S.O.
3   CLARKE, R. V. G. and MARTIN, D. N. (1971). *Absconding from Approved Schools.* London: H.M.S.O.
4   DARTINGTON HALL. *Research Report.* (Personal communication.)
5   GOFFMAN, E. (1961). *Asylums.* Middlesex: Penguin, Chicago: Aldine.
6   HOME OFFICE (1970). *Care and Treatment in a Planned Environment.* London: H.M.S.O.
7   WILKINS, L. T. (unpublished). *Prediction methods in relation to approved school training.* Home Office Research Unit Report.
8   TUTT, N. S., (1971). 'Towards reducing absconding', *Community Schools Gazette.* vol. 65, no. 2.
9   BEHAN, B. (1958). *Borstal Boy.* London: Hutchinson, New York: Knopf.
10   BR. WILFRED, (1970). 'Wanted – psychologist', *Community School Gazette.* vol. 64, no. 1.

11   BROWN, R. (1965). *Social Psychology.* New York: The Free Press.
12   BANDURA, A., and WALTERS, R. H. (1959). *Adolescent Aggression.* New York: Ronald.
13   LUMSDEN WALKER, W. (1968). 'The limits of therapeutic methods in approved schools,' in *The Residential Treatment of Disturbed and Delinquent Boys.* Ed. R. G. Sparks & R. F. Hood. Cambridge: Institute of Criminology.
14   ANTHONY, J. (1958). 'Group therapeutic techniques for residential units' *Case Conference.* vol. 4, no. 7.
15   JONES, H. (1959). *Reluctant rebels.* London: Tavistock Publications.
16   WILLS, D. J. (1967). *Spare the child.* Middlesex: Penguin Books Ltd.
17   TUTT, N. S., (1970). 'In need, in care, in-side', *Community Schools Gazette.* vol. 64, no. 3
18   BERNSTEIN, G., and HENDERSON, D. (1969). 'Social class differences in the relevance of language to socialisation'. *Sociology,* vol. 3, no. 1.
19   HAWKINS, P. R. (1969). 'Social class, the national group and reference'. *Language and Speech.* vol. 12, no. 2.
20   POLSKY, H. W. (1962). *Cottage six: The social system of delinquent boys in residential treatment.* Chichester and New York: John Wiley & Sons.
21   LEWIN, K. (1947). 'Group decision and social change', in *Readings in Social Psychology. Ed.* Newcomb & Hartley. New York: Holt, Reinhard, Wilson.
22   YÁBLONSKY, L. (1962). *The Violent Gang.* London: Macmillan, New York: Penguin.
23   WEST, D. J. (1967). *The Young Offender.* Middlesex: Penguin, New York: International Universities Press.
24   JANIS, I. L., and KING, B. T. (1954). 'The influence of role playing on opinion change', *J. abnorm. soc. Psychol.* 49, 211–18.
25   GOFFMAN, E. (1968). *Stigma.* Middlesex: Penguin, New York: Jason Aronson.
26   HINES, B. L. (1968). *Kes.* Middlesex: Penguin Books Ltd.
27.   REVANS, R. W. (1964). *Standards for morale, cause and effect in mental hospitals.* Published for the Nuffield Provincial Hospitals Trust. London: Oxford University Press.

Chapter V

1   GOFFMAN, E. (1961). *Asylums.* Middlesex: Penguin, Chicago: Aldine.
2   POLSKY, H. W. (1962). *Cottage Six.* Chichester and New York: John Wiley & Sons.
3   FIELD, E., HAMMOND, W. H. & TIZARD, J. (1971). *Thirteen-year-old approved school boys in 1962.* H.M.S.O.
4   DARTINGTON HALL RESEARCH TEAM (1972). A comparative study of eighteen approved schools which explores their stylistic variety and the commitment of boys and staff. Unpublished.

5   HOME OFFICE (1970). *Care and Treatment in a Planned Environment.*
6   H.M.S.O. (1967). Williams Committee Report. *Caring for People.*
7   ALDRIDGE-MORRIS, R., *et al.* (1971). 'An analysis of the relation-
     ship between intelligence, personality, occupational motivation
     and job satisfaction in a sample of residential care workers'.
     Community Schools Gazette. Vol. 65, No. 3, 107–116.
8   BALLARD, R. (1971). 'The 1969 Children's Act – where from here?'
     Community Schools Gazette. vol. 65, no. 1, 16–18.
9   TUTT, N. S. (1972). 'A study of attitudes expressed by field and
     residential social workers'. *Social Services News,* March.
10 TUTT, N. S. (1972). 'A study of attitudes expressed by Social
     Workers'. *Community School Gazette,* vol. 66, no. 9.

Chapter VII

1   WILLS, D. (1971). *Spare the Child.* Penguin Books.
2   POLSKY, H. W. (1962). *Cottage Six.* Chichester and New York:
     John Wiley & Sons.
3. HOMANS, G. C. (1950). *The Human Group.* Harcourt Brace.
4   TOSH, N. D. F. (1964). *Being a Headmaster.* MacLellan.
5   GOFFMAN, E. (1961). *Asylums.* Middlesex: Penguin, Chicago: Aldine.

Chapter VIII

1   LITTLE, A. (1971). 'A sociological portrait: education'. New
     Society, 23 Dec.
2   POWER, M. J., ALDERSON, M.R., PHILLIPSON, C.M.
     SHOENBERG, E. & MORRIS, J. N. (1967). 'Delinquent schools?'
     New Society, 19 Oct.
3   HARGREAVES, D. H. (1967). *Social relations in a secondary school.*
     London: Routledge and Kegan Paul, Highland: Fernhill.
4   FARRINGTON, D. (1972). 'Delinquency begins at home'. *New
     Society,* 14 Sept.
5   GOODLET, G. (1972). 'Classroom behaviour'. *New Society,* 6 April.
6   NEILL, A. S. (1967). *Summerhill.* Middlesex: Penguin, New York:
     Hart.
7   FIELDS, E., HAMMOND, W. H. & TIZARD, J. (1971). *Thirteen-
     year-old approved school boys in 1962.* H.M.S.O.
8   SULLIVAN, P. T. (1971). 'Quality and quantity – specialist provision.'
     Community Schools Gazette, Oct.
9   HARGREAVES, D. (1972). 'Staffroom relationships'. *New Society,*
     2 March.
10 HUMANITIES PROJECT. (1970). *An introduction.* Heinemann
     Educational Books.

Chapter IX

1   WEST, D. J. (1967). *The Young Offender.* Middlesex: Penguin,
     New York: International Universities Press.

2   FRANKLIN, M. E. (1945). *The use and misuse of planned environ-mental therapy.* Sussex: Palnned Environmental Therapy Trust.
3   WILLS, W. D. (1971). *Spare the Child.* Middlesex: Penguin Education.
4   DARTINGTON HALL RESEARCH TEAM (1970). Personal communication.
5   McCLELLAND, D. C. (1967). 'The urge to achieve'. *New Society,* 9, 227–229.
6   McCLELLAND, D. C. (1961). *The Achieving Society.* Princeton: Van Nostrand.
7   MORENO, J. L. (1946). 'Psychodrama and group psychotherapy,' *Sociometry,* 9, 249–253.
8   KELLY, G. A. (1955). *The Psychology of Personal Constructs.* vol. II. New York: Norton.
9   JANIS, I. L. and KING, B. T. (1954). 'The influence of role playing on opinion change', *Journal of Abnormal and Social Psychology,* 49, 211–218.
10   DAVIDS, A., KIDDER, C., and REICH, M. (1962). 'Time orientation in male and female juvenile delinquents', *Journal of Abrnormal and Social Psychology,* 64, 239–240.
11   LEWIN, K. (1947). 'Group decision and social change, in Newcomb, J. M., and Hartley, E. L. Eds. *Readings in Social Psychology.* New York: Holt, Rinehart and Winston.
12   REIMER, E. (1971). *School is Dead.* Middlesex: Penguin, New York: Doubleday, Gloucester: Peter Smith.
13   H.M.S.O. (1970). *Statistics relating to approved schools, remand homes and attendance centres in England and Wales for the year 1969.* London: H.M.S.O.

Appendix

1   FIELD, E., HAMMOND, W. H. & TIZARD, J. (1971). *Thirteen-year-old approved school boys in 1962.* H.M.S.O.
2   TRENAMAN, J. (1952). *Out of Step.* Methuen.
3   FIELD, *et al. op cit.*
4   COHEN, A. K. (1955). *Delinquent Boys: the Culture of the Gang.* New York: Free Press.
5   GIBSON, H. B. (1967). 'Self reported delinquency among school boys and their attitude to the police.' *British Journal of Social and Clinical Psychology,* 6, 168–173.